PRESSURE BUST PIPES

Rex T. Pelote Jr.

REX T. PELOTE JR

(Pressure Bust Pipes)

Illustration done by Burie Garrett

Copyright © 2016 by (Rex T. Pelote Jr)

Dedication

I would like to dedicate this book to my brothers and sisters from another who I lost in the struggle along the way. Ebony (E.B) Burgees, Tamika Hill, Vanessa & Damon Clarke, Otis (O.T), Melvin Kearney, Antfernee (T), Edward (loose boost) Foley Jr, Mckenzie (Kenz), Auburn, my cousins Ray-Ray & B.O.B, Carlton Fisher, and my lil brother Kenneth (Kenny) Grimsley Jr, who was and still is everything to me. Man, I would give anything to see all y'all again. Just know that my love & loyalty will never waiver and that I carry y'all in my spirit. And last but not least, I would like to dedicate this book to a young girl by the name of Myesha Lowe who lost her life at the age of fifteen to a senseless act of violence. Although I never met you Myesha I want you to know that every day I think about the tragedy that took you away from this earth too   soon.

Acknowledgements

First off and most importantly all praise is due to Allah the highest. Secondly, I would like to thank my beautiful wife who has been nothing but supportive, because of her all of this is possible. She even threatened to put my book out without my permission if I didn't stop changing scenes and second guessing myself lol. Baby, I love you too death. I appreciate and adore your patience your everything a man could ever ask for. I also want to take this time to acknowledge my lovely, incredible, beautiful daughter Reasia Zenith Pelote, who I love dearly and cannot wait to get back to. I can't forget about my over protective parents Rex Pelote Sr. and Lawanda Pelote who sacrificed everything to give me a better life. Mom, dad from here on out I'm going to make you guys proud! And to my uncles Roy & Thaddeus whom I think the world of and can't wait to see on the other side of these gates.

PRESSURE BUST PIPES

PROLOGUE
JEETER'S BARBER SHOP

"Youngin' what the hell he jus' give you?"

Jeeter frowned stepping from behind his swivel chair towering over his barber-boy, who stood confused in the middle of the crowded shop clutching a crumpled bill in his right hand.

"A dolla," the barber boy responded. Jeeter turned around facing the back of the hustler who just left the cheap tip.

"Aye, muthafucka' get back here!" he hollered in his raspy voice getting everyone's attention including the hustler. "Yeah, 'I'm talkin' to your ass. Nigga, you out there slingin' all that shit, and you can't slide my barber-boy nuthin' but a dolla? What kind of business you think I'm running here?"

The hustler didn't take offense to Jeeter's comment because that was his character; he smiled lightly digging in his pocket.

"Yeah that's right, reach in ya' pocket and give that boy some real money," Jeeter said playfully.

The hustler laughed it off pulling out a wad of cash peeling off two ten dollar bills placing it the youngster's hand.

"And don't try no shit like that again," Jeeter said twirling his toothpick in his mouth.

That's how it always went down in Jeeter's shop, although he was often referred to as a vicious bamma for still rocking a jerry-curl in the millennium. Everyone and their mother showed him, love. Jeeter migrated to Nation's Capital from California right after the Watts riot in the early sixties. With only barbering skills, his shop would later become a city's landmark. The preeminent salon was often occupied by some of the city's most notorious gangsta's. Luxury cars aligned its front on a daily basis. Jeeter had one rule with no exceptions no gun play in or around his shop, it was a rule that everyone respected.

"I appreciate that Mr. J," said Fray the young barber-boy who often referred to Jeeter as Mr. J.

"Ah, don't mention it. Hell if it wasn't for your pop's I don't know if Lavish Kutz would still be in business."

Jeeter reflected back when he had fallen on hard times, and could barely afford to keep the shops doors open. After being denied repeatedly by the banks, he reached out for help from the many drug dealers who visited his shop, they too denied him. It wasn't until one late night during closing that big Frank came strolling inside. Jeeter protested by informing him the shop was closed. Big Frank sat comfortably in the chair and demanded a shave.

Jeeter had never seen the unfamiliar face before, but rather than argue he broke out the clippers. Amazingly he found the slick gentleman company soothing. Within minutes of cutting his hair, he began to confide in him, telling him all about his woes of keeping his shop open. To his surprise, after sweeping the hair off the man's back, Frank told him not to worry that he would have the money delivered to him the next morning. Jeeter froze not believing his ears. He was speechless. He suspiciously eyeballed the stranger still unable to speak big Frank smiled taking that as a thank you. At that moment, a friendship was bonded for life. Jeeter learned that big Frank was the biggest heroin pusher in the city, that was over a decade ago. However, even in Frank's absence Jeeter still remained loyal to his friend who had fallen victim to the chain gang. Rather than seeing Frank's son travel down the same road he employed him as a barber-boy.

"I'll see you later Mr. J," Fray said interrupting his thoughts as he pulled on his fitted hat just as the last customer exited. Jeeter normally would close the shop around seven or eight o'clock, but today he had a funeral to attend.

"A'ight, baby boy you be careful now, ya here?"

Jeeter yelled as he rinsed his hands off in the sink. After removing his jacket from the hook, Fray noticed there was still a jacket dangling. He immediately cut his eye over at Jeeter who had still been washing his hands, he knew it couldn't belong to him because the jacket looked too expensive. Thinking quickly on his feet he knew it had to belong to the last customer. His eyes swept to the huge glass front window, there he observed the customer chatting away on his cell phone walking to the driver side of a white Porsche. Fray watched as he lowered himself into the car. Not wasting another minute he snatched the jacket off the hook dashing out the door.

"Aye, you forgot your coat," Fray said tapping on the passenger window. The customer shook his head at his own carelessness. He placed his phone on his lap and rolled down the window.

"Good lookin' out shawty," he said pulling his coat inside through the window. He then opened his glove compartment, which contained a zip lock bag filled with cash, and a big block of white substance. Fray knew exactly what the white substance was. He was so focused on the white stuff that he didn't see the outstretched bill that the hustler was attempting to give him. After realizing what the youngster was looking at the hustler slammed his glove compartment door shut.

"Everything ain't for e'rybody shawty," he frowned. "A lot of heartaches and sleepless nights come with this game here," he said handing Fray fifty dollars. "Now you think about that, and why you're at it make sure you hit your man off wit' some of that."

Following his eyes, Fray looked over his shoulder. His best friend

PRESSURE BUST PIPES

Ashley was leaning up against the wall with his basketball. He hadn't noticed him when he first ran out the shop. Fray thanked the hustler and stepped back on the curb allowing the car to pull off.

"Man, you heard what he said, he said split half of that wit' me." Ashley reminded Fray as they dodged cars crossing the busy street of Benning Rd.

"Damn nigga miss sumthin sometimes," Fray said.

They cut down a side street in the back of the Benning Court apartments making a right on Rosedale Street, heading towards 18&D. Once they reached their neighborhood people were scattered everywhere, which wasn't unusual for the rundown residential street.

"You still going wit' me to shoot some hoops up Eastern right?" Ashley asked once they neared Fray's two-unit apartment building.

"Yeah, I'm still going, but let me change my clothes first," he took off leaving Ashley standing at the bottom of the steps. Upon entering the dimly lit building he was shocked to find himself staring down the barrel of a gun.

"Oh, Shit...Don't shoot"

He ducked covering the top of his head with his hands.

"Damn, Fray! How many times I gotta tell you to watch how you come through that door. Suppose I woulda' shot your ass!" Rico said lowering the gun, stuffing it back in his waistband. Rico couldn't have been any more than three years his senior.

"Man you don't even live here, and why you always so paranoid!" Fray shouted while holding his hand over his racing heart.

"Shid, nigga you would be too if you was makin' the kind of

money I'm making, but you wouldn't know nuthin' bout that barber-boy," he chuckled adjusting his diamond chain, and watch pulling out a knot of money wrapped in a dirty rubber band. "And to think, you Frank's boy."

This wasn't the first time someone compared him to his father, so instead of doing what was expected of him he chose to sweep floors and brush the hair off customer's backs. On the other hand, he knew Rico was right, he could never save that kind of dough sweeping floors. Humiliated, he brushed passed the arrogant Rico and climbed the wooden creaking steps to his apartment. Once inside he read the note that was attached to the refrigerator.

"Fray I'll be working late tonight. I separated your clothes and placed them in the washing machine, make sure to wash them and warm up the leftovers for dinner. Don't stay up late playing that game. I love you."

For the third day in a row, his mother wouldn't be home. He tossed the letter and grabbed a bottle of Deer Park water out of the refrigerator, then headed down the hall towards his bedroom. After stripping off all his clothes he heard chattering voices from outside his window. He took up his position prying through the blinds so no one could see him. His window served as his own HBO special of the wire. As soon as he peeked out the blinds he saw someone willing a dirt bike up the street, the females screamed in amazement. When he looked closer he saw Rico exiting the building motioning to the fiend on how to wipe his car down.

Fray admired the brand new pearl white Q45 with peanut butter-colored interior. From the outside looking in, the drug world seemed so much better than sweeping floors, or any job for that matter. For years, his mother worked every day including extra shifts and still struggled to pay bills, which is why he always visualized what life would be like to become a hustler. Fourteen-year-old Fray Pascal never knew what it was like to want for nothing, that is until the feds came knocking, arresting his father.

PRESSURE BUST PIPES

The days of lavish shopping sprees and expensive trips were a thing of the past. Fray sat staring out the window watching several hand over fist drug transactions, life had to better than this he thought.

FRAY

The rain had come and gone leaving behind a heavy fog,
meanwhile, Fray frantically weaved in-between abandon cars
ducking behind trashcans, as he tried desperately to elude the
police. Besides a few barking dogs, the only thing that could be
heard were hard slaps from his black Timberlands splashing
through puddles as he raced through the alley in search of a hiding
place. He looked over his shoulder several times making sure the
undercover officer wasn't behind him. The officer wasn't anywhere
in sight, he figured he must've lost him. He bunny-hopped over a
fence landing in someone's backyard he then crawled underneath
the porch. Just as he was about to stash his drugs and gun he heard
movement next to the gate.

"Come in rookie, we lost sight of you, what's your 20?!"

PRESSURE BUST PIPES

The crackled message came over the officer's radio. With his service weapon drawn he carefully stepped in the fog. Unbeknownst to him he stood one house down from where Fray was hiding. He placed the radio to his lips.

"I'm not sure Sgt. it looks like the suspect led me into a crack infested alley," He said noticing the many syringes and crack pipes scattered on the ground. He resumed his search in efforts to locate the suspect. Fray could hear the officer's faint footsteps approaching as well as the static from his radio. From his stooping position, he tried to steady his breathing. The officer now stood right outside the gate. Looking through the fog the only thing Fray could make out was the officer's dangling gold badge around his neck.

The rookie looked around nervously. There was only one house that remained before the intersection. He figured the assailant couldn't have made it across the busy street without drawing patron's horns. Following his instincts, he unlatched the gate to the house in front of him. Fray began to panic and perspire heavily as he watched the fog slowly fade. He tightened his grip around the butt of his chrome 44 revolver that rested in his hands. The officer had just stepped foot inside the yard when a nervous, and scared Fray slowly raised his gun with his finger on the trigger. The officer took two more small steps then stopped when he detected movement through his peripheral. He jerked around wildly with his gun raised high ready to fire. His eyes widened at the charging pitbull who was violently yoked out the air by his secured chain.

"Jesus Christ!" he proclaimed. Had the chain been any longer the officer would have been dog food. The dog was barking and growling uncontrollably. Still shaken up he disregarded his supervisor first attempt of reaching him.

"I repeat…do you read me, rookie?"

"Go ahead Sgt."

"We could use a hand up here this crowd is becoming hostile."

"Roger that, I'm in route."

He raced back up the alley. Fray took a deep breath, allowing his head to rest on the wall before crawling from underneath the porch. He dusted himself off checking the perimeter before heading back up the alley.

"Helen Monae Smith, hurry up and finish that cereal so you can get out of here," her mother yelled from the top of the stairs. Helen ate the last spoonful of her cheerios and sat the bowl in the sink, placing her backpack on her back then exited out the front door. The brisk fall morning slapped her in her face. This was the part Helen hated about walking to school. Minor elementary school was only a ten-minute walk from her house, but she decided to take the forbidden shortcut that would get her there four minutes early. Helen skipped joyfully up the alley while humming her favorite Disney channel song.

As she skipped further into the alley she was caught off guard by a rattling sound coming from her right. A man wearing a dirty peak coat was rummaging through the garbage cursing like a sailor. He toppled the trashcan over, when he looked up he was startled by the little girl's presence. Helen stood face to face with the dingy fiend. His hair was matted to his head and alcohol reeked through his pores. With glossy eyes, he looked ten-year-old Helen up and down. She instantly mistrusted him, frozen with fear she didn't know whether to scream or run. The fiend rubbed his hand over his nappy fro as if he was trying to impress her. He reached into his coat pocket and retrieved a melted Hershey Kisses with lent attached to it. He started to advance towards her.

Helen let out a loud scream as the stranger reached for her, she tried to run but tripped over her untied shoelaces. Within seconds he was on top of her, dragging her malnutrition body behind an abandoned car, she clawed at his gloved hands.

Fray continued to proceed through the alley with caution. When nothing happened he began to relax. All of a sudden, he heard a muffled scream. He searched the alley for any signs of life, but only stray cats moved about. As he continued on his way he stopped in his tracks, he was certain he heard screams this time. Up ahead he noticed a pair of black and white Mary Jane shoes protruding from the rear of an abandoned car. He approached the car with vigilance.

The man ignored Helen's pleas and desperate attempts to get free. Her forty-pound frame was in no way a match for his. He held her hands above her head with one hand hiking her uniform dress up with the other. He began to tug at her underwear. With one last burst of energy, Helen let out a frantic scream that was met with a forceful backhand knocking the fight out of her. The swift smack split her upper lip leaving her temporarily dazed. The fiend began to unfasten his pants; he never saw Fray appear behind him. What Fray saw sent him into a rage, and before he knew it he had already eased his nickel plated snub nose .44 from his waist. He locked eyes with the battered girl for the first time.

The fiend was just about to ram himself inside of her when Fray raised the gun. The sun reflected off the glistening gun catching the fiend by surprise. *Boom!* Fray squeezed the trigger. A mist of blood splattered on him and Helen. At the sight of blood, the little girl began to scream hysterically. Fray had seen plenty of people die before, but never by his own hands. He stood paralyzed at the realization of what he had just done. His mind seemed to have blocked out the little girl's struggles and screams. This was a life changing event for the both of them.

Helen was finally able to wiggle from underneath the lifeless body of the fiend. She looked at her attacker's killer wondering if she would be next. Fray remained motionless with the smoking gun in his palm. Helen sprinted towards her house never once looking back. The blaring sound of sirens brought Fray back to reality, he took off running. Ronnie was awakened out of his sleep by the banging at his front door. Squinting his eyes, he read the clock on the wall it was 8:45am. Annoyed, he wiped the saliva from the side of his mouth before rolling off the couch. He didn't bother to look out the peephole before yanking the door open. Fray stood covered in sweat and blood.

"What the hell happened to you?!" he questioned stepping aside so that Fray could enter. Ronnie went straight to the kitchen and poured a glass of cold water. "Here drink this," he passed him the glass of water. After gulping down the water, Fray checked all the windows worriedly.

"Nigga, would you chill. My grandma still up there sleep."

Once Fray was sure he wasn't being followed he began to explain what just took place. The two had been friends since grade school.

"What about the lil girl? Do you know who she is?" Ronnie asked. He was still in awe by the news his friend just laid on him.

"Naw, I never saw her before until this morning. Ronnie, I swear we gotta take this shit to our graves. I don't want Shay or Ashley to know."

The two made a pact to keep Fray's secret a secret.

THE CREW

Ronnie walked the track alone, he had matured a lot since his incarceration. He was no longer that little boy who walked through those gates at sixteen. Tall, dark skin, and skinny he wore a 5'oclock shadow. The day had finally come when he would be free. As he continued to walk the track, he wondered what the hell was taking them so long to release him. He reflected back on something his last celly Chucky said before he went home, "these muthafuckas are quick to lock a nigga up but slow as hell to let you go when your time is up." Ronnie had to agree with that thought. Outside of him being released, he had other things on his mind as well.

Ronnie replayed the conversation he had with Ashley the other day in his head. He sometimes questioned his friend's loyalty for their dealings with Derek knowing the history. Ashley tried to assure him that their affiliation was business and nothing more. Derek was a successful drug pusher for many years, but what Ashley failed to mention was the father-son relationship Derek developed with Fray over the years, he would soon let Ronnie find that out on his own. The last time Ronnie was on the street he awoke in a hospital cuffed to a bed. When the cops arrived at the scene they found him unconscious. Upon conducting a search for his I.D they discovered a loaded firearm in his possession, they ran his name through their database. Not only was he in violation of a firearm, but he was also a suspect in an earlier shooting. The bullet had left the right side of his face paralyzed. Ronnie stopped on the track rubbing his wounded right cheek remembering that night...

"Man, my point was six!" Rico fumed springing upward from his knee as Derek raked his money up off the ground. The crap game was flooded with hustlers.

"Nigga, you trippin' you burnt dice, your point was four," Derek lied matching Rico's aggression. Derek had a thing for pressing young hustlers in the hood. He felt like he put in so much work in the late 80's early 90's he deserved to be praised. For years, he lived off of his old reputation, which put fear in many people, but had the youngsters investigated his background a little deeper they would've discovered his putting in work was a myth, and that his three older brothers who were now serving life sentences were the actual killers.

"Man, you got me fucked up! I ain't goin' like that. Put my muthafuckin money back on the ground!" Rico demanded.

The dice game fell silent. It was unusual for someone to speak to Derek in such a way. Rico was cut from a different cloth the more his gun went off the more confident he became.

PRESSURE BUST PIPES

"And if I don't what'chu gon' do lil nigga?" Derek said closing the distance between them, getting all up in his face. Rico took a step back.

"You know what, you got that. You can have that Lil bit ass money," he backpedaled away.

"Just like I thought," Derek said dropping back down to one knee picking up the dice. "I need a fader."

Ronnie stepped up to the plate.

"I gotcha big-boy," he dropped a twenty.

"What the fuck is this! Nigga, we shootin' a hunnid or bet-," Derek never finished his sentence. The first shot pierced the night whistling past his ear. Everyone scattered trying to get away from Rico as he busts shots into the crowd. In the end, Ronnie was the only one who would suffer. Just thinking about that night made the right side of his face tingle. He acknowledged a passing jogger on the track. He hated Derek for that night, if it wasn't for him he wouldn't have been confined in the first place. He had to admit his friends hooking up with Derek was a smart move.

During his entire bid, he wanted for nothing, and not to mention every time he encountered someone who had just left the streets, they couldn't stop boasting about or dick riding his friends. Ronnie heard just about all the rumors about how Fray, Ashley, and DeShay were out there getting it. His friends seemed too had gained notoriety becoming hood celebrities. Some of the inmates called him bluff when he would mention the trio as his friends. To shut them up he brought his photo album out to the rec yard proving his point.

Even with his friends in a good position in the drug game he still found it hard to accept Derek. The first thing he wanted to do when he touched down was to go see Rico, but that was a dead issue Rico's body was found slumped over in a car, he had been shot multiple times. His thoughts were interrupted by his name being called over the intercom. A half an hour later he was stepping through the steel gates and into the parking lot.

"Oh, my lord!" Ms. Watson smiled touching her chest. Ronnie's grandmother was a very religious woman. She attended church almost every day out the week. His grandmother was the only living relative he had left, at least, that's what he liked to tell himself. He never knew his father and his mom was strung out on crack. He was awarded to his grandmother by the state. Besides a few new strands of gray hair, she still looked the same.

"Come here child let ol' Granma take a look at cha," she smiled cupping his face into her wrinkled hands.

"Hi you doing Granma," he blushed.

"Better now. The Lord has finally answered my prayers and brought you home."

Ronnie didn't talk much on the ride home. For the most part, he stared out the window lost in his own thoughts.

"Honey, you okay? You haven't said a word since we left that place."

"I'm cool grams. I'm just takin in the scenery tryna adjust to being back out here."

"Well remember, put the Lord first and he shall show you the way. He knows I don't want you back out here doing what you were doing before you went to that place."

She gave him a stern look before cutting her eye back on the road. "Oh, I almost forgot. Fray stopped by yesterday and dropped some things off for you, he's such a nice boy, he use to stop by all the time to check on me." She beamed.

Ronnie smiled at the thought of Fray. Although, DeShay and Ashley talked to him on a regular, Fray stayed down from day one. It didn't matter if it was writing letters, working the three-way, or visiting, which DeShay and Ashley couldn't because of their criminal records. Fray made sure everything was taken care of. They cruised in silence the rest of the way home. When Ms. Watson pulled her Buick alongside her house, Go-Go music could be heard blaring from the car's speakers parked in front of them.

"What in the Lord's name?" she frowned adjusting her bifocal glasses.

"You know them Granma'?"

Before she could respond, Ashley jumped from the black tinted SS Impala brandishing a bottle of Rose'. He didn't drink, but he knew Moet was Ronnie's favorite.

"Slim come give a nigga a hug!"

Ashley hollered with his arms outstretched. His brown Bob-Marley locks hung down to his stomach. If one looked closely you could see curls mixed in with his locks. He was short and stocky with muscular features. Ronnie was out of the car embracing him in no time.

"Ashley if you don't turn that ruckus down!"

Ms. Watson bellowed walking from the driver's side of the car.

"Oops…my bad Ms. Watson," he reached inside the car turning the music down. Ashley loved go-go music he had the dance moves to match it. "Man, your grandmother still mean as hell," he chuckled passing Ronnie the bottle of Rose'. "Welcome home nigga."

"Thanks, brah, but where e'rybody at?" Ronnie asked.

"Man, this joint been hot is shit today. The police been hawkin' all morning. "You know ain't nobody tryna play with them peoples, so e'rybody hit up the casino."

Ronnie was disappointed that he would have to wait to see Fray and DeShay, which didn't go unnoticed by Ashley.

"Man, why the long face? Smile nigga you wit' your boy," he tried to uplift Ronnie. "C'mon let's take a ride," Ashley said.

"A'ight, hold fast. Let me get out this prison shit first."

Ronnie stepped out wearing some dark blue fitted Levi jeans, a Giorgio Armani t-shirt, and some Prada loafers. The t-shirt fit his slender frame perfectly. The hard life he lived growing up made him appear older than what he was. To the visible eye, one couldn't tell the right side of his face was crooked unless he smiled. Over the years, he fought just about every day when someone made fun about his face. Ashley eased away from the curve with no specific destination in mind.

"How long you had this joint?" Ronnie asked checking out the tan interior.

"About a month," Ashley responded.

"Slim, I want you to know that I really appreciate all the shit ya'll did for a nigga while I was in. There were some niggaz in there who couldn't afford to buy quarter soups because they had no support out here. I want y'all to know that I'm thankful for that."

"C'mon man, you ain't gotta thank us for none of that shit. Just because we was out and you were in our code ain't never change. We still live by and die by that shit (no man ever left behind)."

PRESSURE BUST PIPES

The sincerity in his voice touched Ronnie's heart. After being crammed in a box for four years surrounded by so much hate, envy, and deceit Ronnie felt good to be back amongst the people he knew really loved him. Ronnie was just about to recline his seat when they neared K Street, the thought of unfinished business registered in his head.

"Ash you strapped?" The question took Ashley by surprise as he scanned the crowd trying to figure out what Ronnie saw. As requested by his friend he pulled his Smith& Wesson 9mm from underneath the seat. "Slide through the Cordas right quick I gotta take care of somethin'," Ronnie said as they cruised past Temple Courts apartments. Ashley was skeptical about giving his friend the gun knowing that he had only been home for a few hours. The look on Ronnie's face spoke volumes, Ashley made a right into the Sursum Corda market.

"What'chu got beef wit' one of these niggaz or sumthin'?" Ashley said.

"Sumthin' like that. When I first went in two niggaz from down this joint jumped me." His eyes were scoping out the cuts on the deserted block.

"Fa real! Man, why the fuck you ain't been say nuffin' we could've taken care of this shit before you came home."

"Naw, this shit is personal my nigga. Plus, one of the niggaz is already dead somebody smoked his ass at the halfway house as soon as he came home, and the other nigga Nut supposedly crashed out on some robbery shit in Maryland."

"If one of the niggaz is already dead, and the other one out Maryland, what the fuck we doin' down here now?"

"Cause I later found out the nigga supposed to gave his time back…still don't know how true that is, though," Ronnie said watching the market.

What was supposed to be a simple ride turned out to be a full stake out. The duo had been parked for over two hours when Ashley finally received the text he had been waiting for. He flipped his mobile phone closed and started his engine.

"Slim, we goin' have to finish this later. I gotta meet somebody in a few."

Ashley pulled up on H Street N.E with Ronnie in the passenger seat. cars were parked on both sides of the street.

"C'mon nigga get out the car," Ashley chuckled looking back at Ronnie who still sat in the car.

"For what ain't shit out here."

"Nigga jus c'mon," Ashley walked towards the run down building. This has to be a joke Ronnie thought as he looked at the run down building that had been vacant for years. He joined Ashley as they made their way inside the pitch black building. Feeling uncomfortable, Ronnie started tugging at the back of Ashley's shirt pulling him towards the exit when someone flipped on the lights.

"Surprise!" the countless smiling faces yelled from the crowd. Ronnie's heart nearly jumped out of his chest. It took him a minute to register what was happening. To Ronnie's surprise, the building was no longer vacant but now Club 12. Fray and DeShay were amongst those in the crowd both of their mocha-complexions glowed under the disco balls and spot lights. Ronnie playfully bear hugged Ashley hoisting him in the air. The crowd immediately swarmed him! There were a lot of familiar faces as well as unfamiliar faces.

PRESSURE BUST PIPES

More women than men turned out for the celebration. His friends planned the event thoroughly reserving the up and coming nightclub for the night. They hired his favorite go-go band along with the R&B singer Mya. Working his way around the club Ronnie dapped up and hugged everybody while Mya performed her hit single Ghetto Superstar. Ashley was doing what he did best entertaining the crowd dancing his ass off. Ronnie now accompanied Fray and DeShay at the bar. Fray didn't drink or smoke so he settled for a bottle of water.

DeShay's shoulder length locks complimented his slanted eyes and flat nose. One of his more attractive features to the ladies was his thin lips, which drove them crazy. Medium build, 5'7", he was without a doubt a lady's man. He wore a black and gray Solbiato hoodie as he sipped his Hennessey blowing exotic smoke into the air. Fray and DeShay were cousins only one month apart but more like brothers. They differed in many ways. DeShay was wild and outgoing also a hot head. Fray, on the other hand, was more observant, mature, level headed and the thinker of the two.

"It's nice to finally see you on the other side of the gate," Fray smiled humbly embracing him. His well-groomed beard shined with oil flowing like the rapper Stalley. He practiced the Islamic religion which is why he wore a beard. Five foot eleven, one hundred and ninety pounds, a low hair cut with waves he too was a magnet to the ladies with his baby face. His demeanor often came off as arrogant and or a pretty boy.

"Yeah, nigga we missed you. Now the first thing we gotta do is get you some ass!" DeShay laughed embracing him with a hug passing him the blunt. Ashley emerged from the crowd with two big breasted nicely shaped women. The taller of the two had a bigger backside wearing liquid leggings with no panties and a sheer top. The shorter one was prettier she wore a plaid skirt with a variety of tattoos on her thighs.

"Kitty, Michelle this is the man of the hour I was telling you about," Ashley said handing them over to Ronnie.

"Sweetheart, I jus' have one question," Ronnie smirked focusing on the shorter one. "Why they call you Kitty?"

"Because I lick my men clean," she purred like a cat.

"Damn, why ain't nobody let me know y'all was havin' a party?" Rick walked up stealing the moment. His locks were long, broken off and unkempt. The bar fell silent everyone's mood changed except Ronnie's.

"Ricky Lanier is that you?" Ronnie smiled recognizing the old timer from around the way, "Somebody' told me you had thirty years."

"That's why you can't believe e'rything you hear," Rick said loud enough for the trio to hear. If looks could kill he would've been dead already. Picking up on the vibes he decided it was time to go.

"Aye, Ronnie I'ma get up wit' you later."

"A'ight man, jus' say the word, I should have a phone by tomorrow."

"Ladies, would you excuse us for a second," Ashley said sending the ladies on their way.

"Don't fuck wit that nigga slim, he got a fucked up bone on his name right now," Ashley said now facing Ronnie.

"What kind of bone?" Ronnie asked confused.

"A hot one!" DeShay chimed in.

"Oh yeah, who he supposed to told on?"

"Some nigga from down the west," Ashley said.

PRESSURE BUST PIPES

"Y'all read the paperwork?"

"*Paperwork!* C'mon Ronnie man don't tell me you went in and forgot how the streets work. The nigga who said it screamed on him down the Farms tournament when he first came home, and he didn't straighten it out."

"And he ain't got no plans on straightening it out either!" DeShay blurted out once again. Fray remained silent throughout the debate.

"So let me get this straight. Y'all haven't seen any paperwork and y'all going off another nigga's word who we don't even know." Ronnie shook his head in disbelief. Fray finally broke his silence.

"And that's all we need," he said in his high-pitched voice. "We watched that man bitch Rick down the farms holmes. Now when you walk away from a situation like that without sayin' nuffin' it makes us question if you really did what he accused you of."

"Slim, I feel where y'all comin' from and e'rything but I'm still not sold," Ronnie said.

"And you don't have to be," Fray said cutting him off. "Look all were tryna' do is put you on point, if you decide to still fuck wit' slim then that's on you."

Ronnie let his friend's words sink in.

"Now we didn't bring you here to argue," Fray smiled. "Let's party…"

SPINGARN HIGH SCHOOL

Fray yawned just before the bell rang ending History class, he was feeling the aftermath from Ronnie's party. He closed his notebook and gathered his belongings. Fray's days in school were pretty much always the same females practically throwing themselves at him or just dying to get his attention. Some even went as far as leaving notes behind on his car after school only to never receive a call. After turning them down with a smile, or two words the girls in school deemed him as being conceited. He was having small talk with some of the guys from around his way when he noticed a female he had never seen in school before. She appeared to be lost as she looked back and forth from the paper to the classroom. She was stunning he just had to get her attention.

"I'll catch up with y'all later," Fray said as he swiftly made his way down the crowded hallway catching up with her when she unexpectedly turned around to go in the opposite direction.

"Hey! Watch where you're going!"

She collided with Fray. Katie stooped down to pick up her books that had fallen. Fray kneeled down commencing to help her.

"My fault, I wasn't even looking."

"I can see that," she replied sarcastically.

The two made eye contact for the first time. Katie's beauty was breathtaking, he found himself gazing into her eyes. He held on to her chemistry book longer than he should have. The pint-size, caramel complected beauty was shaped like Xscape's R&B singer Tiny. She was 5'2 with a broad nose, luscious lips and high cheek bones. Fray found her features to be distinctive. Her two-tone brown locks fell to the middle of her back. She ran her manicured hand through her neatly twisted locks pushing them from her face, Fray looked as if he had stumbled upon a goddess.

"You can let my book go now," she smiled showing her silver braces.

"My bad," he said releasing his grip.

He found himself at a loss for words he figured he should say something rather than just stare at her.

"I'm Fray, you new here?"

"Uh, yeah it's my first day. I'm Katie," she said readjusting her books. "Well, I betta' get going." She said.

He watched her disappear through the double doors with a smile on his face. Katie was steadily grinning when she rounded the corner.

"Bitch, where you been smiling like you just got laid," Unique joked. Unique was Katie's best friend.

"Ha, ha very funny don't be a dick Nique. Some guy just knocked all my books out my hand."

"And who is this guy?!" Unique seethed ready to rumble.

"Chill out missy it was an accident he helped me pick them up."

"I still wanna know who this mystery man is, jus' so we don't have this problem again."

"Well if you must know, I think he said his name was Fray or something like that."

Hearing Fray's name Unique's manner softened.

"You know him?" Katie asked.

"*Do I!*" Unique exaggerated. "Girl, every girl in here is tryna holla at him."

"Including' you," Katie snickered.

"Mm-Umm boo not my type. He's too much of a pretty boy and he's arrogant as hell. You know I like them wild and thugged out. Now his cousin DeShay, that boy can get it!" she laughed.

"Nique, your ass is crazy." Katie snickered as well. "And jus' how in the hell do you know his cousin?"

"He goes here too, well whenever he feels like showing up, but on the real though Katie I could see you and Fray hookin' up."

"*What!* Excuse you?"

She hated when Unique tried to play matchmaker.

"Don't even fake and act like you weren't checkin' him out Kee! Go ahead and lie."

"He a'ight!" Katie said rolling her neck.

"Bitch ya lying! Even a blind bitch could see that boy got it goin' on."

Fray's handsome face was still on her mind. Just the thought of him made her feel shy.

"A'ight you got me, girl, he did have it going on," Katie admitted. "But that still doesn't mean I'm going out with him."

"Well, look at you acting all snobbish," Unique said. "For someone who says she hates workin' at the beauty supply store as much as you do you would think that you would recognize when a bitch is tryna put you on!"

Katie stopped Unique before she uttered another word.

"Now I know you then bumped your head. I don't give a fuck how much money he has; you know that's not how I get down. Unlike others, I don't sleep around because of what a nigga got!"

"Excuse me!" Unique said rolling her neck. "Did you just take a shot at me? Well, you can miss me with all that good girl shit. A bitch like me ain't gonna' continue to work at the beauty supply store. The last time I checked your stuck up ass come from the projects just like me, so unless you plan on stayin' in the projects you better wake up!"

Katie let out a fake laugh.

"And that's exactly why you go through what you go through."

Ashley sat parked outside Spingarn High School in his shiny black

PRESSURE BUST PIPES

Impala listening to Juvenile's 400 degrees CD when Unique stormed out. She was still upset about the argument she had with Katie. Ashley eyed the attractive slim beauty as she walked down the steps onto the sidewalk with her firm physique, and shoulder length hair. He went crazy blowing his horn getting her attention. Unique adjusted her specs with an attitude looking in the car's direction.

"*Aye Shawty!*" he hollered signaling for her to come over. At first, Unique was hesitant, but seeing the light brown skin, stocky dread head emerges from the car she thought twice. She turned her sexy walk into overdrive.

"I hope this his damn car," she mumbled underneath her breath before reaching Ashley.

"My fault baby for blowin' at you, but as good as you look I had to get your attention," he smirked becoming aroused by the gap in-between her sexy legs.

"Is that right," Unique face lit up seeing the diamond encrusted chain around his neck.

"I'm Ashley by the way."

"And I'm Unique by the way," she giggled. "So what brings you up here, because I know you didn't just stop when you saw me."

"Naw, I spotted you when you first came out. I'm actually here to pick up my man Fray you know 'em?"

"Yeah, I know Fray ass, as a matter of fact I jus' passed him at his locker he should be on his way out."

Fray pushed his way through the front door stopping at the top of the concrete steps as he witnessed Ashley and Unique talking.

"Gold diggin' bitch," he said to himself. Unique was still laughing at something Ashley said when Fray walked up behind them.

"Oh hey Fray," she jumped.

Fray nodded nonchalantly before opening the passenger door.

"Well, you got my number. I'll be expecting your call," Unique said as she walked off.

Katie was just coming out the building when she saw Unique walking away from the black car.

"Man, that bitch is anything I know at least five dudes in school that hit her already," Fray said as they drove away from the school.

"Shawty out there like that huh?"

"Man, not only is the bitch out there but money hungry as well all kinds of big boy whips be scoopin' her up after school."

"Damn, shawty coulda' definitely tricked a nigga lookin' all innocent and shit wit' her glasses on," Ashley said as they approached a red light. "Well, shid her background ain't got nuthin' to do wit' me I got a baby-mamma at home, so it's not like I'm tryna' wife the bitch, but man did you see that gap on her? I gotta fuck shawty." He laughed.

Over the past few weeks, Ashley and Unique had become exceptionally close. Although he was still involved with his baby mother it had been awhile since a side piece had him pussy whipped. He sexed Unique during the day and played house at night, his newly found relationship had cut into his time with his friends and making money on the block. Whenever he did slide through Unique was always riding shotgun. Light rain fell from the darkening sky as Ashley parked his Impala on D St.

"Hand me that hoodie from the back seat," he gestured to Unique who complied with his demands. She watched him slip into his sweatshirt before asking her question.

"I thought we were going out to eat."

"We are, I jus' gotta make up some of this money," he said pulling his hood on his head stepping away from the car.

Usually, around that time of the hour the block would've been empty, which is why he chose to slide through, but tonight the block was the total opposite of that. Fray and DeShay stood in the middle of the crowd wearing their Helley Hansen ski-suits when they noticed Ashley crossing the narrow street heading in their direction, Ashley felt tension.

"Whassup wit' y'all?" Ashley spoke.

"Ain't shit," they replied in unison. An awkward silence fell between them.

"I see you got the hooker wit'chu," DeShay smirked nudging his head towards Ashley's car. He too shared Fray's views of Unique.

"Why don't you nigga's stop hating!"

"Hating!" DeShay repeated. *"Nigga that bitch anything. I coulda' been fucked her."* He barked.

"Man, fuck you, Shay!" Ashley based back snatching off his hood. To him, Unique wasn't anything like Fray and DeShay described. Fray stepped in-between them before things could escalate.

Ronnie had just stepped from one of the buildings when he saw the argument taking place. As he looked down from the top of steps he saw a female sitting in the passenger seat of Ashley's car. Something seemed vaguely familiar about her, but for some strange reason, he couldn't quite put his finger on it. He then turned his attention back to his friends.

"Y'all chill out wit' all 'dat bullshit!" he said descending from the steps trying to smooth things over. DeShay and Ashley immediately calmed themselves.

"Man, fuck what these two nigga's talkin' 'bout, shawty got any friends?" Ronnie asked.

"Yeah, this one broad name Katie. Brah shawty bad as e'muthafucka." Ashley boasted.

"Well hook a nigga up then," Ronnie smiled throwing his hands in the air.

At the mention of Katie's name Fray did a double take, "Naw it can't be," he thought. Ever since he and Katie's awkward encounter he had yet to see her again. Fixing his gaze on Unique "There's only one way to find out," he thought walking towards Ashley's car.

Katie stood in front of the oval shaped mirror in her bedroom conducting her nightly hygiene routine while she listened to Troop (I Will Always Love You) song. She slowly maneuvered her hips to the music when she was interrupted by Unique barging through the door frightening her.

"Damn do you know how to knock Nique!"

"Bitch please it's not like I'm gonna catch you here with a man." She joked flopping down on her bed. Katie flipped her the bird and went back to tying her hair down.

"What are you doing here so late anyway? In case, you forgot we gotta work the morning shift tomorrow." Katie said.

"Yeah, yeah I know but anyway I came over to share some

good news."

Katie grabbed her oversized stuffed bear from the chair, pulled back her comforter, and climbed in the bed.

"I can't believe you still sleep with that thing," Unique shook her head.

"Unique would you get on with the story so I could get some sleep."

"Oh...well since you put it to me like that, I might've found you a date."

Katie popped up from her resting position piercing through Unique as if she just did the unthinkable.

"Before you blow a gasket jus' hear me out this one is different," she said with confidence.

"Hmm, I heard that one before," Katie said laying back down. "In case you forgot Unique you don't have the ultimate track record when it comes to playing matchmaker."

"I already know your talkin' about Rashad's broke ass. Can you believe his ass is still catching the bus?" Unique snickered then abruptly cut it off.

Katie didn't find the situation to be humorous.

"Kee, fa real I promise you this one is not like that. He actually likes your stuck up ass."

Katie was far from stuck up. She just wasn't interested in going out with the guys Unique tried to hook her up with.

"Hol' up Nique what do you mean he like me? who in the hell have you been discussing me too?"

Their attention was drawn to a soft knock at the door.

"It's open," Katie yelled. Her sister Anita poked her head in the door, "Unique you have company downstairs."

"Unique who the hell did you bring to my house?!"

"Well, I figured you wouldn't agree to go out with him so I invited him over so you could personally tell him yourself," she smirked jumping up off the bed running to the door. Katie immediately jumped up pulling her scarf from her head.

"Y'know for someone who acts like she doesn't want to meet him you sure don't act like it. I'll send him to come up."

"Unique I'm goin' to kill you!" she said launching a pillow at her just before she closed the door.

Katie crinkled locks fell just past her shoulders she slipped into a pair of comfortable pajama pants and a wife beater. She nervously checked herself out in the mirror before answering the tap at her door.

"Come in." Katie was surprised to see Fray walk through her bedroom door. Although he was dressed in all black like a gangsta she still found him very attractive.

"Oh, god not you again." she giggled. Fray was taken aback by her reply his smile slowly faded.

"Not who you were expectin'?" Fray said.

"Oh, I didn't mean it like that. I'm jus' glad I didn't turn around and you were directly behind me."

"I see you got jokes. I told you I was sorry about that."

Katie couldn't help but blush, Fray was exceptionally handsome.

"How about we start over? I'm Fray," he smiled extending his hand.

PRESSURE BUST PIPES

"Katie."

She said playing along softly shaking his hand. And just like their first encounter when Fray found it hard to let go of her text book her hand was no different. He was mesmerized by her beauty.

"You can let go now," she snickered.

"Oh, my bad," he said embarrassed. "I'm sorry for poppin' up on you like this, but I had to see you again. I know we don't know each other very well, but ever since that day, it's been hard for me not think about you. I don't want to live with any regrets and not asking you out would be one of them."

Katie was impressed by his mannerism she felt her hormones rising. When she finally mustered up the correct words to say Unique interrupted her yet again with Ashley trailing her.

"How are you two love birds getting along?"

She teased causing Katie to cut her eye at her.

"Pardon our intrusion, but Derek jus' called he said it's important," Ashley said.

Fray retrieved his cell phone from his ski pants pocket two missed calls from Derek displayed on the screen, he looked up at Katie.

"You never answered my question, Ms. Katie. Will you go out with me?"

All eyes seemed to rest on Katie as Unique mouthed yes quietly in the background.

"Sure I'll go out with you…,"

THE SETUP

Bike week was held annually in Myrtle Beach, S.C. Attracting
hundreds of spectators from all over. Live store fronts, women in
bikinis, and plenty of intoxicated people participated. Motorcycles
took over the city as bikers showed off doing tricks up and down
the strip while being cheered on by men and women. It looked like
a Ruff Ryders convention. The sun was blazing out when a thick
red-bone made her way down Ocean Drive. She jogged at a steady
pace. Her white sports bra matched her turquoise leggings that
clung to her crotch area displaying her camel toe. She was built like
a Straight Stutin' vixen she jogged past a small group of bikers
making eye contact with one. The bikers looked on in admiration
when the one she chose got off his bike, placed it on the kick stand
and went after her. The woman was a 5'9" Amazon what she lacked
in looks her body made up for it.

"Damn, shawty slow up!" Said the biker.

The woman stopped and began to jog in place, as she watched him play catch up she noticed he was out of shape and could barely breathe.

"Damn, baby you tryna kill a nigga out here in this heat." He wheezed.

"You don't work out much I see," she said placing her sunglasses on her face.

"Well, I guess that's why I ride a bike."

"You're not from around these parts are you?"

Her southern accent was sweet and sexy.

"Naw baby I'm from D.C," he said watching the sweat roll off her breast.

"Oh, how I would love to go to the city! the country is all I know!"

"Is that right," he smiled with a cunning look on his face. He began to envision himself deep inside her country pussy.

"Well, that could be arranged, sweetheart. Put my number in your phone and save it under Broadway, and what's your name?"

The tall, slender light-skinned gentleman came off as cocky. From the sound of his voice, it was obvious he smoked plenty of cigarettes in his lifetime.

"Oh I'm Anna-Mae," she flirted paying full attention to the diamond bezel Cartier on his wrist.

Next week couldn't have come fast enough, Broadway wasted no time flying Anna-Mae to the city. He sat parked outside in his white Lexus in the back of his honeycomb hideout. The Tyler

House had its share of crime which is why the property manager hired security officers. Still, the high rise back entrance was almost always unguarded. The two had spent all weekend together, however, getting in Anna-Mae's draws wasn't as easy as he thought. Anna-Mae head was spinning from the Vodka she consumed at the bar.

"That's it no more martinis for you," Broadway drunkenly laughed as he helped her from the car. He slung his MCM book bag over his shoulder staggering toward the building with Anna-Mae. His hands were all over her curvaceous figure. Anna-Mae's drunken laughter echoed throughout the narrow halls as Broadway stuck his key in the door. The smell of PCP slapped them in the face as soon as they crossed the threshold. Anna-Mae heard movement signifying they were not alone. Gino and Mousey looked up from the dining room table upon hearing the door open. A gallon of PCP and empty vial bottles was scattered along the rectangular table.

"Hol' what the fuck you doin'! Who is this bitch!"

Gino scrunched up his face jumping up from his chair.

"Man, she a'ight. She wit' me," Broadway slurred placing the book bag at their feet. He and Anna-Mae then stumbled down the hall to the back room.

"Fucks up wit' your man?" Gino frowned.

"Slim, chill. Her country ass don't know nobody." Mousey replied.

Meanwhile, three gunmen sat casing the back entrance of the building in a tinted Crown Victoria. They watched Broadway enter the building with his female acquaintance minutes earlier. Hulk didn't have to say a word he simply pulled the drawstrings on his black hooded sweatshirt masking his bald tattoo head. His tattoos served as a constant reminder of the victims who had fallen prey to his gun over the years. After winning several cases in the court of law, the media dubbed him as the "Undertaker."

They slipped from the car making their way towards the back of the building each one wearing all black. Entering the poorly lit building they drew their guns and moved silently up the cast iron steps. Bullet and Chucky took up the opposite sides of the door of apartment 211. Hulk pressed his ear to the door listening for sound, and movement the television was loud he carefully turned the doorknob it was locked. He gave a hand signal signaling it was locked. They discreetly made their way back down the stairs and out the building. It was time for plan B.

The trio now peered inside the open trunk of their Crown Vic, replacing their hooded sweatshirts with chain badges, blue and yellow DEA hats and tactical vests. Gino had just sealed the last cap on the vial bottle when Mousey dumped the stacks of money from the book bag onto the table. Bullet and Chucky took up their same positions at the door while Hulk chambered a slug into the Mossberg.

"Police!

They yelled storming the apartment. Gino and Mousey were caught off guard neither of them went for their guns on top of the table.

"You hear sumthin'?"

Broadway jerked his head upward from Anna-Mae's wet pussy.

"Um…mm don't stop," she moaned trying to force his head back down. He stopped her in midstride swatting her hand away. He stood up yanking the door open. Mousey and Gino laid face down flexi cuffed on the carpet. They swung their guns in

Broadway's direction he instantly put his hands in the air.

"Damn! It took y'all long enough. I thought I was gonna' have to fuck that nigga," Joyce frowned pulling her pants up emerging from the back room. Her country accent was gone.

"Sorry cuz. We had to improvise," Hulk said waving his gun kissing her on the cheek. It was at that moment Broadway sobered up. Rage filled his body knowing he had just been set up. Unknowingly, it was all a set up stemming from bike week. Outside of running a salon, Joyce made a living by setting up drug dealers for her cousin Hulk.

"Go wait for us in the car," Hulk said

Joyce knew it would be the last time she would see the men alive she took one last look at a helpless Broadway and winked. Bullet, Hulk, and Chucky bagged the money and drugs up in no time. The three gagged men squirmed on the floor already knowing what was next to come. On Bullet's command, all three gunmen raised their gun firing rapidly. The sun was just starting to tuck itself behind the clouds when the trio made their way back to their car. They spotted a police cruiser heading in their direction.

"Hey Harry, looks like some of our guys," said the officer in the passenger seat as he took in the DEA attire.

"You think they could use a hand?" Harry asked.

Without warning, the trio raised their guns upward. All hell broke loose! They showered the squad car with bullets.

"Jeezus. Get the hell outta' here Harry!"

The officer ducked his head under the dashboard while his partner frantically reversed the car screeching away from the scene...

The money machine hummed in the background as Fray and Fat Derek wrapped rubber bands around thousands of dollars placing them in neat stacks. The twosome sat in the cramped living room of Momma Gee's hot one-bedroom apartment. Every Saturday morning, she would make pancakes and scrambled eggs.

"What'chu got somethin' to do or sumthin?" Derek asked curiously as he observed Fray checking his watch every five minutes. Rolls of fat hung from the sides of his wife beater. Derek was brown skin, bald head with a round face. Standing at six-feet tall he weighed over three hundred pounds. Fray didn't notice his anxiousness was evident.

"Kind of. Man, to keep it all the way one hun'nid with you I'm s'posed to be going out wit' this lil broad this afternoon. Not that I'm tryna duck out on you or anything, but I was tryna run home right quick and change."

"Ah, I see," Derek smiled moving his head up and down. "Jus' when I was startin' to worry about you. In this lifestyle, all hustle and no play can become stressful. Well look, go 'head and enjoy yourself I can handle this right here. You jus' make sure I meet this young lady who's able to get your ass off the block even if it is just for a few hours." He chuckled. "As a matter of fact, here…take the keys to my truck, you want to impress her right?"

"Naw, I'm good. I got my Lincoln, plus I don't think this girl is caught up on materialistic things."

"Bull-shit. Every woman has a price remember that," Derek said passing him the keys.

"You sure you got this?" Fray asked fixing to leave.

"Yeah, I got it but, you might want to tell Gee that you'll be missin' breakfast."

Fray's first stop was the florist shop he purchased two dozen of long-stem red roses, his next stop was home. Katie soaked her petite frame in a hot bubble bath while the sun rays crept through the shutters. She fondled with her firm nipples while squeezing soap suds from a loofah onto her 34DD's. Boys to Men "On Bended Knee" filled the air. She closed her eyes picturing Fray inside her. She slowly moved her hand past her stomach, bypassing her neatly trimmed pubic hairs slipping her finger inside her now moist vagina. A soft moan escaped her lips. It had been nine months since she was touched by a man. Just as she was feeling the urge to climax her phone rang ruining it.

"What is it! She yelled, answering the phone.

"Who called and pissed you off this morning?"

Unique's voice came to alive on the other end.

"What do you want this early in the damn morning Nique"

"Well aren't you in a shitty mood. You must be tired of getting your rocks off wit' that rubber dick." She joked.

"Bitch fuck you!" I know the next thing that comes outta your mouth betta' be why you're calling so damn early or I'm hanging up!" Katie hated when Unique made fun of her celibacy.

"Damn, Kee it's not that serious. I was calling to make sure you didn't oversleep. What time did Fray say he was coming again?"

Katie pulled her phone away from her ear looking at the time, it was 10:30am Fray would be there in two hours.

"I have more than enough time to get ready is that all you wanted?" Katie asked annoyed.

"Nope, it's not. Guess who showed up at my door last night?"

Unique said excitedly.

"Who Unique," Katie said nonchalantly knowing it was to many to choose from.

"Girl, Bullet. He came home the other night I was so surprised!" The more Unique talked about Bullet the more Katie became irritated with Unique's conversation. Katie rolled her eyes in her head, Bullet was Unique's on and off boyfriend for years when he wasn't locked up or with other women. Whenever Bullet decided he wanted to break Unique's heart Katie was always there to console her. There were times when he would try to manipulate Unique and turn her against Katie, which is why Katie hated him.

"So, what about Ashley?" Katie asked.

"Katie, don't start okay. You already know Bullet is my heart, so if Ashley doesn't like it he could step the fuck off, but how I see it I could benefit from them both, so, therefore, I'm going to continue to fuck them both ain't no shame in my game."
Katie shook her head at her friend's disposition. Unique had always had that attitude. It didn't matter how many flings or one night stands she encountered Bullet was always her number one.

"Nique, I gotta go. I'll call you later." she disconnected the call sinking further into the water.

Fray guided the silver Range Rover Sport down, Downing street making a right on 15th street. The area looked different now that the old projects had been torn down and remodeled. Fray was still finding it hard to believe that Katie actually grew up in the projects. It was the way she carried herself that was different from your average project chick. However, he wondered if the good girl persona she put on was a front, he parked in the first empty spot.

Katie stood in front of the rectangular mirror in the bathroom pulling bobby pins from her hair. She then dabbed herself with

Paris Hilton's fragrance perfume. She rocked a white t-shirt with the late rapper Tupac on it in red, dark denim Levi stretch jeans, and some cheetah print stilettos. The vibration from her cell phone on the dresser pulled her attention away from her admiration of herself in the mirror. Fray's name flashed across the screen seconds later she was grabbing her red clutch heading out the door.

Katie's caramel skin stepped out onto the porch drawing stares from the surrounding hustlers. Everything seemed to stop as she pulled her house door closed. Over the years, the neighborhood guys watched Katie grow from a shy pretty young thing into a sexy voluptuous woman, but her appeal didn't just stop there. From her independence, humbleness, and light-hearted demeanor the low-key cutie next door had grown into a banger. Fray sat watching Katie turn heads as she looked around in efforts to locate him. She looked so innocent, he smiled to himself before getting out the truck grabbing the roses. His taste in clothes always meshed well together. Sporting a short-sleeve white Gucci polo shirt with the signature colors on the collar, white linen pants, low-cut Gucci sneakers and the platinum Rolex Derek had given him on his eighteenth birthday. Katie wasn't expecting him to bring flowers she lowered her head in bashfulness as she approached.

"You look nice," Fray smiled pecking her on her cheek handing her the roses.

"Thanks so do you," She smiled walking around to the passenger door.

"Wait, let me get that for you," Fray walked around opening the door for her, helping her inside the truck.

"Are you always this charming?" Katie asked.

"Honestly no. I never had anyone special in my life until now."

Katie's heart fluttered as she searched for a response.

"Boy, whatever I bet you tell all the girls that."

"I don't know about any other girls, but what I do know is the only one that's worthy enough is sitting right here," he placed his hand on top of hers.

Katie embraced his touch. Fray was definitely a smooth talker and quick with his tongue.

"So where are we headed?" Katie asked kindly.

"I was thinkin' we could hit the harbor and then shoot over to Moe's afterward. That is if you like seafood?" he said bearing left onto New York Avenue. Katie turned the radio up relaxing in her seat.

"I'll take that as a yes." He said looked over at her smiling.

The hotel's headboard squeaked as its occupants put it to use.

"Take this dick bitch, take it!"

Derek had Isis face buried in the pillows as he pounded her from the back. His three hundred plus pounds dripped with sweat.

"Ah… Yes, fuck me you fat muthafucka!"

Isis moaned throwing her ass back. The two had been going at it like wild animals for the past ten minutes, Derek's body tensed up just as he was about to cum. She scooted away from his grasp causing his dick to slip out of her. She turned around and lowered herself before him cuffing his balls and groping his swollen dick that was covered in her juices, she looked up at him and started deep throating him, sucking him dry. Derek's body stiffened. With his eyes closed tightly he exploded in her mouth. After catching his breath, he laid down and was fast asleep.

PRESSURE BUST PIPES

Isis was Ashley's first cousin they grew up together, and against her cousin wishes, she continued to see Derek behind his back. Though she would never call Derek her man the two got together often. Derek's obnoxious snoring was earsplitting as Isis pretended to be asleep. She eased her body from underneath his tiptoeing in the direction of Derek's jeans that was draped across the chair. Just like always she searched through his pockets whenever he was sound asleep. Without warning, the ringing of his cell phone in his pocket had awakened him.

"What the hell you doing!"

Derek was enraged at what he saw. At the sound of his voice Isis's heart raced, dropping his pants to the floor she turned around. She looked frightened.

"I... I...I was jus' lookin' for my panties." She stammered.

"In my pockets!" He boasted. "Y'know I ain't the smartest man in the world, but to me, it looks like you were jus' stealin'."

"Naw, baby you got it all wrong. I would never do that to you," she began to plead.

"Oh yeah, well what's that hangin' from your bra?"

She didn't have enough time to stuff the money all the way in her bra. Derek rose from the bed charging in her direction.

LOVE IS LOYALTY

Laughter could be heard throughout the Baltimore Harbor as citizens walked hand in hand with their loved ones chasing after their kids. Numerous of stores lined the port, The Baltimore Aquarium was their first stop. It was Katie's first time, she pointed out everything to Fray pulling him along the way she was ecstatic. Even though Fray had been before he still enjoyed the visit just as much as she did. The peach colored sun appeared to be sitting on top of the water as Fray peddled the white swan boat. Katie was hesitant at first to climb aboard due to her fear of not knowing how to swim. However, Fray eased her mind by telling her he would never let anything happen to her if she was to fall over he was coming in after her. She sat next to him tossing bread to the wandering ducks. Fray stopped pedaling allowing the boat to float on the waves.

"So what's the deal with you and Unique?" He turned facing her. "I mean cause y'all definitely are nothing alike," Katie smiled hunching her shoulders. She was use to being questioned about her and Unique's friendship.

"Unique's a good person Fray. Yes, she has ways that I don't agree with, but I'm quite sure you don't always agree with your friend's choices either. So despite what people may think about our friendship she has always been there for me."

"So your loyalty to her is what keeps the glue. I can dig that." Fray said nodding his head as a family of ducks swam by.

"Do you have a favorite place to go?" Fray asked

"Yes, I love to go to Haines Point and watch the planes land. So, Mr. Fray. It seems I been telling you about myself all day, and I hardly learned a thing about you."

"What would you like to know?"

"Well you can start by telling me what's with the beard, is it some kind of fashion statement or sumthin?"

Fray chuckled at her remark.

"I'm Muslim."

"Oh! Sorry, I didn't know that," Katie said embarrassed.

"I'll cut it if you don't like it." Fray gave a half smile.

"*Oh God no!* That's your faith. I couldn't ask you to do that. I actually like it. Are your parents Muslim too?"

Fray's smile immediately vanished.

"Did I say something wrong?" Katie asked unsurely.

"No, you didn't. It's jus' that whenever the topic of my parents come up I get emotional."

Katie reached over touching the side of his face.

"If you don't wanna talk about it, you don't have to."

"It's a'ight. My pops is servin' twenty years in prison on a drug conspiracy, and as for my mother," his voice trailed off. "She's a college professor at Southeastern University."

"I don't understand. If she's a professor, why the long face? At least, you have one of your parents to be proud of. I lost both of my parents when I was young."

"I'm sorry to hear that," Fray said with sympathy.

Silence lingered between the two.

"I haven't spoken to my mother in over a year."

"Can I ask why?"

Fray looked at her and sighed.

"She gave me an ultimatum. Either I leave the streets alone or I could no longer stay underneath her roof."

"So let me get this straight. You chose the streets over the woman who birthed you?"

"Kee, you don't understand. After my pops went to prison we lost our house and had to move back to the hood, at that time more bills than money was coming in, and then my mom's work hours were cut back shortly after. I really had no choice it was either hustle out here on these streets or live on them."

"No offense Fray, but what you're telling me right now have me second guessing you. If you're willing to put the streets before the woman who carried you for nine months what makes me any different?"

Fray took her by the hand and looked her dead in the eyes,

"Because I won't..."

"Isis, what the fuck happened to your face, and where the hell is your car?!" Ashley scowled her after noticing the gash underneath her eye and scratches around her neck. After delivering the beating Derek took her car keys leaving her stranded at the hotel, with no one else to call she called her cousin to come pick her up. Had she had other means of getting home her cousin would've never been called.

"We're not pullin' off until you tell me what the hell happened."

"Ashley jus' leave it alone. I don't wanna talk about it okay?"

As much as Isis wanted to tell her cousin the truth she feared for his life had he stepped to Derek wrong. What she didn't know was her cousin wasn't her little cousin anymore his gun was now going off in the streets.

"Jus' leave it alone!" He repeated. *Man, do you hear yourself? You're my cousin more like my sister, ain't no nigga out here gon' be puttin' his hands on you. With that being said I'm goin' to ask you one more fuckin time who put their hands on you!"*

Isis put her hands to her face and began sobbing heavily.

"It...it was Derek..."

The night was pleasant with the temperature just right Fray and Katie walked hand in hand conversing. After accompanying Katie inside the truck, he now sat on the driver side looking in his phone twenty missed calls displayed on his screen. The majority of the missed calls were from Ashley, and the rest of them were from the crew as he continued to scroll two of them were from Derek. He decided he would call them back after he dropped Katie off, he started the engine. After leaving the harbor he and Katie shot over to Moe's to get something to eat before getting back on the road.

When Fray looked over Katie's head was pressed against the window Kem's soothing voice had put her to sleep. Throughout the ride, he stole glimpses of her while she slept. He pulled up in front of her house and put the car in park. He looked over at the sleeping beauty beside him he knew then that he would protect her heart forever.

"Wake up sleepy head," he pulled on one of her locks softly, he blushed. Katie sat up straight glancing at the digital clock on the dashboard it was 9:00 pm. She was saddened the night was over so soon with a forced smile she said, "I really enjoyed myself tonight Fray."

"Sweetheart, the best is yet to come." He reached over squeezing her thigh, followed by an unexpected kiss. Twenty minutes later Fray was pulling around D Street. The neighborhood was a ghost town. Just as he was about to pick up his phone and call Ashley he spotted Ronnie standing underneath the porch light of his grandmother's house. Fray then made a right turn and started backing into an empty parking space. He quickly slammed on brakes when a shadow moved swiftly behind him.

"Fuckin' cats," he said aloud then proceeded to park the truck. Crickets chirped as he planted his feet on the pavement. He watched Ronnie recklessly make hand gestures as if he was a referee.

"Hol, hol, hol y'all dats Fray!" he yelled from across the street. Perplexed, Fray looked back to see just who Ronnie was talking to.

He soon realized that the bolting shadow in the back of the truck had been no other than Ashley, as he crept around the truck with a mac-11. As if on cue DeShay popped up from behind two aluminum trash cans getting his attention as well. Judging by the bulkiness in his shirt he guessed his cousin packed a handgun with a thirty round clip. The fear of knowing how close to death he was sent chills through his body. The duo dressed in all black while Ronnie played decoy.

"Damn Fray, what'chu doin' wit this nigga's truck? We almost killed your ass!" Ashley barked tucking the mac-11 in the front of his pants. Ronnie walked over joining them.

"Would somebody tell me what the hell is going on?" Fray asked looking at each of one them.

"You ain't get none of my messages? I was tryna reach you all day. Where that bitch ass nigga Derek at?"

"Why whassup?" Fray asked confused.

"Because I'm a crush that nigga. He put his hands on my cousin today, not only does she have a black eye he took her car and left her stranded."

Fray knew this day would come from the moment he caught Derek sneaking around with Isis it was an accident waiting to happen. Looking at his friends he knew what time it was murder was all they had in mind. He shook his head at the predicament he was placed in as he tried to come up with a solution.

"What did Isis say happened?" Fray asked.

"He accused her of stealing."

It was no secret amongst the foursome that Isis was a cold-blooded thief, so they knew Derek's accusation could have very well been true.

"Well did she," Fray asked.

PRESSURE BUST PIPES

"It doesn't matter if she did or not!" Ashley snapped. "Look, I'm not askin' for your permission to handle my business holmes, I was simply puttin' you on point because I know this nigga been like a father to you. Fray this nigga then crossed the line one too many times." He pointed to Ronnie's face. "And now this? Slim, like it or not he's got to be dealt with, and if you're worrying about losin' the connect our man Ronnie may have stumbled across sumthin' better." He smirked.

DeShay and Ronnie remained silent for the duration of the conversation. It seemed as if his friends had already made their minds up.

"Slim, my baby mother's aunt introduced me to the man today! Ronnie said amped. "Fray when I say this nigga got that paper, this nigga got it fa real."

Teresa was Ronnie's girlfriend from around the way.

"And Derek ain't fuckin' wit em." DeShay chimed in.

"Fray I know you're tired of being bird fed, which I know Shay and Ashley are I say we go ahead and knock your man off, and go into business with the Jamaicans," Ronnie said dapping up DeShay and Ashley.

Fray saw a war brewing if they tried to wipe Derek out the picture and missed.

"I understand y'all eagerness, but what y'all asking me to do right now is compromise my loyalty that's jus' sumthin' I can't do."

"What! Isis ain't family no more?" Ashley questioned with an attitude.

"C'mon Ashley man I would never say that."

"So what are you sayin' then Fray?"

"All I'm sayin' is give me some time to think things over, and in the meantime, I'll get your cousin's car back."

Ashley wanted to object but Ronnie interrupted him not wanting to cause any more confusion.

"You got it brah," Ronnie said slapping a five with Fray pulling him in for a hug. Fray began to walk to the truck, as soon as he opened the door he heard Ashley call out to him.

"Fray. Don't take too long homie cause this thing goin' down one way or another."

"You're back early," Unique said cradling the phone to her ear.

"Well, what did you expect for me to pull one of your moves and give up the coochie on the first night," Katie's laughter filled the other end of the receiver as she undressed. She couldn't wait to get back to fill Unique in on all the juicy details from her night.

"Oh, you got jokes huh? Well, at least, one of us is gettin' the real deal out here your life, on the other hand, revolves around vibrating dicks." Unique fired back.

"Unique you're a bitch I hope you know that," Katie sucked her teeth.

"You started it. So how was your day anyway?" Unique asked.

Katie smiled when she thought of Fray. She blushed all over again. She began to tell Unique all about her electrifying night making sure she didn't leave anything out.

"I'm so happy for you now you can finally get some real dick and act normal." Unique joked. "I'm just kidding girl lighten up but, I have some not so good news. Guess who I ran into at the mall today? Pebblez and Gigi bitch," Unique said answering her own question. Pebblez and Gigi were old friends of Unique's.

PRESSURE BUST PIPES

Between Unique and the girls, there was an eight-year age difference. They took a young Unique under the wing when she was fifteen. They were the roots of Unique's gold digging ways and fast lifestyle. It wasn't long after that the two had her clubbing, smoking, drinking, and dating older men for materialistic things.

Pebblez and Gigi played major roles in several divorces. Their reputation spoke for itself you had to have deep pockets in order to date one of them. It wasn't unusual to run into the pair dining at an elegant restaurant or spot them parading around known social events. Their model looks and video body's had every hustler chasing after them showering them with expensive gifts from foreign luxury vehicles, Chanel bags, condominiums, and out of town trips. The women had their way in the early nineties that is until they were exposed for their deceitful ways. As an end result, they were forced to acquire their means elsewhere.

Gigi started stripping in nightclubs, Pebblez wasn't willing to settle for less she took her gold digging schemes out of town where she landed in Houston Texas. One evening she returned home to find her boyfriend Jose' lying face down on the carpet in a pool of blood his throat had been slit from ear to ear. She immediately rushed upstairs only to find his safe empty. Besides a few rare diamonds, her designer wardrobe, and Benz wagon, she returned back to D.C with nothing.

"Kee, I don't even have to tell you how scandalous those bitches are. I found out the hard way by trusting their crutty asses in the same room with Bullet."

Pebblez and Gigi hooked Unique up with Bullet but fail to mention Gigi had been sleeping with Bullet beforehand. Their fling abruptly came to an end when Unique returned home from work early one afternoon. A woman's moans could be heard coming from the bedroom. Gigi wasn't bothered by Unique's presence in the doorway. In fact, she thought Unique was going to join them beings though she and Unique had their own sexual encounter. Unique was infuriated at what she saw she rushed over to the bed delivering an ass whooping to Gigi. Unique felt like Pebblez knew about the infidelity that was going on behind her back she cut off all communication with her as well.

"I'm confused. What does running back into Pebblez and Gigi have to do wit me again?" Katie asked.

Unique sat quite for a few seconds as she contemplated if she should tell her or not.

"Katie, I told myself that I wasn't gon' say nothin', but seeing that you fellin' ol' boy I'm jus' gon come out and say it. Did your lil prince charming mention he has a secret admirer that jus' so happen to be Pebblez?"

Katie felt a lump in her throat as she swallowed hard. Just when she thought Unique couldn't ruin her night she sprung the unthinkable.

"Girl, I overheard Gigi telling Pebblez how she accompanied Fray and one of his friends to the All-Star game last year in L.A. She then went on to say how Fray was doing his thing out here, and that she thought him and Pebblez should meet. I hope I didn't t mess up your night wit' all this?"

Katie downplayed the situation masking her true feelings, the two women conversed for another five minutes before disconnecting. Katie now lay awake in her bed wondering if she could trust Fray.

PEBBLEZ & GIGI

A celebration was taking place at the 1st district police precinct as officers chanted, clapped, and pumped their fist in the air patting the super-cop on his back as he walked down the aisle. The hardnosed detective didn't know whether to smile or take a bow so he maintained his game face. Detective Joseph Harrison also known as Joe wasn't your ordinary cop. His signature look was an unfaded-bold cut, gauges in both ears, vintage t-shirts, jeans ripped at the knees and chains hanging from his belt. There were times when he would wear a sleeveless black leather rag & bone motorcycle vest with trooper boots. He looked more like an outlaw breaking the rules rather than a cop upholding it. His biker attire created a mix-up every time he showed up to investigate a crime scene. Despite his delinquent looks, Joe was the best detective

MPD had ever seen.

The chatter ceased as captain Burnette swung his office door open sticking his pudgy frame in its threshold.

"Joe, in my office…now!" He ordered.

"You wanted to see me cap."

Joe tapped on the open door making his way in, closing the door behind him. Burnette was hunched over his desk with both his palms flat on his desk.

"You got damn right I wanted to see you. Joe, please tell me how you managed to destroy half a city block?"

"Cap. I can assure you that the street was under construction all week."

"Do I look like I'm in the mood for games?"

"No sir." Joe said.

"Well wipe that stupid grin off your face."

"Sorry, sir."

"Son, do you even have a brain functioning up there?"

Joe cocked his head to the side waiting for an answer.

"I beg your pardon?" Joe said unsure of what he was asking.

"Joe, did you really have to send your Harley Davidson crashing through the bank's window?" Burnette said.

"Sir, the suspect left me no choice. He took hostages threatening to kill them so it was either act now or start doing a body count."

Burnette cringed at Joe's cowboy antics. He had to admit if it hadn't been for Joe reacting when he did the bank robber would have gotten away. Although, Joe was a pain in his rectum the thought of firing him never crossed his mind. He knew Joe was a good cop. Gangsters and hustlers knew whenever he was around the streets were no longer safe.

DC JAIL...

"Pascal!"

Frank had just stepped out the shower with his shower shoes and towel wrapped around him when he heard his last name being called. He walked over to the female correctional officer.

"You have a visit." She said.

Frank took the pass from her and proceeded down the tier to his cell. It took him ten minutes to get ready before heading out the block. He was called back to the jail by a friend on a writ he was now able to see his son for the first time in five years. During his incarceration, he heard all about his son's hustling activities. The thought of his son following in his footsteps pained him. Just about every day he argued with his wife about Fray's drastic change, and what she was doing to prevent it. He spotted Fray in the waiting area of the visiting hall. Fray cracked a smile upon seeing his old man, he took a seat in front of the Plexiglas.

"Assalam alaykum," Fray said into the phone.

"Wa Alaikum Salaam son. How long you been waiting?"

Fray couldn't help but smile showing all 32 teeth. He was beyond nervous.

"It's no big deal I'm good pop."

"Are you really?"

Frank's question threw him for a loop, and it showed in his facial expression.

"Your mother tells me the two of you haven't spoken in a year. Care to share?"

Fray lowered his head unable to meets his father's eyes. Frank didn't stop there he continued with the next question.

"I hear you in the streets now. Who you workin' for…Derek?"

Fray got wide-eyed upon hearing Derek's name. He had no idea his father knew about him hustling in the streets. Frank felt himself getting worked up at the thought of Derek putting drugs in his son's hand, had it not been for his religion the beast in him would've been touched, Derek.

"Fray look at me." He waited until his son's eyes met his before he continued. "Son this is not the life for you. You're probably thinking your gonna learn from my mistakes, and master the game. Well, I'm here to tell you there is no mastering the game. There's always going to be people who envy you, and just when you think you got it all figured out some new bullshit is thrown in the game. You will without a doubt lose a major part of yourself in those streets."

"Oh yeah, well what did you lose dad?"

"My family," Frank responded bluntly.

Fray had just wiped the last tear when the elevator doors opened on the 1st floor. He checked out the suffocating prison by exchanging his visitor pass for his I.D. His father ended the visit with a warning message for Derek and ordering him to fix things with his mother. When Fray opened the door to his car his phone had just stopped ringing, checking it, seconds later a voicemail message popped up, that's something Derek rarely done. He pressed 1 listening carefully to Derek's recorded message marked urgent telling him to meet him downtown at Ruth Cris. Right away Fray's antennas went up, he hoped his friends didn't try to retaliate on Derek and failed. With paranoia getting the best of him he figured his life was in danger. He removed his twenty-one-shot Colt .45 from underneath his seat and placed it on his lap, started the engine, and pressed down on the accelerator.

The restaurant was crowded. Derek checked his watch for the third time since his arrival, he had been waiting on Fray when he spotted a waiter ushering two familiar faces in his direction.

"I'm sorry to interrupt your sir, but are these two women with you?" The waiter asked.

Derek chuckled to himself. Pebblez and Gigi were still up to their old tricks. There was a two-hour waiting window and there was no way the duo was going to stand around and wait. They spotted Derek sitting alone from the door.

"It's okay there with me," Derek said shooing the waiter away. "Look at you two still up to your old tricks."

"Derek we hope were not disturbing anything, but it's been a year since Pebblez had Ruth Cris spinach dip."

"It's okay, I was jus' waitin' on my lil man to come join me, and as a matter of fact, I haven't eaten myself."

Fray pulled around the corner from the restaurant his right hand still gripped around the chrome .45. He stuffed the gun in his waist before slipping from the car making his way to the front entrance. The restaurant was jammed pack when he entered, Derek had chosen a table in the back facing the door so he could see everyone coming and going. He immediately signaled for Fray to come over and join him and his two lovely guests. Fray seemed a little uneasy about the women's presence, Gigi recognized him from the All-Star game last year in Philly. Fray cut his eyes over to the pretty faced, dimple-cheek, cinnamon complected woman wearing her natural hair in kinky Erykah Badu inspired afro. Derek broke his blatant admiration of her.

"Fray this gorgeous thing here is Pebblez, you already met Gigi."

At 5'5" with tight abs and a combination of petite yet dangerous curves in all the right places, Pebblez was a bad bitch in a hood sense. Judging by her expensive jewelry and expensive apparel Fray got the idea she was definitely high-maintenance. With time, she was just as fine, although she didn't look her age, her persona signified a seasoned vet. Fray acknowledged the two women with a nod before pulling his seat up to the table.

"It's nice seeing you again Fray," Gigi smiled sipping her wine. Silence filled the air. "We'll y'all excuse us while we go to the lady's room," Pebblez said getting Gigi attention. Gigi hesitated before getting up following suit.

"Why didn't you tell me he was a teenager," Pebblez said heatedly, fixing her mascara in the mirror.

"It's not like I'm askin' you to marry him. Girl this might be what you need. I'm tellin' you with a little guidance you can mold him into the man you want him to be. And besides how many nineteen-year-olds you know rock a presidential?"

Pebblez had to admit the boy looked like he was getting it. With that thought alone and Gigi persuasion, her mindset was already cashing in on the young Fray.

"Girl, I can't believe you got me all the way back up here to turn me into a cougar." Pebblez laughed.

Fray wondered what the hell was taking Katie so long as he stared through the obscured balcony glass in his spacious one-bedroom apartment. The storm had intensified; he was beginning to wonder if she had changed her mind about coming. Since their first date, the two had become inseparable. Fray would sometimes meet her at her job to have lunch, or simply pop up just to ask her how her day was going. Fray tried advancing her on several occasions only to be turned down. Katie told him she had been celibate for almost a year, and wanted to make sure what they had was real before pursuing sex. Frustrated, Fray had no other choice but to respect it, it wasn't every day a woman his age went a year without sex.

There were moments when he didn't know how much longer he could hold out with all the advances Pebblez was making daily. Fray's own celibacy was becoming harder to control. A knock at the door startled him. He looked over the preparations then himself one last time before answering the door.

"You gon' jus' stand there or let me in?" Katie blushed pushing her wet locks from her face shaking off the excess water. No matter how many times Fray saw her he still couldn't get over how beautiful she was, he stepped aside so that she could enter. Scented vanilla candles were the only source of light in the apartment. Changing Faces song (Do You Mind If I Stroke You Up) played softly in the background. Dinner plates and glasses set for two sat neatly on the dinner table. One glass was filled with Welcher's grape juice and the other Sangria wine.

"Babe you cooked!"

Katie smiled as he took off her coat. Once seated she saw that he prepared pink salmon, broccoli & cheese laid over a bed of mix rice, and a bottle of honey was on the table that she eyed suspiciously, right away Fray picked up on her curiosity.

"I like my fish sweet." He smirked.

After digging into their meals and great conversation things started to heat up between them. Fray had his hand underneath Katie's shirt fondling her breast as they kissed passionately. He attempted to use his weight to push her back gently while he unbuckled her pants.

"Hold up…wait not like this." She said, pushing him off. Fray exhaled out of frustration he dreaded those three words.

"Are you mad?" Katie asked.

"What'chu think." He snapped looking over at her. "Kee, it's been six months, I don't know what else I gotta do to prove to you that sex is not all that I want."

"Fray I jus' need some-."

"Time." He said finishing her sentence for her. "Look let's jus' enjoy the rest of the night.

"Baby don't be like that," Katie said feeling guilty.

"Don't be like what!" He frowned turning his attention back to the television. She picked up her oversized duffle bag and stormed in the direction of the bathroom. Katie returned a short time afterward only to find Fray sliding the balcony door close as the rain blew inside. He heard her when she entered the room, his intentions were to turn around and apologize when her soft voice beat him to the punch.

"Come show me how frustrated you are."

Fray's eyes widened when he turned around seeing Katie half naked, barefooted in an edible-skittles bra & thong set. She and Unique found the sexy lingerie while surfing the internet and thought it was perfect for the occasion. He was pleased to know he had been bamboozled in a good way. This was the moment he had been waiting for as he speedily walked over to her, kissing her neck, and palming her ass. Katie wrapped her arms around his neck when she felt herself getting wet, she let out a soft moan. Her five foot two stature peered up to his five- eleven frame.

"You wanna see if I taste better than a rainbow?" she whispered seductively in his ear.

"You damn right I do."

He pushed the skittle thong aside slipping his finger inside her hot wet pussy while nibbling on her earlobe. He was erect and breathing heavily. He kissed her neck down to her stomach, getting on his knees placing her right leg over his shoulder all while fingering her, he slipped another finger inside her. He rested his forehead on her stomach while he listened to how wet her pussy was as his fingers went in and out of her. Katie pressed his head further into her soft skin as she rocked onto his fingers out of pleasure. She leaned her head back and began to moan louder. Fray pulled his fingers out slowly, he noticed thick white creamy cum on his fingers. He ripped the candy thongs off her sending skittles flying everywhere. He kissed her set of pussy lips before tongue kissing her clitoris. He then parted her pussy lips spreading them apart exposing her pink wet pussy. He tickled her clit with his tongue.

"Mm oh." Katie moaned louder this time. He went to work twirling his tongue like a tornado gently pulling on her clitoris with his lips shaking his head wildly, slurping up her juices, she instantly became weak.

"Oh, Fray." She moaned. *"Mm."*

He released her leg pushing her backward on the couch.

"Turn on your stomach." He instructed she did as she was told tooting her ass in the air looking back at him while he ate her pussy from the back.

"Ah, Fray it feels so good baby…*Shit.*"

Fray could taste her sweet juices which were smeared across his face. He slid his tongue from her now soaked pussy to her ass. Katie began to breath unsteady.

"Oo Fray please don't stop, don't stop!" She whined.

"Spread that ass open." He said as he began to finger fuck her while still licking her ass.

"Oh, yes, yes, it feels so good Fray, I want you inside of me now, Fuck me now!"

Fray sat on the couch with a rock hard penis, Katie began caressing, jerking, his penis before sliding her tight pussy on his ten inches. "Ow," She was only halfway down before coming back up. Fray massaged both her breast and began sucking, and biting on her hardened nipples while she found her rhythm. He grabbed onto her waist gradually guiding her up and down on his dick.

"Damn, girl this pussy good," he whispered in her ear as he fucked her from the bottom making sure she felt every inch.

"I…I…I… Fray, I'm cumin," she screamed each time he hit her G-spot. With her pussy muscles gripping his thumping dick she lifted her hips squirting all over him.

"Damn, Kee." He smiled rubbing on her drenched pussy. "Bend that ass over and don't run."

Katie assumed the position on all fours, face down ass up. Fray positioned himself behind her spreading her legs as far as they would go.

"Put it in," he said slapping her on the ass with his dick. Katie reached in between her legs grabbing a hold of his dick placing the head inside her. Fray slid right in penetrating her walls.

"Mm," Katie moaned in ecstasy, she was still drained from the

massive orgasm she had earlier. Hearing her moans, and wetness Fray couldn't hold out any longer he grabbed her locks and started fucking her hard and fast.

"Fray it hurt, stop, stop!" She whined.

He was so deep inside her she was now lying flat on her stomach while Fray rammed himself in and out of her like DMX did Kesha off of Belly.

"Oh…yes…fuck me!"

Katie was on her second orgasm. With one last thrust, he pulled out releasing a large amount of thick white cum all over her ass. Fray held his dick as the last specs of semen trickled out the head of his penis, he collapsed beside her. Katie turned over cuddling underneath him laying her head on his chest, she was definitely worth the wait he thought kissing her forehead before dozing off.

For the time being, Ronnie was getting a little more acquainted with Teresa's aunt boyfriend Kingston. For the past week and a half, they partied at every reggae spot in the city, specifically the Cross Roads. Earlier that week, Kingston introduced his right-hand man Trevor to Ronnie who immediately lashed out at him with hurtful words, he didn't trust him. Ronnie didn't take it personal instead he told Kingston he would link up with him at a later time, the time had come when it was Ronnie's turn to show Kingston a good time and he knew just the place.

THE STADIUM…

It was a full house. There were topless women running around everywhere in various colored lingerie and platform heels. Some served drinks while others conducted table dances. However, the star of the night was a long-hair, six-foot-one slender voluptuous redbone who took the stage. The stallion's stage name was Skyy, Ronnie and Kingston watched in awe as she slithered out of her black fishnet stockings climbing up the pole. She was a professional on the pole as she balanced herself spreading her legs out right, bouncing one ass cheek at a time. The majority of the men in club rushed the stage showering her ten's and twenties. Kingston was just about to stand up from his seat and join in on the action when his eyes lit up like a Christmas tree, "Snitch!" he said aloud. Ronnie heard his loud outburst over the loud music he looked closely in the direction Kingston was looking. A dark skin stocky man with a long beard was his focal point.

"Pussy-boy told on my brotha. I got twenty thousand on his head for whoever!"

At times, Kingston heavy Jamaican accent was hard for Ronnie to make out, but at that moment, he knew Kingston was insinuating the bearded man was a "rat". After studying the man's facial features Ronnie nudged him indicating it was time to go.

Katie kicked back in Unique's tan leather lazy-boy chair, the two had been out shopping all day and decided to retire at Unique's place. It had been awhile since they spent time together thanks to Katie's new-found love. Unique disappeared down the hall into the kitchen, when she returned she found Katie giggling away while texting on her phone. She didn't have to ask who she was texting, she and Fray had been texting back and forth all evening. The more Katie and Fray bonded the further Unique was pushed out the picture, the couple was now discussing moving in together.

An old episode of Martin was watching Katie instead of the other way around, she pushed the send button on her phone. Unique picked up a pillow from the couch sailing it in her direction.

"Ouch! What you do that for?"

Katie complained rubbing the side of her head.

"Because today was supposed to be about us, but you spent all evening texting Fray as if the two of you don't spend enough time together already." She rolled her eyes.

The truth was Unique was happy that her friend had finally found love, but she envied their relationship as well. Before Fray came into the picture it was always just the two of them.

"Aww…I'm sorry," Katie said as if she was consoling a baby tucking away her phone. "Nique, it's not that I been avoiding you it's jus' that your girl is in love and it feels good." She smiled.

Unique was just about to reply when Bullet and his crew barged into the apartment rudely. Katie turned her nose up at the trio, she hadn't planned on being there when Bullet arrived.

"Well if it ain't the three stooges," Katie mumbled.

Chucky's was happy to see Katie, no matter how many times she turned him down he just wouldn't accept no for an answer. He made his way over in her direction, sitting on the arm of the lazy-boy forcing Katie to scoot to the other side. Chucky was biracial black and white, he had red curly hair which he kept trimmed neatly in a gentlemen's fade, gray eyes, light skinned, overcrowded teeth, and freckles on his cheeks. At five-foot-six, he was a slim build with sleeve tattoos on both arms, and although he was small in size Chucky was as deadly as a rattlesnake. Katie grabbed her purse and attempted to rise from the chair when Chucky grabbed her arm.

"You ain't leavin' already are you? Chill wit' a nigga for a while."

Katie looked down at his hand as if he was contagious.

"I'ma give you five seconds to remove your hand before I mace your ass." She frowned.

"I love a feisty woman," he smiled releasing her from his grasp. Katie gathered her shopping bags and headed for the door.

"Man, I'ont know why you keep chasin' that stuck up bitch!" Hulk murmured.

"Excuse you!" Katie said stopping in her tracks. "Nigga I got your bitch!" Katie dropped her bags.

Unique had been in the kitchen with Bullet making out when they heard the commotion coming from the living room.

"Hey…what is going on in here?" Unique shouted upon entering the living room.

"This dusty ass nigga just called me a bitch!"

Bullet snickered.

"Bullet if you can't keep your friends under control then they're no longer welcomed in this house," Unique said rolling her eyes turning her attention to Katie. "Girl, I know you're not leavin' already?"

"I gotta get outta here because if I don't it's goin' to be a serious problem. Call me when your done fuckin' wit' the help," she said looking Bullet up and down before slamming the door.

DESHAY

Allah's Way sat in between the intersection of Benning Rd & C St on the S.E side of Benning Rd. The Masjid was held every Friday.

"Man, you sure that nigga said it's over at twelve," DeShay asked checking his Bell & Ross watch for the third time as he and Ronnie sat parked outside the Masjid. "I'on know why he ain't drive his own car anyway, he be throwin' me off wit' all that paranoid shit," DeShay said.

"Shay, you know how cautious your cousin is ever since we started hustlin' he thinks the whole world is out to get 'em. Like he always says, if you can be seen you could be got." Ronnie chuckled imitating his longtime friend.

The red double doors on the Masjid swung open, and out walked a group of Muslims wearing djellabas and colored Kufis. One Muslim, in particular, gained Ronnie's interest as he watched the bearded man step from the curve approaching a green Expedition truck.

"You know that nigga or sumthin'?" DeShay asked.

"Hell yeah, I know where I know slim from now!" Ronnie said looking over at DeShay. "Slim you remember the nigga I was tellin you about, the one me and Kingston bumped into at the club the other night?"

"The hot nigga? DeShay said looking at the stocky bearded man. "Yea, why whassup?"

"That's the nigga right there with the white Kufi on."

That was all the confirmation DeShay needed, he sprang into action climbing into the back seat searching for something to mask his face.

"Hurry up give me your shirt…who this nigga supposed to told on again?" DeShay asked.

"Some dude from the Southside name Kevin Gray," Ronnie said as he pulled his shirt over his head passing it to DeShay. Although DeShay didn't know the man personally, but with a twenty-thousand-dollar price tag on his head, DeShay would have killed anyone. Neither one of them saw Fray approaching, he hopped inside the Cadillac startling them both as he closed the door.

"Good lookin' out Ron-," He paused looking at DeShay. "Man, what he bout to do?" Fray asked as he watched DeShay adjust the t-shirt around his face like a ninja, grabbing his chrome .40 from underneath his t-shirt.

"I'm about to smash your hot ass Muslim brother that's what I'm bout' to do."

He attempted to open the car door. Fray reached over his seat grabbing a hold of his arm preventing him from doing so.

"Shay, I can't let you do that, we ain't killin' no Muslims."

"You right we ain't bout to do shit, I said I am."

He frowned using his body weight to push the car door open, the two began to tussle. "Why the fuck are you protectin' this hot as nigga?" DeShay fussed, exhausted from all the wrestling. Fray released the hold he had on his cousin, turning back around in his seat. He let out a deep breath, he knew DeShay would never understand his Islamic beliefs.

"Cuz, I already fear what Allah is gonna do to me on judgment day for the things I have already done."

His pleading words were enough to win DeShay over for now. DeShay shook his head in disbelief and slammed the car door shut.

"See dis' dat' bullshit I be talkin' about you always tryna save a nigga," DeShay said uncovering his face.

Ronnie threw the car into drive and eased away from the curve. DeShay studied Umar's face from the backseat as they passed by him.

Katie awoke in her favorite place, Fray's arms. She smiled as she watched him sleep. The room was bright from the sun rays, before rolling out of bed she kissed him on his neck. Her legs were like Jell-O as her pedicure feet sunk into the carpet. Last night was miraculous; Fray took his time exploring her entire body making sure she climaxed multiple times. She was in such a good mood she decided to fix breakfast.

Once in the kitchen, Katie plugged in the waffle maker fetching the eggs out of the refrigerator, she blushed at the sound of the shower water her knight and shining armor was awake. Their relationship strengthened the day Katie decided to share her body with him, that was over two months ago. She hated his street life but had fallen head over heels for him which concerned her more. There wasn't a day that went by that she didn't try to talk him out of that life. She had even gone as far as trying to convince him to invest his money.

Fray hadn't had a clue about investing, so his response was always the same, "Just let me stack a little more." In turn, Katie would scold him for not trying to quit. This is where their relationship clashed. Fray tried spoiling her with lavish gifts only to have them returned. The shower water had stopped, she searched through the cabinets for a skillet when she came across a leather knapsack. She glanced around the kitchen before pulling it out, placing it on the countertop. She unzipped the backpack pulling out a clear Ziploc bag filled with raw heroin, she immediately became furious.

Fray had just dried off and wrapped the towel around his waist. Katie could hear his footsteps marching down the hall, she tried to appear unbothered but it was no use.

"Mornin' beautiful," he tried kissing her, but she dodged the kiss by sidestepping exposing the knapsack behind her.

"Oh." He said taking the bag off the counter.

"Is that all you have to say, is oh?" She rolled her eyes. "Fray how many times do I have to tell you don't bring that shit home."

"It ain't mine a'ight. I'm holdin' it for Derek."

"As if that makes it any betta."

She snapped, turning around to flip the eggs.

Fray knew how much she hated him bringing drugs home. He let his towel drop to the floor. He walked up behind her placing both hands on her waist pressing his penis against her rear-end.

"It won't happen again baby I promise," he said kissing on her neck.

While Fray was busy sucking up to Katie, DeShay had just left the liquor store on Alabama Avenue when a green Expedition truck stopped at the traffic light beside him. DeShay could not believe his eyes it was Umar. The light turned green, DeShay stayed three car lengths behind him, Umar made a right turning into the McDonalds drive-thru. DeShay put on his hazards watching him from the street. He quickly pulled out his cell phone making a call.

Ronnie answered on the third ring his voice was groggy from his drunken slumber the night before.

"Yea, who this?"

"Bruh, how much you say them Jakes had on that duck again?"

It took Ronnie a minute to decipher what his friend was saying. He then sat up in bed, "Twenty, why."

"Well tell them I said have my paper ready," DeShay smiled before ending the call. Several seconds later he was pulling into the McDonalds parking lot. Umar's truck was sandwiched in at the drive-thru. DeShay made a quick observation of the parking lot before pulling on his hood drawing the strings. He parked his car with the .40 in his hand, he began to creep low.

"Welcome to McDonalds can I take your order please."

The female voice said over the intercom. Umar was just about to place his order when he saw someone approaching his truck from behind, his eyes searched the rearview mirror as he instinctively went for his gun, but couldn't reach it in time. DeShay rose up on the driver side of the truck sticking the barrel of his gun inside Umar's partially cracked window. The flash was followed by blood splattered across the interior. Umar was left slumped over to the side in the same position he was reaching for his gun. DeShay made his way back to his car, skidding away from the scene.

STRICTLY BUSINESS

Raindrops fell from the dark spring sky as the black limousine cruised through the city hitting potholes along the way. Kingston and Trevor sat in the back of the limo having a heated argument.

"I don't trust them," Trevor said grabbing a fist full of grapes tossing them in his mouth. He was 6'1 with long locks and midnight complexion. Kingston sparked a cigar exhaling a cloud of smoke. He dressed in his usual attire, a double breast black suit, and black Stacy Adams dress shoes.

"I see you still misconstrue trust with business. I don't have to trust them to do business," Kingston said.

"But correct me if I'm wrong. Weren't you the one that told me all business wasn't good business," Trevor said.

"My bruda those are my fiancé nephews. With them pushing the weight we no longer have to take all the risk, and we will take over the city."

"You mean I no longer have to take all the risk!" Trevor snapped. Umar's death created a bond between Kingston and Ronnie making them even closer.

"You're gettin' too relaxed old man." Trevor was in his feelings. Kingston turned to face protégé.

"Are you questioning my authority, Trevor?" He said with a sneaky smirk on his face.

"No sir."

"Let me tell you something. I haven't stayed in the game for twenty years by being dumb." He blew cigar smoke in Trevor's face.

"Driver pull over up there." Trevor pointed with his outstretched right hand.

The driver did as he was told, Trevor grabbed his door handle.

"The man I once knew would've never considered doing business with Americans."

He slammed the door on his way out.

AUDREY'S CRIB...

"Slim, where Audrey at? Ronnie asked no one in particular as he looked through the refrigerator. He, Ashley, and DeShay stopped by Audrey's crib to meet up with Fray. Audrey was a dope fiend from around the way, they used her place to bag up drugs and hideout whenever the heat was on.

"She went to play her numbers," Fray said turning off the TV standing in the center of the living room.

"Look, uh…I know y'all been waitin' on my decision and e'rything and I jus' want y'all to know I thought long and hard about what I'm about to say." His eyes wandered to each of them. "It's like I said before I don't have it in me to snake Derek out, so I came up with a better solution."

"Why am I not surprised," Ashley interjected. "You were always more loyal to him than you were to any of us anyway." He frowned

"You finish?" Fray said unbothered by his friend sarcastic remark. "First off, you of all people know if anything goes down where my loyalty lies, and you also know when I fuck wit' a nigga I don't fuck wit em half way. Now. I told Derek exactly what the Jamaicans said either we play ball or our money is sure to slow up."

"So what he say?" DeShay cut in.

"He said exactly what I thought he was gon' say. He offered us some money to take Kingston out."

"How much money he talkin'?" DeShay was curious.

"Forty racks," Fray answered.

"That's only ten a piece! them Jakes payin' more than that. You can tell your man he can that forty-grand and shove it up his fat ass." DeShay spat.

"Too late I already took it," Fray motioned his head towards the gym bag sitting by the door.

"You what!" Ronnie snapped springing upwards. *"Slim, did you forget that Kingston is my baby motha's aunt fiancé? This shit is crazy man,"* Ronnie said hyped up.

Fray remained calm throughout the chaos.

"Ronnie, man chill out. What your girl don't know won't hurt her, eventually, her aunt will get over it and move on. And Shay ain't nobody's getting pimped. Startin' today those days are over with. While Derek was busy tryna find ways to pimp us I was busy plottin' my own plan. The way I see it, I say we jack the entire shipment them kill em'." Fray said looking around the room reading their body language. "Now they say they importin' six keys of pure heroin sometime this week, now I'ont know about y'all but that's, at least, a brick and a half a piece for each of us, and ain't no tellin how many times we can step it up." Fray paused to let his words take effect. "So I say again gentlemen, let Derek think he's gettin' over on us when in reality were the ones calling the shots."

The crew was quiet as they tried to see the logic in Fray's idea.

"So, let me get this straight. We knock off the connect for a couple of lousy keys jus' to go back to gettin' bird-fed by your man? Now if that ain't crazy I don't know what is. And on top of that, there's probably more where that came from," DeShay said not sold by Fray's proposal.

"Trust me cuz with the money we stand to make off this move we can always find another connect. We can even get Derek to introduce us directly to his people," Fray said.

"And if he refuses?" Ashley chimed in.

"We shut him down and continue to do our thing." Fray finished.

"Sounds like you covered e'rything, but you forgot one thing. How the hell we suppose to know what day they're makin' the drop?" DeShay asked.

"That's where Ronnie come in at." He motioned his head in Ronnie's direction, DeShay and Ashley turned to face him as well. "Ronnie you're the only one that could get close enough…you in or out?"

The room was so quiet you could hear the refrigerator running.

"What do I tell Teresa and her aunt?"

"You don't tell them shit! All you gotta do is find out when it's all going down, and well take it from there, but we gotta know if you're with us or not." Fray said.

Ronnie pondered the benefits his family would reap had he chose to participate. Fray was right, this was an opportunity of a lifetime.

"Fuck it I'm in." He sighed.

"So it's settled then. Ronnie, you work on finding out the whereabouts of the drop me, Ash and Shay will start plannin' the hit."

With that being said everyone started to disperse. Fray called after Ashley he couldn't let him walk out bitter.

"I know how much you love your cousin, but your cousin was wrong. If you still feel some type of way about Derek after this I won't stand in your way, but I'm hopin' you make the right decision. This isn't just about you any more holmes your judgment affects me, my cousin and Ronnie. It may not seem like it now…but just know e'rybody got a day." Fray dapped him up, pulling him in for an embrace.

"We been playing the bars a lot lately don't you think? What'chu tryna get me in the dog house wit' Kim?" Kingston laughed aloud throwing his arm around Ronnie's neck while they sat at the bar. He tossed back what was left in his glass, slamming it down on the bar-top. The Grey-Goose burned the back of his throat as he sucked on the lime to get rid of the horrible taste. "Another round bartender." He yelled from his seat. Over the course of time, Ronnie spent with him he quickly discovered Kingston was a drunk. Ronnie watched his plan unfold as Kingston gulped down his fifth glass.

"Y'know Roney." He slurred, "I been thinkin' bout making you right hand."

"What about Trevor?" Ronnie asked.

"Ah." he waved his hand dismissingly, "Bartender another round."

The bartender glanced at Ronnie for his approval who in turn gave him the okay. Kingston paused eyeing his vodka before tossing it back.

"Hit me again!" He was intoxicated.

"I thought y'all was partnas?"

"Partnas?!" Kingston scowl. "I'm the H.N.I.C, and to prove it to you…how would you like to ride wit' me the day of the shipment?"

"It would be a pleasure," Ronnie said raising his glass in the air taking his first shot of the night.

It was a lovely day in Petworth, chirping birds carried worms back to their nest, and children's laughter packed the residential streets. Illinois Avenue was in a shape of a circle with row houses on each side. Ronnie's mouth was agape as he occupied the rear of the tinted Volkswagen SUV, this section of DC was nothing like what he was use to seeing. Kingston and two of his henchmen rode in the same car.

"Let me guess…you're wonderin' what we doin' here?"

Ronnie shifted in his seat facing him.

"I see you been reading my mind."

Kingston chuckled at Ronnie's bewilderment.

"My friend…look around you, nothing but rich white folks and money. One thing I learned is that the feds rarely patrol areas like this. Hell, my guy at the post office tells me all the time that they don't bother to inspect packages coming to upper-class areas."

Fray and DeShay sat geared up on their Yamaha's 450's posted up on one of the intersecting side streets, 5th & Illinois to be exact. Fray was ecstatic when Ronnie called him with the location of the drop. However, his excitement wore off when he learned his friend would be so close to the action. He even considered calling it off knowing one mistake on their end could cost Ronnie his life.

"Fuck is takin them so long, they shoulda' been here by now," DeShay said frustrated, he was impatient as usual.

"Man, would you chill? They'll be here. Won't you try focusin' on making sure you don't hit Ronnie wit any stray bullets." Fray reprimanded him.

"You acting like you talkin' to a rookie or sumthin' this ain't the first time I bodied some shit. You jus' worry bout' gettin' your man, cause I got mines!" DeShay spat.

Fray wanted to press on but stopped short when he spotted a convey SUV floating down Illinois Avenue. He tapped DeShay nodding in the direction of the two passing trucks. Ronnie had already assured them that Kingston would be accompanied by security, six guards totaling. The escorting truck carrying four heavily armed Jamaicans while the trailing truck, which Ronnie and Kingston rode in was being chauffeured by two more.

"Boss, I thought you said this place was empty?" Said, the driver of Kingston's truck as they spotted an elderly woman with purple glasses occupying the porch of the house. She rocked back and forth in her rocking chair. Kingston frowned, leaning upward from the backseat.

"That's strange this place was vacant a week ago."

"Maybe the old lady brought the place." The passenger suggested.

"Man would y'all relax. How damn hard could it be to take a package from an old lady." Ronnie interjected.

"Let's see 3414 Illinois Avenue," said the delivery man coasting the Fed Ex van as he glanced at his clipboard. He pulled the truck in front of the house that was being occupied by an old lady. Grabbing his clipboard and package he exited the truck.

"Good afternoon ma'am, it says here that I have a package for a…Mr. James?

"Why certainly dear that's my husband." The old woman smiled.

"Well if I can just get you to sign here I can be out your hairs," he returned a warm smile.

After signing for the package he placed the box at her feet.

"You have a good day ma'am."

Fray and DeShay engines roared to life, pulling back on their throttles they raced down the hill. In no time, they closed the distance on Ronnie, and Kingston breaking off at the last minute drawing their Glock 17's.

"*It's a hit!*" Kingston screamed snatching Ronnie to the floor of the truck. The first shots shattered the driver and passenger's glass. Fray and DeShay began filling the two henchmen with hot led. The delivery man hit the deck!

PRESSURE BUST PIPES

Startled by the pandemonium in the back of them the four heavily armed gunmen attempted to react, but it was already too late. The elderly woman in the rocker was none other than Ashley. He raised the AK-47 that was concealed behind the chair and started spraying a volley of bullets shattering glass and putting holes in anything that was moving.

The assault rifle bullets ripped through its occupants. Petworth was now a war zone as mayhem took over the streets. The children's laughter was replaced with horrific screams as they scrambled for cover. Seeing no signs of life in the truck Ashley scooped up the package, bolting across the street to the getaway van. Fray and DeShay kicked their bikes in high gear. When the gunfire ceased for good Kingston cautiously peeped his head up from the backseat. Smoke lingered in the air. He had to literally blink twice, watching what he assumed to be an elderly woman racing across the street to an awaiting van.

"She's got the package!" he yelled out.

"I know," Ronnie said. Kingston's eyes widened staring down the barrel of a nickel plated .357. Ronnie shot him at point blank range. He quickly assessed the damage to the residential street. The two men who had been riding with him lay face down covered in blood, and the truck in front of him had been swished cheesed. The sound of screeching tires pulling alongside him snapped him out of his surveillance. He then wiped the blood off his face with the sleeve of his sweatshirt stepping from the truck. He and Ashley burnt rubber away from the scene.

The reenactments of today's deadly shooting were plastered all over the ten o'clock news. The media was nicknaming the gruesome crime scene as the "Petworth Massacre." So, far they had no leads or suspects. The foursome watched in suspense, they were relieved that they hadn't left a trace. With seven dead bodies, and the crew on the rise it was sure to be a hot summer.

"Joe in my office now!" Burnette yelled from the threshold of his door. He just ended a phone call with the city's mayor.

"You wanted to see me cap?" Joe closed the door behind him.

"What can you tell me about this Petworth Massacre business?"

"I'm still working on it sir, but if you ask me I'd say it was drug related. I interviewed everybody on the block down to the delivery guy."

"You have a witness?" Burnette looked relieved.

"Well…not exactly. He does, however, report seeing two gunmen roll up on motorcycles…and wait until you hear this. He says that bullets started coming from behind him forcing him to hit the deck. Now the only person he recalls was behind him was the old lady he delivered the package too."

"Well, that explains all the shell casings our people gathered from the porch," Burnette said.

"I know…strange right? And it doesn't stop there. Rumor has it that those Jamaicans we pulled from the trucks were part of some ruthless mob in Jamaica." Joe revealed.

Burnette looked up from his desk.

"Alright." Burnette sighed trying to gather his thoughts. "I got the mayor breathing down my neck. Do whatever it is you have to do to solve this, but do it quietly."

CASH FLOW

"So how you want it king-pin?" Jeeter joked as Fray took a seat in his chair. Jeeter tossed the cover over Fray, brushing his clippers with his comb. Fray had come in for an early haircut to his surprise the shop was empty.

"Go 'head wit' all that Mr. J," Fray said as Jeter pumped up the chair.

"I'm jus' tellin you what the streets is sayin'. Rumor has it that you and your boys are on a huge come-up out there."

Fray sucked his teeth.

"Do me a favor Mr. J. Don't believe e'rything you here."

"I don't! I been around a long time boy for me not to notice the change in the young man that I help raise. Fray, if I hear yall's business all the way in here, just how long do you think it's gon' take the feds to get to you? I tried havin' this same conversation with your father years ago, but he wouldn't listen and we both know how that ended."

"Look I ain't him a'ight!" Fray fumed jerking his head away. Jeeter turned off the clippers.

"Son, all I'm tryna do is prevent you from going down that same road. The cycle gotta break somewhere. If you choose not to listen to a thing I said today, just know that if I were you I would put some money to the side to invest. Don't be like these fools out here ridin' around in $50,000 dollar cars, then in a few years, they broke, and don't have nothing to show for it."

"Invest? He repeated. "Mr. J I don't know a thing about investing, and even if I did I wouldn't know what to throw my money in."

"I'll tell you what. If you're really serious about getting outta these streets, when you reach your quota I'll sell you the shop."

"I can't accept an offer like that Mr. J. This shop has been your life."

"Yeah, but everything must come to an end. I kinda outgrew this city anyway."

"So what will you do if you sell the shop?" Fray asked.

"You mean besides kick back on some of California's sandy beaches. Why I don't know…maybe I'll open up another one down there."

Fray considered the proposition.

"So how much you askin' for?"

On the other side of town, the 640 projects were in full swing, residents and hustlers crowded out front of the buildings, some served fiends while others smoked funnel-jays.

PRESSURE BUST PIPES

*"You shoulda' thought about that shit before you started runnin'
your muthafuckin' mouth…got me and my wife out here beefin' in
shit!"*

Dollar spat into the receiver of his phone as he exited the 640
building. The diamonds in his ears and around his neck glistened
under the sunlight. His well-groomed beard, six-feet stature, and
loud red polo shirt made him stand out amongst the rest. He and
Joyce had been arguing back and forth on the phone.

*"Man, I ain't tryna hear that shit…as a matter of fact, bitch lose
my number!"*

He met Joyce a couple of months ago on the south-side
coming out of her salon. What started out as casual sex quickly
evolved into mixed feelings, at least on Joyce's end. However, she
had no idea he was married. It wasn't until one late afternoon
Dollar's wife came strolling into her salon requesting her service.
After Joyce finished doing the woman's hair, the woman stood face
to face with her tossing money in her face. Joyce employees had to
restrain her from retaliating against the psychotic lady. The woman
screamed all kinds of obscenities issuing Joyce a warning to stay
away from her husband. The thought of Dollar being married
crushed her. She immediately pulled out her cell phone giving him
a call.

After listening to her sob and rant he politely ended the call
without an explanation, she felt betrayed. Right then and there she
knew what had to be done, she called her cousin Hulk and gave
him the run down. She even confessed to helping Dollar count over
seventy-thousand dollars during the course of their relationship.
Hulk chastised her viciously for holding out on a come up.

"Let me hit that." Dollar said reaching for the funnel-jay from
a group of friends. He took three pulls passing it back then headed

down the alleyway passing a battered Buick on Warder street, he crossed the narrow street to his Tahoe. He didn't notice the three gentlemen watching from inside a parked car.

"Let's get em now!" Bullet blurted from the rear of the parked Buick reaching for the door handle.

"Hol' up...wait! Hulk exclaimed from the passenger seat. "Man, you 'ont see all them niggaz over there in that cut? Damn all that cowboy shit we don't need to turn this into a senseless shootout. A nigga's pockets is hurtin' fa real, so let's follow him and do whatever we gotta do in order to get this money."

"We been following' this nigga around all week. I'm tired of all this cat and mouse shit lets jus' grab his ass and get it over wit'!"

Bullet's frustration was evident, they all felt the same way. With the last couple of robbery attempts being duds they had to do this one right, not to mention every time they cornered Dollar somehow he always found a way to elude them unknowingly. They watched as Dollar checked his mirrors before pulling into traffic. Chucky started the Buick's engine and began trailing him. He was always the crew's designated driver whenever they went out on a heist.

"Man, where the hell is this nigga going now?" Hulk spat. They watched from a block away as Dollar searched for somewhere to park outside of Bens Chili bowl, a historic landmark, he pulled into the narrow alleyway.

"Got em. Hurry up and go around the other way...go...go...go!" Hulk spoke in a rushed tone.

Chucky cut the wheel racing down the back of the restaurant turning down the opposite end of the narrow alley. They were expecting to catch Dollar in his truck, but to their surprise, he was already out on foot heading out of the alley.

"Damn.... we missed em." Bullet spat, as Chucky brought the Buick to a stop in front of Dollar's bumper.

PRESSURE BUST PIPES

"So what now?" Chucky asked out of frustration reversing the car next to Dollar's Tahoe.

"We wait em out, as a matter of fact, Chucky go inside and keep an eye on em. Let us know the minute he comes out," Hulk said removing his gun from underneath his seat.

Chucky's eyes danced around the clamorous diner taking in the many civilian faces as they stuffed their faces with chili dogs and cheese fries. He noticed Dollar at the counter placing his order to go, Chucky then approached the counter ordering a soft drink. He watched Dollar accept his carry-out bag and head for the door, he made the call. Bullet and Hulk slipped from the old Buick squatting behind Dollar's truck. They heard the automatic click unlock the doors, as Dollar headed up the alleyway. He was just about to open the truck door when he saw two men come into view from behind his truck dressed in all black wearing ski masks, he took off running in the opposite direction. Bullet and Hulk staggered after him.

"Help! Help!" Dollar yelled frantically crashing into the arms of Chucky almost running him over. He then heard a rustling sound and felt a paralyzing pain in his stomach. His body went limp as everything faded black. Bullet and Hulk were there to catch him as he fell backwards.

"Look like y'all had e'rything under control." Chucky snickered putting away his Taser.

Bullet and Hulk carried Dollar back to the truck. Dollar awoke in the backseat of his truck with an excruciating headache in his wife-beater and boxer's. A strip of duct tape covered his mouth, his hands and feet were restrained by rope, a bald man with many tattoos sat next to him waving a gun.

"Main-man, you've been placed on ice, but if you cause a scene you gon' melt. Now I'ma ask you one time and one time only…where we going?" Hulk said giving Dollar his first and final warning as he ripped the duct tape from his mouth. Dollar winced.

"Look, I got five-thousand in the glove compartment take that and the truck, jus' don't kill me!" he begged.

"Nigga, do we look like some petty ass thieves? We only come out for fifty or betta." Hulk said.

"Well, I'm not y'all man. I'm a small time…*Ah.*" Horse smashed the side of his pistol into his skull silencing him.

"Lie to me again and you gon' wish you were dead," Hulk said through clenched teeth.

"Man, I swear…I wouldn't lie to you." He whined as blood trickled from his head where Hulk struck him.

"A'ight if that's how you want to play it." Hulk stripped Dollar out his boxers pulling a lighter from his pocket.

"What'chu' doin' man…c'mon don't do this man…please!" Dollar panicked.

Hulk rolled the dial back with his thumb igniting the flame. He placed the fire underneath his balls setting them ablaze! Dollar jerked and screamed to the top of his lungs. The pain was so unbearable he blacked out throughout the torture.

"A'ight, A'ight," he said after coming to, "I'll tell y'all what y'all wanna know."

"See that wasn't so hard now was it?"

He put the phone to his ear after calling Chucky who had still been tailing them, giving him the address to Dollar's house. They arrived at the apartment ten minutes later, Bullet and Chucky exited the truck making their way inside the building. After retrieving the safe they carried it back to the hoopty. Once Bullet was back inside the truck Hulk continued his interrogation.

"Now I know you heard me when I said we only come out for fifty or betta. That's only twenty-five in that safe, plus the five from the glove compartment which only makes thirty. So I'ma ask you again…where we goin?"

Dollar looked weary. His silence infuriated Hulk turning him into a mad man, he pistol whipped Dollar repeatedly.

"That's for my cousin." Hulk spat.

Dollar was bleeding profusely no matter how much pain he endured he refused to break. The real money he had stashed away was at his residence where his wife, and kids laid their heads, giving them up wasn't an option. With one eye swollen shut he looked in his attackers face, and said in a voice barely above a whisper, "Y'all minus well kill me cause I ain't given y'all shit else." He spit blood in Hulk's face.

"Suit yourself. Take him down the park." Hulk said wiping the blood from his face. They were at the park in twenty minutes, Chucky pulled alongside them. Bullet and Hulk stepped from the truck leaving Dollar lying across the back seat, they both grabbed gas cans from the trunk of the Buick. Hulk pulled out his gun emptying his clip in Dollar's face and upper torso. After dousing the trunk down with gasoline they threw the empty containers inside the truck, setting it on fire. They watched it burn with the feeling of another failed task.

SURPRISE

"Fray, why do I have to wear this stupid blindfold?" Katie asked as he led her down the stairs.

"I told you it's a surprise," Fray said, standing on her right side holding her lower back and forearm as he led the way. Katie felt the beaming sun on her skin indicating that they were now outside. He paused slightly to admire the sightless beauty before him. It was at that moment that he knew he would die for her.

"We're almost there sweety…watch your step." He led her to the brinks of the parking lot. "Now, stop!" He said removing the blindfold. Parked in front of her with a purple ribbon attached to it was a burnt-orange Volvo C70 two door, four-passenger compact car. *"Surprise!"* He smiled jingling the keys. Katie looked confused, she didn't know whether to scream or be upset as she stared at the brand new car.

"Wow…you brought me a car." She said nonchalantly.

"Is that all you can say, Katie? what did I do wrong this time?" Fray was becoming annoyed by her stand-offish demeanor.

"What more is it to say except I can't take these keys?"

She never wanted to give Fray the impression she condoned in his lifestyle.

"Katie, please don't spoil the moment. I'm jus' tryna make you happy."

"Baby, as long as I'm with you I am happy," she said wrapping her arms around the back of his neck bringing him down to her level, giving him a kiss on his lips. Fray grabbed a hold of her hand kissing her knuckles.

"Kee, I know I been telling you this for a while now, but I think I might have finally found my way out. I promise you if this works as soon as I reach my goal I'm done," he said peering into her pleading eyes.

"You promise?" She asked staring up at him. He then pulled her close, "I promise."

"Well, in that case, give me them keys so I can go pick up Nique." She giggled jumping on him wrapping her legs around his waist.

Ashley had just parked his seven series beamer outside the neighborhood liquor store on D St.

"That's my car!" eleven-year-old Rocky energetically pointed at the brand new BMW from his porch. That was the third time today he had beaten his friend to the punch.

"Ah, Man… You always get all the good ones." PeeWee

complained sitting back down on the stoop. Rocky laughed at his friend's disappointment. Suddenly a mega smile spread across PeeWee's beaver shaped face

"Well if that's yours...then that's mine right there." He motioned to the candy apple red Corvette with mirror tints pulling behind Ashley's beamer. The car was so clean you could see your image in it from the street.

"I told you DeShay was rich." PeeWee began imitating DeShay's signature walk around the front yard. DeShay just so happened to look up and witness the youngster pretending to be him from across the street. DeShay flipped his phone closed and begun to make his way across the street with a mean mug. A sudden chill shot down Rocky's spine as he watched the quick temper ruthless gangsta approaching. PeeWee was too busy mimicking DeShay he didn't see him coming.

"And jus' what in the hell do you think you're doing?" DeShay spat startling PeeWee in mid stride.

The two admirers had never held a conversation with him let alone been that close.

"I...I...," a buck tooth PeeWee stammered. Rocky sat trembling in his boots.

"I asked you a question!" DeShay raised his voice. PeeWee finally found his voice box looking his idol in his eyes. Rocky frightfully moved closer to his house. DeShay noticed Rocky's movement, he doubled over in laughter.

"I like you shawty, you got a lot of heart, your man a scared mutherfucka though," He said in between breaths.

"Man, no I wasn't." Rocky boasted trying to sound brave. PeeWee and DeShay however, wasn't convinced.

"What's you Lil niggaz names anyway?"

"I'm PeeWee and this here is Rocky."

"I'm DeSh-."

"We know!" The boys said in unison cutting him off. Unbeknownst to him, the boys looked at him like a hood celebrity. Not only did they Idolize the foursome, but quiet as kept PeeWee had his reasons for favoring DeShay more. For months, he watched from his windows as DeShay repeatedly refused to serve his mother while she was pregnant with his little sister. However, he couldn't say the same for the others.

"Damn, don't bite my head off. I was jus' tryna introduce myself."

"Damn all that...what we really wanna know is, how much did you pay for the car?"

"Why Lil nigga? You plannin' on buyin' one or sumthin'?"

"When I get my money right I jus' might," PeeWee said.

"Yea cause we got next out here." Rocky slapped PeeWee a high five.

The pair sounded as if they were referring to a pickup game in basketball rather than the streets. DeShay was taken aback by the youngster's reply, but before he could protest Rocky's mother stuck her head out the screen door.

"Dinner's ready, so tell your Lil friend goodnight and get in here and wash-up." Rocky hopped to his feet without telling PeeWee so much as a bye, he squeezed in between his mother and the doorway. PeeWee tried to follow suit.

"I'm sorry baby, but there isn't enough," the woman said in the house coat closing the door in his face. He lowered his head in embarrassment. For the first time, DeShay looked him over. His hair was nappy, his hand me down clothes were too small, and his shoes had holes in them. DeShay instantly felt his pain.

"You hungry lil man? C'mon...take a ride wit' me."

The sun sparkled off the pearl white Lexus as Ronnie pulled out into traffic from the car wash. The trio's newfound fortune had them blowing money fast. Cars, jewelry, houses, partying, however, Fray refused to follow the new trend. Besides a few minor purchases, like putting a down payment on Katie's car he was determined to save every dime, there was no need in upgrading he thought.

Ronnie sparked up his blunt and bobbed his head to Memphis Bleek (I get high) turning onto a side street passing Anternet Gardens. He stopped at the traffic light outside the 24-hour store on Benning road, he watched a dark skin woman with booty shorts from behind his tinted windows, her body was banging. Just as he was about to roll his window down he noticed a group of guys posted outside the liquor, mean-mugging his car. He figured the female must have been one of their girlfriends. One of the guys threw his hands in the air asking him, "What's up." However, Ronnie didn't react off his emotions instead he flickered ashes from his blunt out the window. He then revved his engine when the light turned green.

The loud smoke had suddenly given him an appetite, he slowed down as he neared the Denny's. Gigi stepped out the carry out carrying Styrofoam trays. She rocked a silk black blouse, tight jeans, and red bottoms with her curly black hair slicked back into a ponytail.

"Damn." Ronnie mouthed, cutting his wheel into the parking lot, sticking his head out the window yelling trying to get her attention as she headed towards her car. Gigi made eye contact with the driver of the incoming Lexus. Her petite ass jiggled all over the place. Gigi was the master of mind games. She then slid into the driver's seat of her slightly tinted Acura TL.

"Oh, so it's like that?" Ronnie blushed blocking her in, surfacing from his car. He then tapped her window.

"Can't you see I'm tryna get out?" the Puerto Rican beauty smiled revealing a perfect set of white teeth.

"Damn ma'... I could've brought you breakfast." Ronnie hadn't noticed another occupant in the car until he heard a female voice call out his name. He bent his head in a tad bit peering inside the car.

"Boy, check you out, out here acting like some kind of mack."

"Man Pebblez whassup?!" He said excitedly. He hadn't seen her since Fray ignored her at the Erykah Badu concert when he and Fray accompanied Katie and Teresa.

"So, you like what you see huh?" Pebblez smirked.

"You damn right I do but your friend playin' games wit' a nigga."

Pebblez then whispered something in Gigi's ear which made her chuckle.

"Hey Ronnie, come on this side right quick." He immediately rounded the car.

"Whassup?"

"Well seeing that you see something that you like, maybe you and me can help each other out with something."

"Oh yeah, and what's that...?"

PRESSURE BUST PIPES

"Ewe Bullet you stink!" Unique said barging in the bathroom covering her nose. "Let me see the car keys right quick so me and Chucky can go get something to eat." Unique frowned.

"Man, can't you see I'm tryna take a shit...get out!" Bullet spat closing the magazine with a cigarette dangling from his lips, and his pants around his ankles.

"Boy give me the damn keys and stop playin'." He then fished the keys from his pants pocket. "And make sure you spray some damn air freshener in here." She said before closing the door. "Chucky you ready," she yelled down the hall.

Ronnie had just finished eating the last of his omelet, after getting Gigi's number in the parking lot they parted ways. He dropped the money for the bill on the table and headed for the door. Unique and Chucky we're just pulling up outside the Denny's when Ronnie came out. While Unique scanned the moderate lot for a parking spot Chucky's eyes were glued to the front entrance of the restaurant. He watched a lanky dark-skin gentleman with a low hair cut talk on his cell phone, his face looked familiar.

It wasn't until he got a good look at the man lopsided face that he was for certain, he jumped out the car. Upon seeing Ronnie Unique heart skipped a beat, she hadn't noticed Ronnie until now. She backed the Dodge Charger into the first available parking space praying the tints were dark enough to conceal her identity. She remained in the car watching their interaction from across the parking lot, she could tell the two were no strangers.

"Damn slim I thought that was you when you get out?" Chucky asked excitedly looking him up and down. Ronnie not only look like he was getting it but his persona screamed it as well.

"Well if it ain't my nigga Chuck," Ronnie smiled slapping him a five hugging him. "Was happening slim?"

"Man you know me, still out here on a paper chase," Ronnie said.

"Shid, you don't look like you doin' too bad yourself. What your man and em' cop this joint for you when you got out?"

Chucky gestured to the brand new Lexus LS 430.

"Sumthin like that," Ronnie said wanting to change the subject.

"That's whassup." Chucky nodded.

Chucky had dangerous eyes even when he wasn't on a mission he always looked like he was up to something.

"Aye hold on right quick, let me tell shawty to go and get the food…Unique!" He yelled across the parking lot towards the black Charger waving her over. It was then she knew her cover was blown, but rather draw suspicion to herself she stepped from the car. Ronnie thought he was having déjà vu, he reflected back to the day he stood on 18th and D eyeing Unique as she occupied Ashley's passenger seat.

"Unique, this my man Ronnie we were cellies up Cumberland," Chucky said introducing them.

"Hi, you doing," Ronnie played along.

"Go in there and get us a table while I finish hollerin' at him."

Unknowingly to Ronnie and Unique, Chucky and Horse knew all about Unique, and Ashley's affair. For months in the cell, Chucky listened to Ronnie blabber about how his friends were out there getting it. Not only did he store all the information Chucky secretly studied the trio's faces in countless pictures as well. All of the big money talks had him calling up Horse trying to get the ball rolling early. He then told himself that Ronnie's crew would be his big pay day upon his release, and make good on his promise he would, or die trying.

A few months after his release he and Horse watched Ashley fly past them on the highway in his Impala. They then follow him to a hotel in Virginia. Just when they were about to make their move Horse yanked Chucky back down inside the car, with their mouths ajar they watched Unique climbed from the passenger seat of Ashley's car. Unique's presence was the only thing that stood in their way that night.

"Slim, that's your peoples?" Ronnie asked perplexed after Unique was out of earshot.

"Nah that's my man Bullet folks. I jus' rode with her to get sumthin' to eat...why you ask?"

"No reason." Ronnie waved dismissingly. "She favors this lil broad I know."

Chucky's eyes pierced a hole through Ronnie as he listened to him lie to his face.

"Well look I'm 'bout to step inside here, it was nice seeing you, though, and if your ever in the area feel free to slide through and fuck wit' a nigga sometimes," Chucky said dapping him up.

"A'ight, that's a bet slim, you be easy out this joint," Ronnie said lowering himself inside the car, he couldn't wait to get back around the way to break the news to Ashley. Chucky watched him pull off before making his way inside the restaurant. Unique spotted him as soon as he walked in, instantly she was paranoid. She wasn't so much worried about Ashley finding out, but Bullet was her main concern.

Katie and Unique double parked outside the 1330 building on 7th and O street. It was live as hustlers fired up the grill, and children laughed as they chased after one another on the K.D.P playground. Everybody and they mama was out on this hot sunny day. The surrounding hustlers posted up outside the building looking at the tinted Volvo suspiciously. Unique emerge from its passenger side putting the tensed hustlers at ease.

"Don't shoot a bitch." She joked as she approached a hustler named Marco.

"What took you so long?" He smiled palming her ass.

Unique wore leggings and a revealing belly shirt.

"I had to wait on my girl," she kissed him.

"How much you say you needed again," Marco asked.

"Six-hundred...me and my girl about to hit up the mall."

Marco reached in his pocket peeling off six one hundred dollar bills.

"Thanks, babe, and what's goin' on around here? Everybody's out."

"We cookin' out for my man Reggie B-Day. Speaking of the devil here he comes now."

"Who this?" Reggie asked.

"Unique this my man Reggie, Reggie...Unique."

"Whassup you ain't got no friends," Reggie said hyped.

"I'ont really be wit females I only have one friend."

"Where she at then, put a nigga on!"

"She's in the car." Unique gestured towards the double parked Volvo. Reggie started making his way over to Katie's car, he walked around to the driver side motioning for her to roll down the window. Katie looked puzzled. She then cracked her window halfway.

"How you doin' what's your name?" He asked placing his arm on the roof of the car.

"Katie," she responded not wanting to be rude.

"I'm Reggie. Your home girl thought it would be cool if I came over here and talked to you. You're beautiful by the way, you got a number so I can reach you?"

"Naw I gotta boyfriend."

"I mean how he goin' know?"

"Because I will tell him, we don't keep secrets."

His back against the wall niggers fought like us damn poor Isis that's his momma name momma ain't strong enough to raise no boy what's his father name...

Bobbing their heads to Jay-z's meet the parents DeShay guided his Corvette up N St while Fray sat in the passenger seat. Against Fray's wishes DeShay filled his lungs with marijuana smoke. However, he cracked the window to prevent Fray from catching contact. They had not too long ago left Daddy's Grace. As they approached the broad intersection of 7th street he studied the flow of traffic before pulling out, he wasn't expecting to see what he saw next. Katie's car was double parked a block away on 7th and O, a heavyset man was hunched over talking on the driver side, he tapped Fray.

"Slim, ain't that Katie's car right there?"

Fray rose from him slouching position turning his neck to see what his cousin was referring to. Upon spotting the Volvo his eyes blazed with anger, his emotions were running high as he watched the two converse.

"What the fuck! Man, pull up on them." He frowned.

"Look here baby girl if that nigga starts acting up you know where to find me." Reggie managed to say.

DeShay pulled up on the side of them, sandwiching him in. The look on Katie's face was horrific.

"*Oh...Shit*!!" Unique said seeing DeShay car pull up.

"You know them niggaz? Aye, lil Ray get the joint!" Marco spat, but before lil Ray or any of the hustlers could react DeShay jumped from his car showcasing his mac-11.

"I wish you niggaz would. I'd light this muthafucka up!" DeShay spat.

Back at the car.

"Fuck type of games you out here playin'?" Fray seethed.

"Fray it's not what you think!"

"Yeah slim it ain't even like that," Reggie interjected.

"Nigga was I talkin' to you! Mind your mutherfuckin business I'm talking' to my peoples. As a matter of fact, slide off!" He fumed. Fray didn't have to tell him twice he was out of there. He then turned his attention back to Katie.

"*You keep fuckin' wit this freak ass bitch, get the fuck from around here!*"

Unique hurriedly paced over and hopped in the passenger seat. Katie put the car in drive and sped off. With the Mac still raised DeShay waited until Fray was safe in the car before lowering himself into the car. He then followed behind Katie pulling on a secluded side street. Fray and Katie were both out their cars fussing and yelling. They argued heatedly for all of ten minutes before Fray decided to give up. He walked back to DeShay's car leaving Katie standing in the street.

SEVERAL DAYS LATER...

The Charger roared down the highway. Unique set behind the wheel while Katie rode shotgun.

"Girl you mean to tell me he hasn't said a word to you in three days?" Unique said cutting her eye over at her.

Katie looked depressed as she sat resting her head on her left hand gazing out the window. She had no one to blame but herself. She knew how big Fray was on security. He would sit and lecture her for hours about safety. He had many rules, but the most important ones were to avoid strips and to never bring Unique past the house. Fray wasn't a fan of Unique the more he groomed Katie the more she started to see Unique for who she really was.

"Unique if Fray were to ever leave I don't know what I would do." She said sadly.

Unique new Katie would never point the finger, but deep down she blamed herself for the sudden separation between them.

"Katie you and I both know Fray isn't going anywhere. He just needs some time to himself."

"If we didn't live together maybe I wouldn't stress so much," Katie said shaking her head. Every time she and Fray had a major dispute he had a tendency of shutting down which, Katie hated the most. Unique pondered her friend's situation as she bared off the highway. She was never the one to give relationship advice, but she wanted to desperately help her friend.

"I'll tell you what you can do," Unique smirked.

Katie's was anxious to hear her resolution.

The apartment was partially dark when Katie entered. She sat her purse and keys on the table and hit the play button on the stereo repeating the last song that played before she left the house. Faith Evans "Soon as I get Home" came alive. The unexpected sound of running water startled her, she was unaware that Fray was home. When she didn't see his car parked out front she assumed he was out handling business. Unique's ideology was replaying in her head, she stripped off all her clothes and quietly tiptoed to the bathroom.

Fray had just finished an early morning set of crunches after guzzling down a glass of orange juice he hopped in the shower. At the sound of the door opening he stuck his head from behind the shower curtain, he locked eyes with Katie. Still, with them not communicating her presence was ignored. He pulled his head back behind the curtain. Katie snickered under her breath at his stubbornness. She pulled her thick locks into a ponytail on top of her head.

"Would you like some company?" She asked sweetly resting her hands on her hips.

Fray poked his head from behind the curtain a second time. His eyes surveyed her caramel curvaceous figure. Her perky 34 DD breast were on full presentation. He pulled the curtain back just enough to reveal his erection. Her hour glass figure was flawless as she walked over to the shower. He grabbed a hold of her hand helping her into the half shower.

The water was enticingly hot. She turned her back towards him letting the water hit her face as she pressed her rear end up

PRESSURE BUST PIPES

against his hard dick. She briefly closed her eyes as the water trickled down her chest. He caught a whiff of the almond scent in her hair as he ran his tongue along her neck, and ear. He used both hands to grope her breast as he continued to suck on her neck. Katie felt his growing erection jumping against her behind, soft moans escaped her lips as she reached back grabbing his dick stroking it. Her vagina became wetter with each stroke.

"Umm. Baby, wait, wait...let me wash you first." She moaned. Fray released her from his hold. She turned to face him draping her arms around his neck kissing his lips.

"I'm sorry do you forgive me," she said seductively before pushing him back into the built-in shower bench. She grabbed the bottle of Dove body wash pouring it onto his balls and dick, stroking it with ease until she worked up a good lather. He groaned.

"You like that daddie," she whispered in his ear licking on his earlobe. "Close your eyes." she instructed.

Fray did as he was told leaning his head against the tile wall he felt captive to her touch. She then unhooked the shower nozzle from its base rinsing the soap from his private area. Unique sexual advice played in her head like an old song it was working so far. She placed his manhood in her right hand stroking it, squeezing it tightly all while massaging his balls with her left hand his Mandingo had grown to its full erection.

"Damn baby girl," he said with his eyes still closed. She got on her knees before him inserting his rock hard dick in her mouth, twirling her tongue around the tip. Fray's eyes fluttered open. This was the first time Katie went down on him. She twirled her tongue around in a circular motion while stroking his shaft, his toes started to curl. He placed his hand on the back of her head coaching her.

Katie pushed him further into her mouth making slurping sounds.

"Mm... shit." He mumbled in between breaths. She looked up at him lustfully smacking the head of his dick on her moist tongue. She sucked on his balls, and tried swallowing him, but her gag reflex kicked in.

"Whoa." he laughed. "You not ready for that yet babe," he said holding onto her pinned up locks guiding her back down slowly. She clamped her mouth back around his dick sucking harder than before. "No hands Kee…no hands." Fray said as he watched her suck away while in ecstasy. He placed both his hands on the back of her head gyrating his hips, thrusting himself in and out her mouth she was really working now.

"Ah…you want me to cum in your mouth?" He asked in breathy tone gripping her hair. He and Katie fucked on a regular basis, and not one time could she recall hearing him moan. She bobbed her head up and down even faster. A warm salty liquid substance shot in her mouth, she jerked away quickly spitting the cum on the shower floor. Fray set astonished trying to catch his breath.

"You did that before," he painted.

"Boy no!" she said offensively turning away rinsing her mouth out with shower water. He admired Katie's luscious ass from behind. He rose from the bench stroking his dick trying to get it back up. Once he was hard again he pulled her by the waist onto his stiff manhood planting soft kisses on her neck, reaching in-between her thighs fingering her pussy. She let out a soft moan arching her back, grinding on his fingers. Fray wrapped one arm around her waist to keep her from running while he fingered fucked her harder. He pushed her up against the wet tile, Katie peered back at him spreading her ass cheeks giving him a clear view of her pink oozing pussy. He rammed his swollen dick inside her and started thrashing away.

"Ooo." She cried out.

ALWAYS PLAY YOUR MIRRORS

Branch Avenue was a busy street that consisted of four lanes everything from a low budget motel, skating rink, liquor store, apartments, and a shopping mall could be seen on either side. Capital carry out set secluded in the parking lot looking outward on the busy intersection. The popular eatery was surprisingly empty as Bullets stood on the opposite side of the counter.

"Aye let me get a large scrimp fried rice and two half steak & cheese wit' e'rything on it." He said placing his order.

Chucky and Horse stood posted outside engaging in a deep conversation passing the blunt back and forth.

"So you tellin me Kobe better than LeBron?" Chucky questioned.

"Damn right...and he got the rings to prove it." Horse said.

"Whatever man, you jus' a LeBron hater."

"I'm jus' callin' it how I see it," Horse stopped short of raising the blunt when he noticed the burnt orange Volvo slow down at the traffic light. He nudged Chucky who had been leaning up against the trunk of the car.

"Slim, ain't that Katie joint right there?" He gestured towards the intersection. Chucky looked over his shoulder. A wide smile spread across his slender face, he then poked his head inside the carryout.

"Aye tell em' hurry up wit' that shit I'm tryna' catch Katie at the light."

On cue, the employee handed Bullet a white plastic bag.

"Man, I don't know why you keep wastin' your time chasing behind that Bougie ass bitch, knowing she ain't fuckin' wit' you." Bullet got in the front passenger seat closing the Buicks door behind him. "And you might wanna' slow your roll. Word on the street that lil nigga she fucks wit ain't to be fucked wit," he said unwrapping his steak & cheese.

Chucky sucked his teeth.

"Since when I start caring about a nigga gettin' in his feelings about a bitch? Aye, Horse start this muthafucka up."

Horse eased the Park Avenue out into traffic busting a U.

"Bitch you ain't gone believe what happened to me the other night." Unique shook her head in shame.

Katie cut her eye over at her indicating that she was all ears before pressing on the accelerator.

PRESSURE BUST PIPES

"Girl why the hell I called myself getting dolled up the other night, putting on some sexy lingerie for Bullet only to be disappointed. She pouted.

"What happened? Katie asked.

"Bullet ass came home pissy drunk, so drunk that Horse had to drag him in the house. When I say he was drunk, I literally mean I couldn't get a response out of his dumb ass, and then Horse had the nerve to leave his drunk ass lying on the living room floor," She said rolling her eyes. "Talk about a bitch being mad I was horny as hell, and Kee jus', when I thought things couldn't get any worse Ashley tired ass, texted me saying meet him at a hotel."

"Hold up...wait...I thought you weren't fuckin' wit' Ashley no more when you found out he was havin' a baby?"

"Girl, I tried, but he kept sending me expensive gifts. I had to rethink my own situation. I'm like why in the hell should I be mad at him when I got a man, plus you already know he wasn't willing to let all this go." She said running her hands over her petite frame.

"Girl your ass is crazy," Katie chuckled weaving out of the lane.

"Well let me get back to the story. So I end up sneaking out on Bullet and meeting Ashley at the hotel. He had this little romantic dinner set up, but before I knew it he was ripping my clothes off eating my pussy. Kee, I came at least 2 times," she blushed. "I swear that was the best head he had given me and just when I thought he was going to make it a night to remember, girl tell me why his ass climbed on top of me searching for the whole. I figured I'd help him out a little bit. Bitch do you know he had the nerve to slap my hand away, you are not going to believe what happened next?" Unique said disgustedly.

"What girl spill it," Katie said excitedly.

"I was so wet I didn't feel him put the little motherfucker in. If it wasn't for him speeding up making all these ugly as faces girl I would have been a dead fuck."

"So what you do?" Katie said sounding like she was on the verge of laughter.

"Girl I started thinking about all the money he be giving me and put on a show. If someone walked past the room they would've thought he was killing my ass up in there, and then he gon' have the nerve to say who pussy is this? In my mind I'm like negro please," she rolled her eyes sitting back in her seat folding her arms across her chest. "And to think I snuck out on my man for that shit!"

Katie could no longer hold it in she burst out into laughter with tears welling up in her eyes. The women were so in tune with their conversation they didn't notice the black Buick creeping up on them.

"There she go right there," Chucky yelled excitedly from the rear.

"Moe, fall the fuck back with all that geekin' ass shit in my car." Horse frowned maneuvering the wheel. They were now heading to Waldorf. Normally Katie would have played her mirrors, but the humorous conversation had her slipping on one of Fray's proclaimed rules.

"I wonder where she going?" Horse said to no one in particular. His curiosity was soon answered as he watched her Volvo pull into a gated community. Townhouses filled the moderate parking lot, Katie stopped in the middle of the block turning on her hazard lights. Horse quickly backed into the first empty spot giving them a plain view of the foursome standing in front of 4315. Their cars were lined up in the parking lot one by one.

"Bingo!" Horse said as he flashed Chucky a smile in the rearview mirror. Bullet was oblivious to the pairs excitement. For months, they had been trying to stumble across one of the hustler's cribs. Katie's passenger door flew open, Unique ran and jumped in Ashley's arms wrapping her long slender legs around his waist. He smiled gripping her ass. Fray walked over to Katie's side bending over kissing her. Bullet sat seething. Fury was quickly growing inside of him. Horse nor Chucky was prepared for what happened next. Bullet snatched his gun off his waist and went for the door handle.

"*Hold Moe*! Horse reacted quickly grabbing a hold of his arm.

"*Man, get the fuck off me*!" He struggled.

"Son chill. We can explain," Chucky interjected. The duo wasn't about to let Bullet fuck things up for them. Bullet's movement ceased as he looked at Horse and Chucky suspiciously.

"You mean to tell me you two niggas knew about this?" Bullet frowned.

"It's a long story holmes. We'll school you on the way back." Horse put the car in gear and pulled out slowly. Bullet watched helplessly while the love of his life tongued down another man. In the meantime, Ronnie mean-mugged Unique from the top of DeShay's steps as she played in Ashley's arms. "Fake Bitch," he thought. Unique wasn't sure if Ronnie told, but if he did Ashley was doing a good job at hiding it. Ashley caught wind of the killer stare Ronnie was given Unique. He pulled her aside to talk making a mental note to holler at Ronnie when she left.

"So how much is the bag," Ashley asked.

"Mm…fifteen hundred."

"Fifteen?!" He frowned. "What the muthafucka come wit' a dress and some shoes?"

"Baby stop being so cheap. Besides, I thought you liked me in the best?" Unique batted her eyes already knowing he couldn't resist her.

"I do. It's just that my money been kinda funny lately."

"Please! She whined brushing her breast up against his chest. Before he knew it her right hand was grabbing his dick through his jeans. She softly bit his bottom lip outstretching it. "I promise I'll make it worth it," she kissed his neck. Ashley had a hard on already knowing her head was crucial. He started to pull her in the car and take her up on the offer, but the thought of getting caught by their friends discouraged him. Not wanting to appear whipped, he made sure no one saw him slip her the wad of cash.

"Thanks, babe. I'll call you when we're done." She pecked his cheek before making her way back to Katie's car.

The following day the pesky trio slid back out to Waldorf. They parked four houses down from 4315 in a stolen SUV. The cars that once lined the front of the house were nowhere in sight. Chucky suggested they take the oversized screwdriver and pry the door open rather wait for one of the hustlers to return. They watched the house for hours drawing suspicion from the nosey neighbors as they passed in front of the truck with their dogs. Just when they were about to call it off the once congested parking lot had finally settled. Horse had just grabbed the oversized screwdriver from underneath his seat when a black BMW X6 pulled into the gated community. They watched the vehicle pull up to their mark. Neither one of them recalled seeing that vehicle out there the day before.

The driver door opened and out step an attractive, tall, petite bronze skin woman with reddish brown hair. It was hard to tell the woman's descent, but if the trio had to guess they would say the woman look Indian. They watched her open her back door reaching inside carefully un-strapping her baby's car seat.

"That must be one of the niggaz girl." Bullet said clutching the wheel. With her daughter in hand, she started for the house, leaving the car door open indicating she would make a second trip.

"That's our in right there." Chucky said from the trucks back seat. The woman emerged from the house walking down the concrete steps. She removed two large brown paper bags filled with groceries from the trunk, using her hips to close the door she began walking toward the house again. Bullet shifted the truck into gear slowly rolling up behind her. Chucky and Horse casually got out the truck headed in her direction.

The woman didn't have a clue of the danger that lurked behind her as she crossed her threshold. When she turned around to close the door she was met with a terrifying site of Chucky and Horse spiraling out of control at her. With eyes widened with fear, her heart sank, she tried slamming the door on her attackers. Horse dipped his shoulder colliding with the swinging door sending it flying into her, knocking her to the floor. He was all over her like a cheap suit. He snatched her up by her hair before he knew it the woman had clawed his face.

"*Urr...Stupid bitch*!" He said striking her to the floor.

He was so caught up in the moment he forgot to pull his mask down. The sight of his own blood infuriated him. He delivered a kick to her ribs.

"*Oww!*" She cried out curling up in a fetal position. When Bullet entered the house he heard the baby howling. The woman lied on the wooden floor clutching her ribs. Horse was just about to bring down the butt of his gun when Bullet caught him in mid-air.

"Moe if you kill her, how we suppose to get the dough?"

A masked and gloved Chucky returned from clearing the house, unlike Horse he and Bullet pulled their masks down. Once giving the nod the house was clear Bullet gestured for Chucky to get the crying baby off the couch. Bullet grabbed the bruised woman by the back of her neck standing her up. Seeing the masked man holding her daughter, Aisha reached for her daughter desperately.

"Please don't hurt my baby." She cried. Bullet brandished his gun to her head.

"Now I'ma ask you one time and one time only... Where the money at?"

"It's upstairs." She sobbed.

"Lead the way." Bullet shoved her in her back.

The trio trailed behind her closely up the steps. They came to the center of the hallway where a huge family portrait of the couple occupied the wall. It was then they knew which one of the hustlers they were robbing. Aisha unhooked the family portrait from the wall, the greed smeared across the men faces.

"What'chu waiting on open it!" Bullet upped the gun.

"I don't know the code." She yelped.

Bullet aimed his gun at the baby as she dangled in Chucky's arms. The woman looked on in horror.

"*I said open the muthafuckin safe.*" He fumed.

"*I swear I don't know the code. I don't know it!*" She broke down. All of a sudden her motherly intuition took over as she tried going for her child. She was quickly met with a swift blow to the back of her cranium by Horse's gun. She fell to her knees and blacked out.

PRESSURE BUST PIPES

"Man what the fuck!" Bullet fumed looking down at the unconscious woman before him.

"What?" Horse shrugged. "The bitch moved."

There petty disagreement was short lived as Chucky's attention was drawn down the hall to the couple's bedroom window. Flashing red and blue lights illuminated the sheer curtains. With the screaming baby in hand, Chucky dashed down the hall looking out the window. He watched the police cruiser pull up to the house. The Neighborhood Watch witnessed the entire encounter. Chucky looked on in fear as he watched the neighbors point in the direction of the house. He powered walked back down the hallway with the crying baby in hand, he found Bullet and Horse still arguing.

"Aye, later for all that shit we got company," he said placing the baby down beside her unconscious mother. They drew their guns bolting down the steps hitting the back door. By the time the officers broke down the front door the intruders were long gone. The sound of the baby howling raised their alertness. They carefully followed the cries discovering a baby next to an unconscious woman.

"We need a medic in here now!" The officer yelled out to his partner scooping up the crying baby.

Gladys Knight Chicken & Waffles...

Fray was just exiting the restaurant when Derek pulled into the parking lot. Fray signaled with his index finger one moment as he placed the takeout bags on the passenger seat of his car, popping his trunk. Derek parked alongside him. Fray opened the passenger door on truck lowering himself inside, closing the door behind him.

"That's the five I owe you plus our money for another five bricks," he said passing Derek the duffle bag he had just pulled from his trunk.

Derek was still salty about the youngsters going into business for themselves, but he hid his true feelings.

"Shawty, I might need you to take the ride with me this time. At least, until I'm familiar with this new connect." Fray knew Derek was referring to his new New York connection he met a month ago while vacationing in the Big Apple.

"When you 'pose to meet up wit' em?"

"Sometime later today, but I think it's best we leave now if we plan on beatin' rush hour."

"Damn, why the short notice?" Fray frowned.

"That's how the new people like to play."

"How long do you think we'll be gone," Fray asked.

"Two days max."

Fray Wrestled with the thought. The truth was he was only supposed to be running out to pick up something to eat, and head straight back to the house to spend time with Katie and her nephew. However, he had got more than he had bargained for when he secretly called Derek to cop. Although he and Katie didn't have children of their own Sunday served as their own personal family day.

"C'mon baby-boy I need you on this one. I don't trust these people no further than I can see them." Derek pressed on, Fray already knowing Katie was going to be upset with his decision he sighed heavily.

"You owe me big for this one. Follow me back to my crib so I can pack," Fray said hopping out the truck.

PRESSURE BUST PIPES

Twenty-five minutes later Derek was watching Fray get out his car, and head towards his building.

"I'ma wait out here," Derek said lowering his window.

No sooner than Fray entered the building Katie pulled in the back of Derek's truck. Her ten-year-old nephew was full of joy upon seeing Fray's car parked outside. Anton leaped from the car running towards the building. Katie called after him stopping him before he could enter the building.

"Get back here and help me with these bags," she said popping the trunk. After grabbing the bags, they walked to the building together. Derek blew his horn getting her attention.

"What's up Kee?"

Looking back over her shoulder she noticed Derek, she was perplexed as to why he was parked outside their house. Katie didn't care for Derek much because he always made her feel uncomfortable, she waved anyway.

"Fray were home." She yelled out.

She found Fray walking towards them carrying a gym bag as if he was preparing to leave. She dropped the bags at the door folding her arms across her chest, guarding the door. Anton didn't seem to notice the tension around him as he jumped in Fray's arms.

"Woe, lil man!" Fray smiled as Anton almost ran him over. He was crazy about Fray.

"Whassup Uncle Fray? You ready to play me in some basketball?" He said excitedly.

"I wish I could lil man, but I gotta go out of town." He said breaking their embrace.

"Awe man...I thought you were staying."

"Anton, let me talk to Fray. Go in the room." Katie interjected. Disappointed, Anton pouted down the hall with Fray watching him.

"I guess that explains why Derek is parked outside."

"He asked if I could ride with him to New York to handle some business."

"To handle some business?" Katie repeated. "Fray you don't even go out on Sunday's, or did you forget today was our day?" She fussed. Fray knew how Katie could get when she was upset, he searched for the right words to say.

"I promise I'll make it up to you," he said reaching for her hand.

"Try making it up to that disappointed ten-year-old boy who thinks the world of you," she avoided his touch, picking up the bags that she dropped, walking to the kitchen. Fray was right behind her. Katie slammed the contents from the bags on the counter.

"Kee, what do you want me to do?"

"Cancel," she said with attitude.

"You know I'm not about to do that. Besides, I already gave him my word that I'll go."

"So why would you ask me what you should do if you already had your mind made up? Why do I always come second to the streets Fray, huh?"

"Katie you talkin' crazy now."

Fray picked up his bag leaving out the kitchen

"What about your word to me and Anton? I guess that doesn't mean shit!"

Fray was at a loss for words.

"Y'know if the streets is that important go...go!" She yelled shoving him. She was on the verge of tears.

"Kee I-," she silenced him with her hand. He gave her one last look before turning to leave out the door. Katie broke down. She headed straight to the bathroom to gather herself before going to check on her nephew. Anton was sitting on the floor at the foot of the bed playing Madden. He was really looking forward to hanging out with Fray.

"Mind if I play?" Katie asked sitting next to him on the floor. He shrugged. She figured just because Fray broke his promise didn't mean she had to do the same, she picked up the extra controller. With a forced smile he said, "Girls don't play video games."

"Oh yeah...says who?" She said.

"Uncle Fray."

Katie was always up for a challenge.

"Oh, he did...did he? Well, I'm jus' goin' to have to prove him wrong." She smiled.

Five minutes into the game Katie was leading 6-0. A familiar melody drew her attention away from the TV, it was coming from down the hall.

"Pause the game right quick Anton. I'll be right back," she got up and followed the sound. Young Joc's "Dope Boy Magic" ringtone was coming from the living room. Fray's cell phone was plugged in the wall still attached to the charger sitting on the table.

"Serves his black ass right." She said aloud before answering it. "Hello."

Click! The phone hung up.

Taken aback by the caller hanging up, she removed the phone from her ear looking down at her picture on the screensaver. She checked the last call the number wasn't saved. Thinking a hundred miles per minute her antennas went up. She called out to Anton who came trotting down the hall.

"Call this number back for me. Ask if somebody just called Fray." Anton eyed his aunt suspiciously as she hit the talk button putting the phone on speaker. A woman picked up on the third ring.

"Somebody call Fray?" Anton asked.

"Yea, Pebblez…hold on right quick," Gi-Gi said.

Katie's eyes enlarged at the caller's name. Seconds later a different voice came alive over the phone.

"What's up handsome?" Pebblez beamed.

Katie was so caught off guard she didn't realize she had snatched the phone from Anton.

"Aren't you a hard man to catch up with," Pebblez continued.

"Bitch this ain't Fray! And what the hell you doin' wit' my man number anyway?" Katie snapped taking Pebblez by surprise.

Pebblez didn't know whether to hang up or toy with the young girl's mind. Pebblez knew all about Katie. She did her own investigation after meeting Fray for the first time.

"Lil girl ain't it past your bedtime? So run along and put your man on the phone." Gigi couldn't help but to overhear the conversation, "Whassup youngster!" she taunted in the background.

"I know you washed up bitches ain't jus' come for me." Katie spat refusing to back down.

PRESSURE BUST PIPES

"Washed up!" Pebblez frowned. "Lil girl you 'ought to respect some boss bitches like us. You would think Unique's tender box-ass woulda' gave your green ass some game by now. Who am I kidding it's in you two bitches' nature to try and lock a nigga down."

"You know what, I'm not even about to go back and forth with a whack bitch like you, but you betta' pray we never bump into each other in the streets."

Katie hit the end button slamming the phone down hard on the table. She felt like her heart had been ripped out of her chest. She had been nothing but a good woman to Fray, and for the second time today she wept overwhelmingly.

Fray sat fidgeting in his seat while Derek pushed his truck down Baltimore-Washington Pkwy.

"You lost sumthin'?" Derek asked briefly taking his eyes off the road.

"Yea, my phone," Fray said reaching in-between the seats.

"Here call it from my phone." Derek passed him his cell phone, Fray dialed his number from his phone. He was startled to hear Katie's voice on the other end.

"Hello?" she answered dryly.

Fray frowned at the realization of what he had just done. Had it not been for Katie nagging him he wouldn't have forgotten his phone.

"When were you going to call and tell me I forgot my phone."

"So we playin' games now?" Katie asked cutting straight to the chase.

"Games? Man, ain't nobody playin' no games wit' you."

"Don't play dumb. You know damn well what I'm talkin' about. I'm talkin' about that bitch Pebblez calling your phone." She barked.

"Pebblez?" Fray said dumbfounded. *"Man, I 'ont know how that bitch got my number."*

"Fray really? Your number didn't jus' fall out the sky and into her phone."

"Look, man, I jus' told you I 'ont know," he said but Katie wasn't convinced.

"So she just popped up with it...yea right."

"Kee I don't talk to that bitch!"

Fray was adamant about pleading his case. Katie wanted to believe him badly, but Fray didn't have the best track record. The bigger he got in the drug game the more drama she had to deal with from other females. Nothing seemed to surprise her anymore, she heard everything from Fray getting someone pregnant to females claiming him as theirs. With no solid proof of the accusations, Katie decided to make it work each time. This time was different, Pebblez was the straw that broke the camel's back. Fray could hear muffled sobs through the receiver.

"I can't do this anymore." Her chest heaved up and down.

"Kee, you can't do what! I'm tellin' you ain't shit goin' on with me and that bitch." He pleaded.

Silence filled the line.

"Goodbye, baby." She whispered in the phone.

"Kee don't do th-," The phone line disconnected. Fray removed the phone from his ear staring at the blank screen. He tried calling her back several times only to be sent to the voicemail. Fray sat in a state of confusion trying to figure out how the hell Pebblez got his number.

"Woman problems?" Derek asked.

"Slim, you gave that bitch Pebblez my number?"

"Hell no! I wouldn't do no shit like that without your permission." Derek looked at him like he was crazy.

"Well if you didn't…who then?" Fray said more so to himself.

He placed both hands over his face leaning his head back on the headrest as Derek continued on New Jersey turnpike…

BLOOD IN MY EYE

DeShay stormed through the sliding doors accompanied by Ronnie and Ashley. The hospital was in a frenzy. The trio approached the receptionist desk only to have their presence blown-off by a short hair, long fingernails, fake eyelashes, ghetto receptionist sitting behind the desk popping gum. They stood there waiting for assistance as she continued her personal conversation on her cell phone. Already irate DeShay became hostile by the woman rudeness. He reached across the counter snatching her cell phone out her hand tossing it on the floor.

"Oh no, you didn't jus' take my phone out my hand. Are you fuckin' crazy!" she frowned.

"Oh yes I did bitch, and I'll show you just how crazy I am if you

don't tell me what room Aisha Williams is in." He spat.

The woman assessed the three men who stood before her, judging from their demeanor she could tell they were about business. She picked up her clipboard scanning over the patients' name until she came across the name she was looking for.

"She's in room 313," she said slamming her clipboard down. DeShay gave her a menacing stare before stepping onto the elevator with Ronnie, and Ashley.

"We goin' wait out here," Ronnie said as DeShay pushed the door open to room 313. Aisha was asleep when he pulled the curtains back. The rattling from the curtains woke her from her sleep. He forced a gentle smile.

"Where's our daughter?" she asked groggily.

"At my mom's she's fine." he kissed her on her lips.

Tears began to roll from the corner of her eyes. DeShay sat next to her pulling her up into his arms. Once she regained her composure she gave him the rundown. Fifteen minutes later he was stepping back outside the room.

"How is she?" the pair asked in unison.

"She suffered a minor concussion. She'll be out in a week."

"Did she get a look at the niggaz faces?" Ashley blurted out.

"Yea, one of em. The other two had on a mask." It was a slight pause. "That nigga Fray still ain't call yet?" DeShay asked.

"Hold that thought," Ashley said stepping aside to answer his buzzing phone. "Hello," he whispered. He listened closely to the frantic hysterical caller on the other end. "Fa real?" he frowned. "A'ight. I'll hit you when we leave the hospital." Ashley ended the call. "That was Katie. She said she moved out."

"What!" Ronnie and DeShay said surprised.

"She said something about Pebblez calling his phone." Ronnie's heart sunk to his stomach at Ashley's revelation.

"Oh yeah, and Fray's in New York, by the way, she said he left with Derek this morning."

"New York? Fuck he go up there for?" DeShay asked.

"What you think?" Ashley said cocking his head to the side.

"Well we'll jus' fill him in when he gets back," DeShay said.

As soon as the words left his mouth they spotted a pot-belly detective heading in their direction.

"Hi, you doing kid? I'm detective Nash I recognize you from all the photographs around your house."

The officer extended his hand but was left hanging.

"What do you want?" DeShay said rudely.

"Can we go somewhere private to talk?"

"Anything you got to say you can say in front of my friends."

"Very well…what's in the safe? I mean it's gotta be something worth value to nearly get your girlfriend killed."

"You got any questions you can contact my lawyer Douglas Woods," DeShay said handing the detective his lawyer's card.

"Hey, hey take it easy no one's treating you like a suspect. I was simply asking if I could have a look inside the safe?"

"You got a search warrant?" DeShay asked. He took the officer silence as a no. "Like I said if you got any questions contact my lawyer. Until then leave me be so I can finish talking to my family." The detective nodded his head making his departure towards the elevator.

"You know you gotta clean out the safe," Ronnie said as they watched the detective step onto the elevator.

"I know." DeShay agreed. "Well look, I'ma let y'all go 'head and get outta' here. I'm spendin' the night with Aisha. And remember to keep y'all ears to the streets. The minute y'all hear sumthin' call me. This shit is personal."

They slapped fives giving him a hug before parting ways. Ashley was just about to stick the key in the ignition when he remembered he had to call Katie back, he retrieved his phone from his pocket.

"Who you calling?" Ronnie asked.

"Katie, so I can try and straighten this shit out with her and Fray. To tell you the truth I didn't even know he was fuckin' wit Pebblez." He commenced dialing her number. Ronnie knew it was now or never.

"Hold up before you do that I gotta tell you sumthin." Ashley looked at him puzzled. "Now before you judge me let me say this. I didn't know me givin' Pebblez his number was gonna fuck up his happy home." He revealed.

"You did what!" Ashley said confused.

"It's a long story and I rather not get into it right now, just know I was the one who gave out the number."

"Man," Ashley lowered his head shaking it. "You did anything."

"How the hell was I supposed to know his dumb ass was goin' leave his phone around Katie," Ronnie spat, trying to justify his actions.

"Yea, well you betta' hope Katie don't leave his ass, because if she do." He paused. "It's gonna be trouble, trouble." Ashley joked imitating Bernie Mack from "The Players Club."

PRESSURE BUST PIPES

The Barry Farms Tournament served as D. C's own Rucker's bringing out some of the NBA's biggest stars from Gilbert Arenas, Steve Francis, and Kevin Durant just to name a few. The annual b-ball tournament consisted of some of the city's known urban wear boutiques that sponsored teams and concession stands.

"Yaay!" The crowd went wild as Curt "Trouble" Smith shook left, crossing over right hitting a three pointer putting All Daz up 55-53 over The Madness Shop with 1:30 to go. Trouble Smith and D-Nice had been going at it all game. Ashley and DeShay stood on the sideline in a separate crowd engaging in a crap game.

"Shake the muthafuckin' dice next time!" DeShay spat, frustrated he was down a stack. The old-timer Charlie was locking the dice. Various hustlers stood around with knots of cash in their hand. Two of the men the duo knew such as Pimp Charlie and their one-time childhood friend Brian.

"Gate what you hate young-boy." Pimp Charlie said from his stooping position in his linen shorts scooting the dice. He had two bad broads standing behind him. Scooping the dice from the ground, clutching them in his big hand not shaking them he rolled.

"Sat em' down," DeShay said, blocking his shot.

"Scared money don't make no money." Charlie barked, running his ring filled hand over his perm hair. He then scooped the dice back up, exaggerated shaking them so DeShay could hear them before releasing them from his grip, snapping his fingers.

"Snake Eyes!" DeShay boasted collecting his bets as the dice landed on 1 & 1.

Chucky and Horse had just stepped foot inside the gate. They scanned the many faces in the crowd for potential prey and enemies. Horse nodded his head in the direction of the crap game.

"What y'all shootin'?" Horse asked approaching the game.

"Got Damn young boy what got you in the face." Charlie blurted out causing everyone at the dice game to look up. The nasty scratches were visible on Horse's check. Horse was taken by surprise by the stranger putting him on the spot, masking his feelings he responded.

"My girl like to play rough."

DeShay eyed the stocky gentlemen hesitantly.

"Let me go back?" Charlie said peeling a hundred-dollar bill from his knot gathering the dice.

"Go head," DeShay said matching his bet. The ringing of his cell phone had his undivided attention. "Hello." He answered listening intently to the caller on the other end. "A'ight. I'll meet you out front of the gate," he said disconnecting the call. "Aye, look I gotta step outside the gate right quick…Ash make sure that nigga shakes the dice."

Aisha was parked outside the ten-foot black fence when she spotted DeShay stepping through the opening of the gate.

"What the hell you doin' down here Aisha?" He asked upon entering the car. I thought the doctors said for you to rest?"

"I'm scared to be in that house alone, what if they come back" she cried.

"I talked to the realtor today. The house will be listed next week."

Aisha wiped her tears with the back of her hands looking past DeShay, through the holes in the fence, and into the crowd, a chill ran through her body. Horse's face jumped out at her as he stood up from the crowd, arguing with another gambler about a bet. She tried to speak but nothing came out. Confused by the horrific look on her face, DeShay looked over at the group of men. Looking at each one them warily he said, "Whassup? What's wrong?"

Still at a loss for words, she pointed out Horse.

"What'chu know that nigga or sumthin'" He tightened his face.

"Shay, that's the guy who broke in the house!" she finally uttered. Out of the blue, his memory was refreshed when he thought back to Aisha encounter with him, the dude with the scratched cheek. He reached for the door handle, Aisha grabbed his arm.

"No baby please, let's just go." She begged.

"Man, get the fuck off me!" He jerked away getting out the car. *"Get the hell from down here Aisha,"* he said slamming the door. Murder was the only thing on his mind as he stepped back through the gate, biting his bottom lip. DeShay had tunnel vision as he pushed his way through the crowd. Ashley noticed the sudden change in his friend's character. He tried to hand DeShay his winnings, but DeShay brushed by him. Knowing his friend all too well he instinctively positioned his hand on his Sig Saucer that was concealed underneath his shirt ready for action.

Stepping in the circle DeShay found Horse on a bended knee shaking the dice. DeShay's towering presence made him look up. For the first time, he looked death in the eye. In one swift motion DeShay whipped out his P97 Ruger from his waist, aiming it, the first shot froze everything. He continued to squeeze the trigger rapidly. Disorder erupted as spectators trampled one another desperately trying to get through the gate. DeShay's course of action set Ashley into motion as well. He drew his gun chasing after the fleeing Albino. He managed to let off a round before Chucky blended in with the crowd. Being a careful shooter, Ashley bolted to the car not wanting to hit any innocent bystanders.

DeShay stood over Horse's lifeless body filling his head and chest with led. He continued to pull the trigger even after the gun was empty. Ashley's car horn snapped him out of his psychopathic-state. He ran towards the awaiting beamer leaving Horse's riddled body behind.

"Did you get the other one?" DeShay asked once inside.

"Nah, that lil muthafucka got away! What the hell was that all about?" Ashley asked moving his beamer down the highway, occasionally peeking in his mirror for the cops.

"Them was the niggaz who hit my spot. Aisha got a look at the nigga when I was in the car with her."

"Oh yeah, so what now?" Ashley asked ready to put in some work.

"You already know. Take me around the way to get one of them choppers. I'm 'bout to put the niggaz whole strip on no movement." He seethed.

But he would never get the chance, not even two hours later the feds had apprehended him.

"Fuck you mean they killed Horse!" Bullet grabbed a weeping Chucky around his collar. *"Where the fuck was you niggaz guns at?"*

"Horse thought it would be a good idea if we left 'em in the car because all the undercover police that be out there." Chucky sobbed. Bullet released him from his grasps. His legs felt heavy. He took a seat on the sofa and began bawling. A war had just begun.

ALL RATZ MUST DIE

"Kee, you been moping around this house for the past three days," Unique said as Katie climbed back into bed.

"I don't know why you jus' don't call him. I mean Ashley did say it was all Ronnie's doing."

Katie looked at her like she was crazy.

"Really, Unique what else was he supposed to say? You even overheard Gigi saying she was gonna hook them up," Katie said clutching her bear.

"I did say that, but Kee maybe that's not the case. I'm telling you I know how those two bitches play," Unique said sincerely.

Normally Unique would've been the one to encourage Katie to cheat, but seeing how happy Fray made her friend she learned to accept it. Ever since Fray returned home from New York he had been desperately trying to contact Katie. His calls were unanswered and never returned. He was surprised to return home to an empty apartment. He went so far as popping up over her sister's house but was turned away by her guard dog Unique. As soon as he returned home he was hit with the news about DeShay, which put his chase of Katie on hold.

"Damn after e'rything we built all it took was three lousy ass days for it all to come crumbling down." Fray thought as he sat parked outside of DC Jail. He was still battling with his break up with Katie, and on top of that, he had to deal with DeShay mess. With the cops locking DeShay up for Horse's murder Ashley went into hiding. Fray pondered how he was going to clean it up to protect his cousin's fate. He asked Allah to forgive him for his soon to be actions he knew he was about to take.

After filling out the visitor's form he submitted his I.D to the police in the bubble and proceeded to the elevator taking it to the third floor. The visiting hall always smelled like stale cigarettes. There were visits already taking place when Fray found an empty seat. He glanced at his watch, hoping DeShay would hurry up, so he wouldn't get caught in the count. The electric door slid back making a loud clanking noise. DeShay handed the C.O working the door his pass. He stepped in with his collar popped on his orange jumpsuit. Fray stood up and proceeded towards the two-way phones separated by Plexiglas.

"Whassup?" DeShay smiled pressing his fist on the glass cradling the phone to his ear. Fray didn't return the smile.

"I 'ont know cuz you tell me. I mean you in there and I'm sittin' out here."

From the moment DeShay stepped through the door, and laid eyes on his cousin he knew he was in for an earful.

"Look before you say anything…,"

PRESSURE BUST PIPES

"Man, what were you thinkin'! Down the Farms though holmes?" Fray's frustration was visible as he thought how packed the tournament could be. *"I told you before this is a thinkin' man's game,"* he tapped his temple *"That hot-headed shit don't get a nigga nuthin' but a rack of time."* DeShay lowered his head in shame.

For years, Fray had been telling him to control his temper.

"Cuz, I already know you fucked up at me. Sumthin' in me just snapped." DeShay lowered his head.

Fray watched his cousin defenselessly, with one foot in the game, and the other on Qur'an there was no way he was going to allow anyone to make it to court, his cousin's life was on the line he would do anything to free him.

"You holla' at your lawyer yet?" Fray asked taking a softer approach.

"As a matter of fact, he came to see me today." DeShay held up two fingers indicating that the government had two witnesses. With a Kool-Aid smile on his face, Fray knew his cousin knew who the witnesses were.

"Oh, yeah?" Fray said relieved the government only had two witnesses, which made his job easier.

"Make sure you get at Tee asap," Fray said.

"Oh, and before I forget, your lil man Pee-Wee asked about you the other day," DeShay smiled thinking about his young protégé.

"Whassup wit em?" DeShay asked.

"Shid, we had to damn near run his lil' ass off the block the other day for tryna sell demo's." Fray laughed.

"Fa real!" DeShay frowned. "Man, I swear if I beat dis' joint I'ma take shawty under my wing."

Over the years, DeShay had taken a liken to the youngster and his best friend lil Boo.

"Hmp...good luck," Fray chuckled.

The C.O signaled time was up.

"That's your visit." The chubby officer said staring back at him.

"Got damn big boy give a nigga another ten minutes." DeShay protested.

"I gave you enough time. Now 'dats your visit." The officer spat turning to exit the visiting hall.

The pair then stood saying their goodbyes bumping their fist on the glass.

"Don't forget to get a Tee," Fray said before returning the phone to its base.

The following night Fray sat parked outside his building conversing with Tee on his throw away phone.

"Hold on, you sure he said the second name was Charlie?" Fray said in disbelief already knowing the answer to the question. He and Charlie gambled together regularly, however, he wasn't surprised to learn Brian was one of the witnesses. Brian had grown up with the foursome around D Street, N.E. to say that he was friends with them would be highly mistaken. They use to bully Brian when they were younger.

At dawn, Fray called his partner Wax from Lincoln Heights asking about Pimp Charlie. He was astonished at how much insight he obtained with one phone call. Wax put him right at Charlie's doorstep. Already knowing Brian's mother still owned the house on 17th & C street, there was no need to do any homework on him. Lincoln Height's comprised of over five different territorial sections divided by the street crews. There was the valley, the circle, the basketball court, 51st and the maze. With all the different sections the flow of the traffic was always on the go. It made it easy for someone to slip in and out unobserved.

Fray pulled his car next to the curve parking in the Valley. He sat examining the crowd of fiends through his tinted window as they stood in line waiting for their morning fix. He grabbed the today's newspaper from the passenger seat, zipped up his black Helly Hanson ski-jacket, and exited the car pulling his hood tight, he was met with a cool morning breeze. He tucked the newspaper under his left armpit and proceeded up the broad concrete stairs with black handrails leading into the circle. Fray let out a yawn as he climbed the stairs fighting the temptation to stay awake. He was exhausted. He was relieved to find that section of the projects was still empty prior to him cruising by.

"Jus' like Wax said," he thought looking at Charlie's Caddy parked right out front of his building. He scanned his surroundings looking for a spot to lay low. He spotted a milk crate sitting in front of the building parallel from Charlie's. Fray decided to take his position from there. Sitting down on the crate he eased his P97 Ruger.45 from his black Helly Hanson Ski-pants resting it on his lap. He pulled the newspaper from under his arm flipping to the metro section. He began to read as he periodically glanced from the paper to the many windows. DeShay picture was on the front of the metro section. There was an entire article about his case.

Tournament killer captured last week without incident. Authorities arrested twenty-year-old DeShay Mills from the 600 block of D street N.E. Authorities believe he, and another assailant whose identity has yet to be determined because he is still at large shot, and killed thirty-one-year-old Horace Smith...

Fray looked up from the paper at the sound of a car's engine turning down the circle. *"Shit,"* he said frowning, lifting the paper up, pretending to be reading as the car inched closer. His first thought was to get up and leave, but rethinking it he stayed glued to the crate peaking over the top of the newspaper. He watched the Honda Accord come to a rapid stop beside Charlie's, the door flew open. Out jumped a white woman with blonde hair, a tight black jacket, body dress, and thigh high stripper boots. She looked to be hiding something behind her back. Sitting opposite of them Fray could see the driver of the vehicle was a Caucasian woman as well. Out of nowhere the woman in the leather jacket raised her arm, cocked it back, and threw a brick through Charlie's window.

"Dis bitch 'bout to make shit hot." Fray scowled watching the shattered glass fly everywhere triggering the alarm. Both women were laughing as she hopped back into the passenger seat. They skidded off in a hurry leaving black skid marks in the street. Charlie came storming out of his building with concern on his face. Dressed in tan slacks a wrinkled wife beater, and a matted bush he held a baseball bat. Touching his key ring he silenced the alarm. He began examining the damage to his car unaware that he was being watched.

Fray sat looking over the top of the paper from his target to the sheet covered windows. Charlie stood ten feet away from him. Turning on his heels, Charlie noticed a man sitting on a milk crate with his face buried in the newspaper. Without second-guessing he headed in Fray's direction hoping for answers. Fray chose to capitalize on this just like a lion whose gleaming eyes covered by tall grass stalks his prey. Fray secretly watched him approaching as he peeked over the rim of the paper.

"Aye, my man did you happen to see who just bust my damn window?" Charlie asked still unable to see the person's face. Slowly

PRESSURE BUST PIPES

Fray lowered the paper from his face. Charlie looked as if he just seen the grim reaper taking a step back, his heart skipped a beat. Fray rose from the crate, .45 in his hand, aiming it at Charlie's chest he tried to protest. As soon as his mouth opened Fray squeezed the trigger putting a bullet through the right side of his cheek. Blood splattered landing on Fray's face and clothes. Charlie was dead before he hit the ground. Fray stood over top of him pumping two more hollows into his chest. He dropped the newspaper he had been reading on Charlie's lifeless body. DeShay's picture turned upwards he bolted towards the steps heading to his car in the Valley…

TWO DAYS LATER …

Charlie's murder spread through the city like a wildfire. Loved by many, and hated by few. No one knew the particulars of his premature death or the identity of his killer. Everywhere you turned someone was trying to piece together his or her own version of why he was murdered. The only people who knew the truth was the arranger, the killer, and Charlie. The cousins intended on keeping it that way.

The sun hid behind the clouds on the residential block of 17th & C street. Cars drove up and down the two-way street separating the row houses on both sides. Fray and Ronnie sat parked across the street from Brian's mother house in Ronnie's Lexus. With the steady flow of traffic, they had no choice, but to change their plan.

"Man, don't light 'dat shit up! We on a muthafuckin' mission, and we ain't got time for no fuck up's." Fray barked looking over at Ronnie who sat in the driver seat sticking his cigarette in a twenty-dollar capsule of PCP.

"What the fuck you talkin' bout I can function off dis shit!"

Ronnie shot back.

"Aye holmes," Fray said lowering his squeaky voice. "My mutherfuckin' cousin is sittin' in a box right now, and you gettin' high off that shit goin' up in there tripping ain't goin' do him, or Ashley no good."

"So what am I supposed to do the shit already dipped?"

"Personally, I 'ont give a fuck what'chu do wit' it, but you ain't 'bout to get high, and go around 'dis dude's moms like that. She don't have shit to do with it." Fray frowned thinking the worse that could happen while inside with Ronnie high off PCP. "Now quit stallin' and c'mon we wasted enough time already," Fray said opening the car door on Ronnie's Lexus crossing the street heading towards Brian mothers' house. After putting the un-smoked dipper (PCP) in the ashtray Ronnie followed suit.

"Now remember let me do all the talking," Fray said ringing the doorbell. After a few seconds of waiting a woman's voice bellowed from behind the door.

"Who is it?"

Fray and Ronnie knew exactly whom the voice belonged too.

"It's Fray Ms. Riley."

"Who?" she repeated.

"Fray." Ms. Riley said to herself before unchaining the locks. She hadn't seen them since they were kids, and now they were all grown up. She didn't recognize them instantly. Pulling the fiberglass door open the elderly woman appeared in the doorway. She had a huge mole on the side of her nose. She stood looking through her bifocals trying to make out the two people before her.

"Umm…yes?" She asked looking confused. Figuring she may not recognize him with his full beard Fray gave a warm smile. It was then his youthful appearance appeared before her. "Fray baby is 'dat you?" she blushed.

"Yes, it's me, Ms. Riley." He continued smiling.

"Awe baby don't jus' stand there give me a hug. I almost didn't recognize you," she smiled embracing him.

After breaking their embrace Fray asked, "You remember Ronnie don't you Ms. Riley?" he gestured.

"Wait…Ms. Watson grandson?" She answered eyeing Ronnie in a quizzical manner. Ronnie smiled crookedly. "Boy if you 'ont get over here and give me a hug!" She smiled pulling him close. As the two shared a squeeze Fray noticed a little boy peeking from behind her. The boy couldn't have been any more than three years old. He had a big ass head just like Brian. After Ms. Riley and Ronnie broke their embrace Fray decided to ask about the little boy behind her. Already knowing the answer.

"Who's 'dat lil fella hidin' behind you Ms. Riley?"

She looked over her shoulder locating her bashful grandson.

"Well I see you already met Brian Jr," she smiled at the little boy at her side. "Say hi baby these are your daddy friends."

At the mention of his father lil Brian mustered a smile. Ronnie stood eyeing them with all kinds of wicked thoughts running through his head.

"Give me a five lil man!" Fray smiled extending his right hand breaking Ronnie out of his daze. Lil Brian slapped the palm of his hand.

"Speaking of 'dat no good daddy of his y'all know he isn't here right?" Ms. Riley said. Fray had an instantaneous comeback.

"Yeah, we know he told us to meet him over here," he lied.

"Oh why didn't y'all say something sooner come on in." She stepped aside so that they could enter.

Sleek contemporary furniture and Asian rugs adorned the living room. There was a sleeping baby on one of the two sofas.

"And 'dis lil feisty heifer here is my granddaughter isn't she precious?"

"Yeah, she looks 'jus' like you," Fray said stroking her ego.

"Oh, boy stop." she blushed tapping his arm. "So what'chu boys been up to y'all have any kids of ya' own."

"No I don't, but Ronnie has two a boy, and a girl," Fray said. "Ms. Riley we didn't interrupt you or anything did we?"

"Well, I was jus' about to put another load in the washer until you showed up. Would y'all mind sitting here wit' them while I go down in the basement?"

"Of course, we don't take your time," Fray smiled swatting her off.

"Thanks, baby, y'all are too sweet." She disappeared into the basement.

Five minutes later the two made themselves right at home. Fray crawled around on the rug playing horsy with lil Brian saddled on his back. Ronnie sat on the sofa holding Brian's now awakened daughter in his arms. Brian was sure to flip upon walking through the door seeing them playing with his kids, and holding down the fort in his mom's house. Ronnie placed his P89 on his lap pulling his Polo hoodie' over it. They heard the locks turning on the front door. Looking towards the entrance they watched the knob turn, and the door open. Dressed in blue jeans, Nike boots, and a red t-shirt an obese Brian strolled in.

"Daddy look at me I'm a cowboy!" Lil Brian laughed.

PRESSURE BUST PIPES

Brian froze. Taking in the view he nearly blew a gasket.

"Man what the fu-, " ...Aye, ma! Fuck you niggaz doing in here and give me my muthafuckin' daughter slim!" Brain said heatedly rushing in Ronnie's direction. Ronnie calmly lifted his sweater allowing the burner that rested on his lap to show, stopping him in his path. Lil Brian watched his father from Fray's back bemused. Carefully pulling him down, Fray rose to his knees so that he was now eye level with him. Fray gripped both of lil Brian's shoulders looking at big Brian.

"Hey, lil man how about we play a new game do you like hide and go seek?" Fray smiled. Lil Brian looked from his newfound friend to his father for his approval. Fray gently turned the little boy face back around to face him. "You go upstairs, and hide I'ma count to ten and come find you."

Gleefully lil Brian took off giggling as he headed up the spiral staircase. Fray stood to his feet turning his attention to Brian Sr.

"Dat ain't how you treat old friends now is it?" Fray said.

"Friends? Man, you niggaz ain't no friends of mine, and what the fuck y'all doin' here!"

Ronnie had enough he gripped the butt of his gun with his free hand.

"Fray let me smash this nigga!" he said placing Brian's daughter down beside him rising from the sofa.

"Chill." Fray blurted lifting his hand holding him off. "I think you know exactly why we here unless you want to end up like that nigga Charlie I suggest you come clean."

"Yeah nigga, or I'd be more than glad to smoke your hot ass along with everybodie' in this bitch!" Ronnie interjected.

Brian now knew who was responsible for Charlie's death. Even with the lives of his family in danger, he still wasn't ready to confess.

"Slim, what y'all talking bout'?" He whimpered.

Fray's face flushed with anger.

"Slim, 'dats how you wanna play it?" Fray asked stepping closer to him.

"I'm sayin' Fray I 'ont kn-," *Smack!* His words were cut short by the forceful backhand Fray delivered to the right side of his cheek.

"Bitch nigga you know the business!" Fray seethed. Brian held his cheek backing up into a corner. "Nigga you betta' think twice before you lie again cause I ain't got no problem goin' in 'dat basement, and putting a bullet in Ms. Riley head," Fray said praying that Brian did not call his bluff. Looking from an unbalanced Fray to an enraged Ronnie who stood with his gun drawn inches away from his daughter. Brian started to tear up.

"Fray Please don't let him kill me. I'd do anything!" he got on his knees sobbing at Fray's feet.

"Now that's the Brian I know." Fray kneeled to where Brian laid sobbing profusely placing his hand on his back. "I ain't gonna' let him kill you, but why'd you do it?"

"You promise," Brian said looking up at him wiping his face.

"You got my word now stop bullshitting and spit it out."

"Dis nigga anything let me crush 'em and get it over wit!" Ronnie was beyond furious.

"A'ight, A'ight…jus' don't let him kill me!" Brian panicked. "Man, a couple of months ago I got pulled over wit' a blah-zay blah-zay."

Fray looked to Ronnie for comprehension, but he didn't seem to know either.

"Hold on, hold on, hold on, slow up. What the fuck is a blah-zay blah zay?" Fray asked mystified.

"Oh, my bad it's jus' a lil slang we say on my block."

"Yeah well speak English to me then nigga." Fray was blunt.

"Them peoples pulled me over wit' a half a joint in the car when I was on my way to hit a nigga. They told me to step out the car, and I was like for what? They already had my driver's license, and everything was legit." Brian continued looking amongst the two men. "They must've called the homicide detective from our area while they were running my name because he pulled up while I was still in the car. The detective comes over and starts asking' me a lot of questions. Like, where I be and all that. Then he starts askin' me about y'all I mean 'dis dude really had it out for y'all."

"What detective?" Fray butted in.

"He said his name, Joe."

At the mention of his name Ronnie, and Fray cringed Joe was legendary.

"He had pictures of y'all and everything so I jus' gave him a lil bit so he can let me go. I had no idea they had plans on using me in the future. Fray you know that would've been my third strike I was looking at football numbers. He told me all I had to do was be his eyes on the streets. I was jus' goin' give him some petty cases I swear! The day 'dat shit happened with DeShay he called me outta' the blue. I'm so sorry slim I didn't know they was gonna lock him. up!" He began to sob again.

Once the rabbit was out the hat it took everything in Fray not to hit Brian's head right there. He knew that if he killed Brian he would have to kill everybody in the house. He didn't have that in him.

"Say sumthin' Fray. You ain't thinking about killin' me now are you?" Brain started to panic.

"Nigga, if I wanted you dead you'd be dead!" Fray blurted out.

"So what'chu want me to do," Brian asked sadly.

"You gonna meet wit' them peoples and recant your statement, and if I even think you playing games 'dat hide out you, and your wife got in Clinton." Fray didn't even have to finish. Brian's eyes widened. "And then I'm goin' come back here and pay your moms a visit.

"Fray I swear you won't regret it. I'm on it first thing in the mornin'."

"You bet not be bullshitting. I swear if DeShay's lawyer don't hit me in the mornin' confirming your story, I'ma wipeout everything you ever loved." Fray assured him looking him in the eyes. "Let's go Ronnie, and just like that, the twosome was gone.

Ronnie wasn't feeling Fray's decision to let Brain walk. The whole recanting thing was a surprise to him as well, after cranking the engine Ronnie decided to pull Fray up about it.

"Slim, what type of time you on? You really goin' give 'dis nigga 'dat much credit to talk to them peoples again? Nigga we goin' to jail!" Ronnie was pissed.

Fray looked at him as if he was crazy.

"See if you and 'dat nigga DeShay wasn't so damn hot-headed you would see the bigger picture. Ain't no way we goin' allow 'dat hot ass nigga to walk. If we would've smashed 'dat nigga in there we would've had to kill Ms. Riley, and his son plus wipe down our prints. I ain't wit' all 'dat. If you had been paying attention to our conversation earlier you woulda' heard Ashley say he want 'dat nigga for himself."

🎱🎱🎱

"Jesus Christ Kelly you gotta be kiddin' me! What do you mean you're dropping the case against the tournament killer?" Burnett said not believing his ears.

He and Kelly had been going back and forth for hours over her department's decision to drop the case against DeShay.

"Sir believe me we want to nail his ass to the wall just as bad as you do, but with no witnesses it would be hard for us to get a conviction," Kelly revealed.

"What do you mean you don't have any witnesses. The fuckin' guy murders a man in cold blood in front of a packed court, and you don't have any witnesses!"

"Well, you have your department to thank for that."

Kelly blamed the police for the lack of protection they provided her witnesses. After learning of Charlie's death several days ago, she insisted that the police park a cruiser outside of Brian's house. It wasn't long after Brain left the District Attorney's office recanting his statement he was found murdered, it left the D.A no other choice but to drop their case against DeShay. An infuriated Kelly Anderson greeted a baggy-eyed Joe as she stormed out of Burnett's office rolling her eyes at him.

"Let me guess that was about me?" Joe asked upon entering already knowing the answer to his question.

"Do you really have to ask?" Burnett sighed waltzing behind his cluttered desk taking a seat in his rolling chair.

"Joe, explain to me how in the hell you manage to lose two

witnesses?"

"Cap the men refused to be placed in witness protection, and technically I didn't feel their lives were in any type of danger." Burnette's pale face turned beat red.

"The D.A is blowing smoke up my ass, and you're sitting here telling me what you felt! Quite frankly I don't give a rats' ass what you felt you should've given them the protection Joe!" he yelled slamming his fist on his cluttered desk, papers fell to the floor. "If you weren't so got damn busy chasing a ghost you would notice the whole world is moving on without you."

"This doesn't have anything to do with that," Joe said.

"Like hell, it doesn't!" Burnette snapped, "Admit it you underestimated these boys?" Burnett said forcing the truth out of him.

"Okay so maybe I did, but what have they done up until now to make us believe them to be so dangerous?" Joe said without a care. Burnett ignored his arrogance slightly reclining in his chair placing his index finger on his snow-white temple.

"Sorry to pull you off your high horse Joe, but this isn't the only investigation pending against this crew." Joe stood dumbfounded.

"What are you talking about?" Joe asked.

"The D.A just informed me that they got an inside tip that these boys are the culprits behind the Pet Worth massacre, as well as the Alabama Avenue killings. Now how's that for your jolly apples?" Burnett grinned with confidence.

"You gotta be kidding me!" Joe was in absolute shock.

"Nope Kelly says her source says the youngsters seemed to blow up after a block full of Jamaicans got taken out sound familiar…

THE HEAT IS ON

The sun was at a standstill above the horizon as pigeons flocked to the broken pavement pecking away at bread crumbs. Women who showed up to visit their men on the block dressed in Jimmy Choo heels, Cobalt Manolo's, and Prada. Bright sundresses and tight fitted shorts revealed their camel toe and fat asses. D Street was in full swing as the many hustlers, and various groups of women scattered throughout the block taking advantage of the warm weather. Hustlers sporting cool shades with the latest designer gear moved up and down the block. Some stood atop the outside building steps waving fiends into the run-down two-story building. Others raced to cars handing off single zips of crack, and bundles of heroin as if they had a license. The trio stood in the mix of it all cracking jokes with exotic weed smoke filling the air. Giggling women and bottles of Rose' lined up on the pavement. Within earshot, DeShay leaned up against the neighborhood ice-cream truck passing a jay back and forth to the driver through the service window.

"So, when you goin' to take me out?" the slim girl with the Toni Braxton haircut asked, passing DeShay the blunt as she exhaled the smoke from her mother's ice-cream truck. Tracy and DeShay had been friends since grade school. Nothing ever happened between them sexually, but that still did not stop her from having a crush on him.

"You already know the answer to 'dat," DeShay said placing the jay to his lips taking a long pull.

"What!" She said defensively, looking down at him from the truck.

"You jive be on some other shit," he said.

"Boy please ain't nobody got time for your lil games that you play."

"Oh, well you must ain't tryna' go out then," he chuckled.

"DeShay I'm serious stop playin' all the time." She became agitated.

"Sike nah I was just bullshitting," he said between laughs. "What if your crazy ass baby father sees us?"

"He ain't worried about you, what he don't know won't hurt him."

"See, that's why I don't trust any of you bitches out here now!"

"I can see if me and you were together it would be totally different." She said.

"Oh yeah, and what makes me so special?" he asked out of curiosity puffing the half of jay twice before passing it back to her.

PRESSURE BUST PIPES

"Don't play dumb. I'll bust you in the face if you stand right here, and act like you don't know I been feelin' you since elementary," Tracy snapped at his response.

"Shid, I'm feelin' me too!" he said arrogantly adjusting his red and white Nationals-fitted cap fixing his shoulder length dreads.

"Nigga, you ain't like dat!" she barked.

"Shid, now dats' a first," smiling he ran his hand over his smooth mocha skin.

"Shay you know what...get ya' conceited ass away from my truck!" She fussed.

"A'ight give me my weed then," he extended his hand out to her.

"What weed punk!" She rolled her neck taking another hit of the jay.

"Oh, so you jus' goin' rough me off like 'dat? Well, at least, let a nigga get a snickers or sumthin," he smirked.

"Nope not today holmes," she said hitting him with his own words.

"Oh yeah, that's how you feel? Well, look hit me later I'm bout to go see whassup wit' these niggas."

"I hope it's goin' to be worth my while!"

"Who knows you might jus' get what you been askin' for," he smiled.

"Yeah, 'dat a be the day," she said playfully strutting to the front of the truck with the jay in her mouth, cranking the engine, ringing the bell, pulling off.

"Nigga, keep bullshitting 'dat nigga black goin' kill both y'all asses! Ashley joked referring to Tracy's baby father as DeShay walked up joining the group.

"Fuck that! Black rather check his bitch then to come fuck wit' me," DeShay said bending over retrieving one of the bottles of Rose'.

"Oh shit," Fray said looking up the block.

"What!" DeShay asked unsure of what Fray saw.

"Feds, Feds, Feds!" Fray yelled getting everyone's attention as an unmarked cruiser turned onto the block. The hustlers occupying the steps eased back into the buildings. The others that were standing next to the curve wasn't so fortunate. With nowhere to go the quartet stood in the middle of the block looking for an opening.

"Shit hurry up and put 'dis in your purse!" Ronnie panicked passing his gun off to one of the nearby women.

Joe pulled up, got out the car, and started walking towards the four men. They knew exactly who the detective was and wanted no heat from him. Joe started clapping as he approached them. The group of four and surrounding bystanders looked confused.

"Well done, well done, I gotta hand it to you boys you really had me fooled. However, you made one mistake you picked the wrong case to fuck with."

"It's Open!" Katie yelled from her bedroom, standing in front of an oval shaped mirror as she admired her outfit.

"Well aren't chu' classy tonight," Unique said upon entering Katie's cozy bedroom. The high slit up her thigh showed off her sexy Channel platform heels, and her Monique–Lhuillier gown snug onto her body in all the right places.

PRESSURE BUST PIPES

"You like?" Katie twirled around in a circle.

"Well, you're in a good mood," Unique smiled at her friend through the mirror.

"Girl I am. I'm so glad you convinced me to put Fray's no good ass behind me and start datin' again." Katie said half ass telling the truth. She later learned that it was her fault for the breakup, and that Fray was indeed telling the truth and innocent. This way of thinking didn't come until months later when Ashley spotted her and Unique at club Touché. He exposed the whole truth to her about the Pebblez situation, and what Ronnie did and why she instantly began to feel guilt for the way she treated Fray. After their break up Fray did not go quietly. He called and popped up over her sister house every day sometimes twice a day, but still couldn't reach her. It wasn't until the fourth month he decided to call it quits. Heartbroken and alone he turned to Pebblez.

After Ashley's confession, Katie later became the one on the pursuing end. Her pursuit would not last long when word surfaced that Fray and Pebblez were now a couple. Through it all, she and Ashley remained close friends

"Oh, so you and 'dis guy La-La must really be hittin' it off," Unique said reflecting back to the rugged looking person with the scar on his face, they met several weeks ago while gambling in Atlantic City. For the life of her, she could not understand Katie's attraction to the midnight complexion, pink lips, thuggish looking guy. Not wanting to come off as a hater, she held her tongue while they conversed. The six foot La-La had been gambling with a couple of friends that night when he spotted the beautiful woman draped in olive colored linen pants, a white top accompanied by open toe sandals. He immediately noticed the vixen's entire beauty. Liking what he saw he excused himself from the blackjack table, heading in Katie's direction to introduce himself. It was his personality more than anything that won her over. His character made her overlook the fact that he was ugly; she also ignored the many questions of Unique's disapproval. The two ended up hitting it off and exchanging numbers, agreeing to hook up once they got back to the city.

"Girl he is so sweet. Yesterday we went to the movies and he held me the whole time!" Katie's face was jubilant with happiness.

"Well, I guess it's safe to safe the ugly ducklin' goin' break a world record at gettin' those panties huh!" Unique chuckled.

"Ha, ha very funny bitch. It still ain't that type of party." Katie frowned.

"Kee you know I'm jus' fuckin wit'chu, lightin' up," Unique said.

"Anyway changing subjects. Did you ever go out wit' his friend Mike D?" Katie asked referring to one La-La's friends Unique met while in Atlantic City.

"Bitch please he wasn't even my type!" she frowned. "Dat nigga out here beatin' his feet, he better get his weight up before tryna holla at me!"

"And Bullet so happens to be this prince charming huh?" Katie chuckled.

"Trick you can't talk, because even if the beast had a Bentley I wouldn't be caught dead with his ugly ass!" Unique spat referring to La-La.

"Beast?" Katie said confused before she caught on to the insult. "Don't do La-La like 'dat he cool peoples." Katie snickered.

"Well, I hope you ain't being fooled by all 'dat innocent shit. You know like I know it always starts out that way," Unique was speaking from experience.

PRESSURE BUST PIPES

"Nique trust me after what I went through with Fray, I'm really being careful. La-La knows I'm not lookin' to rush into things, all I was saying is that he's a cool dude."

"Katie, please do me a favor and don't move to fast with him, I can't stand to see you hurt again," Unique said genuinely.

Unique didn't know how to tell Katie that she thought she was rushing into the whole ordeal with La-La. Nevertheless, who was she to give relationship advice?

"I promise everything is going to be fine. Now would you stop worrying? You're supposed to be happy I'm dating again," Katie smiled weakly.

"Bitch you know I am, now get over here, and give me a hug!" The two laughed as they hugged. They were interrupted by a knock at the front door.

"Oh, dats' La-La, and I ain't even ready!" she said breaking their embrace. She rushed over to her dresser anxiously looking for the best fragrance that would suit their evening.

"Chile it's not that serious." Unique frowned, rolling her eyes before slipping from Katie's bedroom, making her way through the ivory colored living room, pulling the front door open finding a tall La-La on the other side. La-La was chewing annoyingly on gum to stop from gritting his teeth, he was rolling off an "E" pill. Wearing dark sun shades at night, a tight fitting Banana Republic t-shirt, blue Lucky Brand jeans and black Timberland boots, he looked the slender Unique up and down stopping at the huge gap between her legs.

"Whassup shawty?" he smirked. His dirty looks didn't go unnoticed. Rolling her eyes, she yelled out.

"Beast here...I mean La-La's here!"

She walked away leaving him standing at the threshold. La-La was taken aback by the blatant disrespect he envied her from that moment on. Katie heard every word from her bedroom. She stood shaking her head in embarrassment. "I can't believe 'dis bitch jus' did dat," she said aloud slipping on her diamond tennis bracelet Fray brought her. She ran her hands over her curves in her sexy glove fitting dress and did a model walk to the living room. Her platform heels made her appear taller than her actual 5'2" stature. La-La stared in awe licking his pink lips hungrily. He sized her up from head to toe. She had French pedicure feet, a thick thigh that protruded through the thigh-high slit, her cleavage spilled out the top of her silk gown. Her chestnut-brown curly locks hung to her shoulders.

"Mm, damn you wearin' 'dat dress!" La-La smiled walking up to her giving her a tight hug. She smelled like Paris Hilton's perfume (Candid). Unique stood there watching with both hands on her hips. Being a team player herself game recognized game, it hadn't been five minutes and La-La was already sizing Katie up the same way he did her, her dislike for him was building by the second.

"Shawty off the no bullshit as good as you look tonight you might not make it back home after dinner!" He flirted.

"Boy behave." Katie giggled pulling away. "I hope I'm not overdressed." She asked taking in his relaxed attire.

Lowering his eyes, he looked from her tempting breast stopping on her small hips and flat stomach. He could literally see her plumped ass peeking from behind.

"Ain't no such thing as being overdressed sweetheart." He sneered dropping his shades to the bridge of his nose winking. Unique watched unimpressed.

"So, you ready to go?" Katie asked.

PRESSURE BUST PIPES

"Baby I was born ready!" he said turning towards the door leading the way.

Katie looked towards Unique

"Don't forget to lock up," she said before exiting her apartment behind La-La.

"Your friend really needs to learn some manners."

La-La was still upset about the smart comment Unique made. They walked on the damp pavement to his old battered jeep, he walked around the truck to open Katie's door.

"Please don't pay her no attention she's just over protective of me, I apologize," she said climbing inside.

Forty minutes later they were crossing a small parking lot heading into Mary's restaurant. It was a moderate up and coming jazz spot. Katie found it quite strange that La-La was wearing sun shades at night. However, giving the fact he was from uptown she knew they tend to be flashy and animated. La-La was more talkative than normal. He was also chewing like a savage on some bubble-gum for the duration of the ride.

The large bay windows added sheek to the exterior of the restaurant. Inside, its light fixtures were faint. The various white table cloth was scattered throughout. The bar was exceptional. It was lit up with assorted colors. Uniformed waiters and servers smiled while refilling drinks, and presenting trays of food covered with sterling silver caps. The light laughter from the customers provided a mellow atmosphere. Being directed by a waiter La-La, and Katie made a beeline to a corner table. Katie was famished. She flipped through the menu settling on the Hawaiian steak. After placing her order, she noticed La-La had yet to touch his menu.

The waiter collected their menus and excused herself.

"You're not goin' eat?" Katie asked eyeing him intently.

"Nah. I'm good I ain't really hungry. I'll just have a drink," he said looking around the crowded restaurant through shade covered eyes.

"Well, can you, at least, take your shades off. Aint no sun in here." she joked.

"Oh I see you got jokes!" he snickered. "Aye, but let me ask you sumthin.' Why you stop fuckin' wit' the dude Fray?"

At the mention of Fray's name, she became a little saddened. She looked at La-La bemused.

"What'chu know him or sumthin'?" She asked calmly.

"Nah, I wouldn't say 'dat, but you know how the streets talk. My man Mike D was down the hill wit' his man Ronnie awhile back. Hold that thought right quick. Where the fuck is the waiter. I been placed an order for our drinks." He looked around agitated. "Hold on boo I'll go to the bar my damn self." He got up and proceeded to the bar.

Katie didn't see what the fuss was about when the waiter left no even a minute ago. When he returned he had a glass of red wine and a blue motorcycle.

"Now back to what I was saying. I saw him out a couple of times he use to come by, and holla at this broad from around my way." He lied.

The thought of Fray fucking around on her while they were together made her blood boil. Fray rise in the streets made him envied by jealous niggas as well. La-La boosted his own ego knowing that he was fucking with Fray's old girl. La-La was a natural born hater, he was also the wolf in sheep's clothing. Judging by the look on Katie's face it was apparent his words cut deep.

"Shawty I know what'chu thinkin' right now, but don't even trip it's his lost. If you was my girl you ain't never got to worry about me steppin' out on you."

Katie grabbed the glass of wine and gulped it down.

"La-La would you excuse me I gotta use the restroom." She said getting up before finishing her sentence.

"Sure." He smiled rising from his seat so she can bypass him. La-La smirked devilishly as she headed across the restaurant. No sooner, their waiter reappeared carrying a bottle of red wine, and Katie's tray of food she also placed two glasses of lemon water on the table. La-La was on his second glass of wine when she emerged from the ladies' room.

"My bad shawty if I upset you," he said as she approached the table taking her seat.

"It's not your fault you just put me on point. You never really know a person until your no longer with them."

"Katie don't let 'dat nigga fuck-up our night you should be happy."

After thirty minutes of venting about Fray, Katie was ready to call it a night.

"Here have a toast wit' me." He gestured to the bottle of wine that sat before her. "Look I know you don't drink, but I figured you might need another glass to cheer you up."

"No thank you. For some reason, my mouth is extremely dry. It must've been that first glass I had." She picked up the glass of water drinking it. "I 'ont feel so good La-La."

She rested her head in the palm of her hand clutching her stomach with the other.

"You a'ight?" La-La asked tossing the tab on the table helping Katie to her feet. "I got you."

He staggered with her out the door to his Jeep helping her inside, he then rounded the back climbing into the driver seat. If only Katie would have of known La-La was slithering snake, and that he spiked her wine when he went to the bar.

"Pull over. I need sumthin' to drink." Her voice was barely above a whisper. La-La continued down the freeway straining his eyes for the nearest hotel.

"I got you sweetheart jus' hold fast."

He quickly bared off making a sharp right turn into the illuminated Days Inn parking lot. He backed in-between two parked cars in the hotel's parking lot. He hopped out the truck bolting inside. After securing a room he was on Katie's side of the truck unbuckling her seat belt. He draped her arm around his neck and carried her from the truck. A cool breeze swept across her face waking her momentarily. Katie looked up and seen the bright sign.

"What are we doing here?"

She blacked out before she got an answer. La-La inserted the key card into the door of room #216. He laid her down on the bed, Katie was incoherent as La-La hands slid up the sides of her dress. The date rape drug seemed to paralyze her limbs preventing her from putting up a fight. To his surprise, she was panty less which enticed him more. He eagerly fumbled with his belt buckle until he was free letting his pants, and boxers fall to his ankles exposing his stiff penis. Aggressively, he jerked her towards him disregarding the Trojan in his back pocket. He raised her dress up above her waist, crawled between her legs, and forced his six-inch dick inside her walls. Her vagina became moist. When Katie felt him enter her she

PRESSURE BUST PIPES

gasped, La-La succeeded at raping her.

UNIQUE

With the heat coming down hard the group of four decided to lay low until things cooled down.

"You call this laying low?" Betty said watching DeShay strain the heroin onto a plate. Betty was dark skin, pudgy, with Asian features in her early fifties, she had been smoking crack since the eighties. "Don't look at me like that Shay. I overheard y'all talkin' the other night."

Through his surgical mask, he said, "I ain't 'bout to let that cop stop my paper. Fray and em niggaz lunchin'." Betty walked away to go answer her ringing house phone.

"Just me DeShay," Betty replied. The mentioning of his name

made DeShay key in on the one-sided conversation.

"So what time y'all coming?" She paused waiting for the caller's reply. "That can be arranged," she said cutting her eye over at DeShay who sat watching her like a hawk. "Boy, what did I just say? Didn't I say I'll handle it," she said placing the receiver back on its base.

"Who was that?" DeShay asked.

She began tidying up the cluttered house raising DeShay's curiosity. Out of all the years, he couldn't recall a time when Betty straightened up the house.

"That was Ashley. Look you gon' have to hurry up I got sumthin' to do."

"So go do it." He said nonchalantly continuing to work.

"I gotta lock up my house," Betty said fiddling.

"Since when I couldn't stay when you had to go out?"

DeShay turned and faced Betty. He knew her better than she knew herself especially when she was lying. Determined to get to the bottom of it, he put the strainer down.

"What Ash' talkin' 'bout?"

"Huh?" Betty responded nervously.

"I said what Ash' want?"

"Oh nothing just small talk," She said as she continued to clean up the house. DeShay wasn't swayed. He took off his latex gloves digging in his pocket pulling out a wad of cash.

"What's it going to take to get the truth out of you," he said unfolding the knot placing a fifty-dollar bill on the table. Craving for a fix with her mouth twitching she could no longer hold it in she gave way. A half an hour later Ashley recovered the key from under the mat as planned. Within seconds of entering the house, he was digging in Unique guts.

"Ah…Yes…Fuck Me! Unique bellowed stroking Ashley's ego as he rabbit-fucked her from the back. His pants and boxers were draped around his ankles. Unique had been faking moans for the past ten minutes as she laid on Betty's bed in doggy style position.

"Mm…yes…beat 'dis pussy up!" She was so wet that Ashley miniature dick kept slipping out. Meanwhile, DeShay stood watching the fiasco from the closet. He listened to Unique's forced moans. He covered his mouth to hold in his laughter. It was the perfect opportunity to prove to Ashley Unique was, in fact, a money hungry whore, and that she would do anything if the price was right. After hitting Betty off, he stayed behind to catch the session. Witnessing the live porn DeShay became aroused watching Unique throw her petite ass back.

"Ooo…Yes!" Her screams became louder. He began stripping off his clothes leaving nothing on but his boots. He then slipped out the closet. Ashley had to double take whipping his head in DeShay's direction. He was completely naked stroking his hard dick signaling for him to let him get behind Unique. With Unique's eyes closed in fake ecstasy, she was unaware of his presence. Still pumping away with his face scrunched up in anger he mouthed, *"What the fuck you doin'? Get the fuck outta' here!"*

DeShay refused still stroking himself.

"Shay, man get the fuck out!" he mouthed nudging his head towards the door, but DeShay still declined to leave he walked around the bed to wear Unique head was. Noticing a change in his rhythm she was just about to slide off of him in fear he was about to nut. She opened her eyes finding herself face to face with a hard big dick.

"Oh, Uh-un what type of shit y'all on!

She looked back and forth between the two.

"Shh. I won't tell anybody if you don't," DeShay said assuring. Pre-cum oozed out the head of his dick. Always wanting to fuck DeShay, Unique looked over her shoulder at Ashley who continued to pump away for his approval. Taking his silence as a yes she turned back around eyeing DeShay big dick eagerly. She reached out for it gripping his dick at the base. DeShay placed his hand on the back of her head edging her closer. With lustful-filled eyes, Unique took him in her warm mouth. Moaning, stroking and making slurping sounds she bobbed away. DeShay winked at Ashley who was still behind her mean mugging. Unique started out giving him slow neck then sped up deep throating his dick, and sucking on his balls. DeShay could feel his knees buckle as he moved his hips fucking her mouth.

"You got a condom," DeShay said pulling out her mouth. Unique used her head to point towards her bag. After retrieving the Magnum, he ripped open the gold wrapping walking to where Ashley was. He then gestured Ashley to move. Ignoring him, Ashley kept stroking away. DeShay was ruthless about the situation as he shouldered him out the pussy disregarding his friend's feelings. Unique was wet and juicy from the previous action. Squatting behind her he took her by her small waist plowing inside.

"Mm-hmm!" Unique hollered feeling his dick in her guts. DeShay pounded away pushing her face down in the pillows. Unique tried to squirm away.

"Stop runnin'…take dis dick bitch."

Pinned to the headboard and nowhere to run the pain soon became pleasurable.

"Yes…I…Fuck Me Shay…Fuck Me Harder Shay…Shit! She screamed throwing her ass back. Ashley watched DeShay fuck the

shit out of Unique. He was amazed at the sounds she was making.

An excruciating headache welcomed Katie the next morning. She was spiraled out on the floor in a smelly pool of her own vomit. Adjusting her eyes to the familiar surroundings, she had the slightest idea how she ended up back at her apartment on the floor, not to mention her vagina was really moist. For the life of her, she could not remember how she had gotten home. The last thing she remembered was sitting across the table from La-La eating Hawaiian steak. She prayed she hadn't done the unthinkable. With her stomach still upset she figured it had to be food poison. She called Unique, but to no avail. She cleaned herself up and did a walk-in at the clinic.

"Ms. Turner!" Dr. Rice yelled from the doorway of her blain office addressing Katie by her last name. She was a woman in her early forties. She wore her hair short and styled like Halle Berry's displaying her dark brown beautiful African features. Her white physician-smock unfastened highlighting a white button up shirt, black pencil skirt and black 3-inch heels. "Are we feeling better?" Dr. Rice asked as soon as Katie was seated in her office comfortably.

"I still have a headache, but, for the most part, I'm okay," Katie said.

"Well that's good to hear," she smiled. "I have your results back, and after reviewing your blood work we found traces of methamphetamines and speed in your system."

Katie only comprehended the word speed.

"But how is 'dat possible. I don't even use drugs." Katie said looking confused.

"Honey believe me when I tell you we have been seeing this kind of thing a lot lately. I can guarantee you that these tests are 99.9% accurate." Katie was still speechless. "Now normally when we find traces of these two drugs together we find them in a date rape drug called MDMA, which is called ecstasy on the streets.

"Ecstasy!" Katie repeated a little louder than she should have causing Dr. Rice to flinch. *"Doc are you sure?"* she asked distressed.

"It's like I told you earlier we been seeing a whole lot of these cases lately. Usually, a guy would slip these drugs in a woman's drink when she is not paying attention. If you like I can run a few more tests to see if you are a victim of rape."

Katie sat flabbergasted trying to piece together the events from last night all. Then it dawned on her. The glass of wine she shared with La-La. She buried her face in the palms oh her hands, breathing heavily.

"I can't believe 'dis happened to me. How could I be so stupid." She thought. Thinking about what Dr. Rice just asked her she decided to speak up. "Umm…no that won't be necessary. I think I know how 'dis could've happened."

Holding back her tears Katie stood to gather her things.

"Sweety are you sure?" Dr. Rice asked concerned.

"Yes, I jus' need to go lay down," Katie replied.

"Well if you change your mind give me a call."

With tears, Katie sat numb and motionless. She felt violated to the highest degree. The vibration coming from her purse indicated she had an incoming call. She retrieved her phone looking down at the screen seeing La-La number sent hatred through her body.

"What the fuck do you want!" she screamed into the phone.

PRESSURE BUST PIPES

"Damn what's wrong wit' you?"

"Nigga don't give me 'dat innocent shit! You know what the fuck your trifling ass did. Is that the only was your bum ass can get some pussy!"

"Shawty who the fuck do you think you talkin' too?" La-La fired back.

"You! I'm talkin' to your dirty dick ass. You oh nasty muthafucka! And to think I took a chance by going out wit' your ugly ass!"

"Bitch Fuck You." La-La snapped.

"Oh, so I'ma bitch now. Yeah, a'ight jus' lose my number, and forget you ever had it."

Katie started to end the call, but La-La maniacal laugh prevented her from doing so.

"You might want to reconsider that. As a matter of fact, check your text messages right now."

Katie heard the messages as they were coming through. She removed the phone tapping on her messages. Her eyes widened as she watched the video of La-La raping her.

"What cat got your tongue bitch?" he laughed as Katie had become silent. "If you ever think about leavin' I'm posting the whole video online. If you watch till the end you'll see where my man come in and have some fun with you. Now do you think Fray gon' take you back after seein' that? He chuckled.

Katie remained quiet while he continued to blabber on.

"I remember the very first time I saw you wit' that nigga I told myself I had to have you at any cost, so now that I got you-you ain't goin' nowhere. I own you!" He spat. "One more thing if you think about tellin' Fray I'ma give that nigga the business myself. I love you boo."

The line went dead leaving Katie in shock while she tried to figure out who this crazy derange person was.

Things were going the total opposite in Fray's life. Though he and Katie's drastic break up crushed him tremendously his life was beginning to take on a new romance. As the saying goes whenever there is rain there's always sunshine. After a few weeks of him and Pebblez flirting openly through text messages she was a good distraction to help take his mind off Katie, even though he was still deeply in love with her. Pebblez had just stepped out of a steaming hot shower moments before. The cool air of her open bedroom chilled her naked body causing her to shiver, and her nipples to harden. Lauren Hill's Pandora station played as she applied coconut milk body lotion to her soft skin.

Her jet-black, curly natural big hair shined from the citrus organic hair spray. She lightly caressed her eraser size nipples as she looked back over her shoulder at her ass through the tall mirror. After kidding around she spun on her bare heels strolling over to her mid-night blue marble dresser with silver trimming. An assortment of perfumes and cosmetics sat neatly on top. After spraying her groin with summer's Eve deodorant spray a light tap at her front door disrupted her. She grabbed her silk robe from her queen-size bed pulling the belt tight as she walked towards the living room.

Looking through the peephole she frowned upon seeing no one there. She yanked the door open with force with an attitude. Shockingly, there was a Sacs shopping bag left on her welcoming mat. Thinking it to be some kind of joke she slowly stuck her head out of the apartment door scanning the empty hall before picking up the bag. She closed the door and placed the light bag on the tan

PRESSURE BUST PIPES

lazy boy looking through its contents. She came across a knee length white body dress with a Deep-V stopping at her belly button. The dress was sure to show off her C cups, and she had the perfect heel to match. She paused briefly checking out the expensive price tag smiling already knowing who the gift came from. The buzzing of her vibrating phone on the rectangular shape table disturbed her brief inspection of the sexy fabric.

"Hello?" she answered excitedly.

"I'm out front." The voice on the other end of the phone said before hanging up.

Pebblez blushed hard placing the phone back on the table commencing to get dressed. When she got downstairs she was breathless as she placed both hands to her mouth. She was met by white rose peddles scattered at her feet that trailed to an all-white stretch limousine. Inside Fray was raising a strawberry covered in whip cream to his mouth pausing upon her arrival.

His muscular body complimented Ralph Lauren's finest. Aviator sunglasses covered his shifty eyes. A classic long sleeve pink linen shirt under a white linen suit jacket with a pink Irish linen square pocket matched his tan trousers, and white and brown Henley 11 saddle shoes. His platinum diamond Bezel Cartier added the final touches. Fray loved the way her body filled out the dress showing off her Serena Williams curves. Fray greeted her by reaching out for her hand.

"I knew it would fit." He smiled.

The two were about to experience their first date since hooking up.

ASHLEY

Ashley and Ronnie stood posted outside of the convenience store leaning against the wall. Ashley planted his right foot on the store wall behind him facing the gravel lot opposite of him. His eyes constantly roamed up and down the block, PeeWee appeared from the cut extending his hand inside a window of an awaiting vehicle. After passing off two bags of weed, PeeWee pocketed the money and crossed the street reclaiming his spot next to Ashley. Ronnie disappeared inside the store leaving the two fussing about sales. Pee-Wee took off running flagging down a sale before Ashley could object.

"*Yeah, yeah...pull over!* How many you want?" PeeWee asked the dread head man in front of him.

"Bring me a twon-ty!" he replied with his back pressed against the tail end of the cab, tossing a chip into his mouth.

"A'ight stay right there," PeeWee said heading across the street to the open lot disappearing through the cut. Ashley stood with his arms folded across his chest eyeing the dark-skinned man who had gotten out of the cab. He could not put his finger on it, but something just did not feel right about the individual before him. His phone began to vibrate in his pocket drawing his attention away from the dread head man. He pulled out his phone looking at it, an incoming call from Katie. "Hello?" he answered. Bullet was the culprit behind the dirty wig, he quickly cast the block capitalizing on Ashley's mistake. With his sweaty palm stuffed inside the potato chip bag, he gripped the sig Sauer 45. Sour cream and onions chips fell to the pavement, he pulled out the gun. He watched as Ashley continued to rap on the phone with his eyes low. PeeWee was just returning when he spotted the man opposite of him raising a gun, aiming it at Ashley. PeeWee froze at the sight of the gun!

"Slim watch out! Pee-Wee yelled.

The terror in PeeWee's voice caused Ashley to quickly look up, by that time Bullet was pulling the trigger *Boom!* The bullet pierced his stomach knocking him to the pavement. Bullet had been standing so close that the hot lead ripped through his flesh exiting out his back. Ashley insides were on fire. He opened his mouth to scream but nothing came out. Looking on in horror, PeeWee finally broke out of his sudden case of shell shock and sprinted back through the open lot. He approached the abandon red Nissan where he kept the .380 stashed that DeShay had given him prior to putting him on his feet. Ronnie was in the process of paying for his items when the single gunshot erupted outside of the store.

His mind raced to Ashley instantly. Looking from the counter through the chicken wire on the glass storefront window he had an outlook of the gunman. He pulled out the Mac 12 from the front of his jeans racing out the store. The chiming bells on the store's door got Bullets attention. Seeing the dreaded gunman standing over top of Ashley sent Ronnie's rage into overdrive! Ronnie's storming out caused Bullet to loose focus of the target. Bullet raised the gun wildly attempting to get a shot off, but Ronnie already had the drop on him. Upping the Mac with two hands he let loose a volley of bullets!

Tat, tat, tat, tat stepping with it as he fired!! Bullet fired back blindly in his direction before diving head first between two parked cars. Seeing Bullet under heavy fire Chucky attempted to exit the driver seat of the cab, but PeeWee came running out the cut shooting from a distance at the open door of the cab. *Pop, Pop, Pop*! Preventing him from getting out. Ronnie turned around showering the cab with bullets as well. Chucky began to ease the cab away from the curve blindly. Being on the other end of the gun was never part of the twosome plan. Ronnie and PeeWee turned their attention to the bullet-riddled cars that Bullet was squatting behind unloading on it. Bullet was outgunned, and in no position to return fire, but he knew if he wanted to make it off of D street alive he had to save some bullets for his desperate retreat.

Listening to the gunfire on the right of him cease, and the shots to his left continue he prayed the man who had been firing recklessly at him gun was empty. Bullet hesitantly peeped out from around the bumper of the bullet-riddled car looking for the second gunman. Seeing PeeWee nowhere in sight he began to panic. He didn't know if the second gunman was closing in on him from a blind angle. He made his move. Looking around nervously he spotted Chucky waving his arm out the shot up the cab. He decided it was now or never. He busts two shots in the direction PeeWee once stood.

Hearing no return fire coming from the right of him he rose to his feet exchanging fire with Ronnie. PeeWee's location was still unknown. Bullet began to peddle back towards 18th street where the awaiting cab was sending hot lead whistling past Ronnie's ear. The close encounter caused Ronnie to side step to the right dropping on one knee so that he could get a better aim at Bullet. Bullet made a run for it. Ronnie started shooting at him once more missing him with every shot but managed to shoot out the back windshield before the Mac went empty. Bullet didn't bother to use the cab door handles he dove in head first through the shot-out rear window of the cab. There were so many holes in the stolen cab Chucky was lucky to be alive. He smashed the gas pedal fleeing the scene.

It was a beautiful day in Nation's Capital especially in West Potomac as Fray and Pebblez stood in the middle of it. His muscular chest pressed up against her back with his arms wrapped around her waist. Her big hair brushing the left side of his face. She leaned back into his arms taking in the beautiful view of the cherry blossoms. The sun was slowly starting to fade into the heart of the clouds. Fray checked the time on his diamond face, Cartier. "Oh look!" Pebblez said excitedly pointing upward at the multi-colored air balloon as it drifted over the Tidal Basin earning curious stares from the countless tourist.

The operator glanced around the crowded mall from the basket of the balloon as if he was searching for someone. The copper complexion man with the handlebar mustache smiled upon seeing the familiar face. Fray smiled grabbing a hold of Pebblez hand pulling her in the direction of the balloon.

"Me friend!" The Mexican operator said in his heavy accent opening the door on the basket.

"Fray oh my…Are you serious?" She snickered.

Fray knew it would be a challenge trying to impress her beings though she dated some of the biggest moneymakers in the city. He decided to do something different by sailing in the hot air balloon with her.

"Fray how did you…when did you?" she stuttered in happiness.

"Shh." he gestured placing his index finger to her lips, "just enjoy," he whispered with his right hand on her lower back extending his left hand to help her inside. After enjoying the view of the city from the air the two headed back to the limo with intentions of going back to Pebblez place. Before the limo could pull off they were all over one another. Fray used his warm tongue to lick on her earlobes, with his right hand he softly massaged the back of her neck. T-Bozes baritone voice mixed with Fray's licks and passionate kisses made her horny.

"Fray what if he looks back here?" A concerned Pebblez asked as he pushed her thong to the side sliding his middle finger inside her. With his middle finger coated in her juices, his dick became hard making his linen pants protrude.

"Man he ain't gon' look back here," he said eyeing Pebblez hungrily. Her hazel colored eyes drifted to his lap taking in the bulge in his trousers. She unbuttoned his pants and reached between his legs pulling out his hard dick. Fray was enjoying the sensation when the thought of Katie crossed his mind. For some reason, he felt like he was about to cheat on her. He started to protest, but Pebblez lowered herself in front of him sensing his resistance.

"I promise you, you won't ever have to hurt again," she said giving him brain. When it was Fray turn he started at her back door, tonguing her ass, sending tingles through her body. With both legs in the air, spread apart, she gripped the back of his head with both hands grinding on his tongue.

"Ooo…yes suck 'dis pussy!" she quivered spreading her fat pussy

lips apart.

He then began alternating his tongue against her enlarged clit and licking her ass hole. With Pebblez now on the ropes, he began forcefully slamming his index, and middle fingers in her ocean of sea while swirling his thick tongue around her clitoris.

"Mm…oww… yes… I'm cummin!" She screamed. Convulsions shot through her entire body followed by squirting of her cunt, Fray continued to perform oral sex with a drenched mouth.

As for Katie, she was adjusting to dealing with La-La who proved to be more than a psychopath. The constant threats of harming Fray was the only reason she stayed. If something were to have ever happened to Fray because of her she would've never been able to forgive herself. On K street was a probation building that sat across from the diminutive size Domino's Pizza parlor. Directly across from the busy two-way street was a U-Haul store. Today was the same as any other day, felons were in and out taking their urines for their probation officers.

It was a nice day to be out, and Katie was enjoying the sunny afternoon. Wearing a white lace halter top, loose khaki shorts, and gold thong flip-flops she looked stunning as usually. Passing cars honked their horns at her as they drove by. She looked closely as the familiar Range Rover slowed down, stopping in front of her. The driver rolled the tinted passenger window down and called out to her. Already knowing the trucks occupant, she began walking to the truck.

"What's going on Derek?" she asked with a forced smile.

Even though she never been to fond of Derek she knew he was like a father to Fray. She nervously approached the sparkling Range in hopes of hearing something about Fray.

"Ain't shit. Haven't seen you in a while." Derek blushed from behind the wheel.

"I jus' been workin' that's all," Katie said.

"You still workin' at the beauty supply store?"

"Mm-hm." She looked to the entrance of the probation building praying La-La wasn't on his way out.

"Why are you standing out here by yourself?" Derek asked following her eyes to the building.

"I'm waitin' on someone," Katie said looking over her shoulder nervously.

"Let me guess the new guy?"

"Derek that's none of your business, and besides your boy moved on first!"

"You mean after or before you cut him off for no reason?"

"I figured you would say that, but I find it kinda strange and ironic that he would start going out with the bitch who actually broke us up. Now if that ain't guilty then I don't know what is."

Sensing their conversation going left field Derek decided to soften his approach.

"Katie to be honest with you the boy hasn't been the same since you left. And the fact still remains that you are the best thing that ever happened to him. No matter who he fuckin' wit right now, at the end of the day you know like I know 'dat he still loves you."

Katie stood silently at that bold statement. She batted her eyes to the ground. Derek noticed her sudden mood-swing. Taking her quietness as an indication that the conversation was now over he decided to channel the conversation in another direction.

"You know we throwin' a fight party 'dis weekend. You're more than welcome to come. Fray will be there and who knows this might be the opportunity y'all need to work things out." He smiled.

"Look who's tryna' play matchmaker. Where y'all having it at?" Katie said.

"At the Hilton downtown. We got the penthouse suite." he boasted.

"I 'ont know Derek. She gon' be there?" Katie asked referring to Pebblez.

"If you 'ont want her there she won't be. You family."

"Well let me think about it, but if I decide to come can I bring my girl?"

"Aye, Katie!" La-La shouted stepping from the probation building. His lanky frame clothed in a tight fitting Giorgio' Armani t-shirt, True Religion jeans and gray New Balance. Fear could be seen on Katie's face.

"Katie you know 'dis joker?" Derek said watching a dark skinned male angrily approaching them. He reached under his seat placing his 357 revolver on his lap. Cutting her eye at the big gun on his lap she said, "Derek that's my friend."

"Bitch fuck type of time you on." La-La fumed grabbing her by the arm, locking eyes with the bald head heavy set man in the truck. *"You know my peoples or sumthin'!"*

"La-La it ain't what you think." Katie snatched away.

"Bitch shut up I'm talkin' to him." he barked *"Nigga you 'ont here me talkin' to you!"* La-La said never breaking eye contact with Derek. It took everything in Derek not to raise his gun and kill the

loud mouth buffoon on the spot.

"Shawty I think you should listen to your peoples," Derek said in a calm voice.

"Nigga what! do you know who you fuckin' wit? step the fuck out the truck, we'll see how tough you are then!"

"You know what, you got that shawty. Katie, it was nice seeing you again," Derek said before rolling up his tinted window pulling off.

"I can't believe you just embarrassed me like that, that man is like Fray's father." Katie frowned.

"Mutha-fuck Fray! Get the fuck down the street." He spat gripping the back of her neck shoving her in the direction of the Corda's.

WHO CAN YOU TRUST?

The weekend could not have come fast enough. Katie turned off Connecticut Ave into the half-full parking lot of the hotel. On the way there she questioned her decision to attend the crew's fight party, but her desire to see Fray made her go through with it. She tried calling Unique several times to accompany her, but in return, all she kept getting was her voicemail. Sitting behind the wheel of her Volvo she coasted the partially dim parking lot searching for a recognizable vehicle. Locating Derek's Range Rover truck she paralleled parked beside it, checking her makeup in the mirror one last time before making an exit.

A light breeze swept across the back of her exposed neck causing her to hunch her shoulders and pick up pace. The hotel's automatic motion-sensor glass door slid open allowing her to enter the lobby. Its large lobby was decorated in sandy hues with orange and yellow highlights, dark wood furniture, and art. The two elevators sat opposite of the gigantic crystal chandelier accompanied by a receptionist desk. Already having the room number, she bypassed the receptionist desk taking the elevator to the top floor. After stepping from the elevator it was awfully quiet for a fight party she thought. Stopping outside of room 800, she softly knocked on the door. Derek answered seconds later. His sloppy frame filled the doorway. Wearing a white button-up shirt, black slacks, and Versace loafers his bald head was freshly shaved.

"I hope I'm not too early?" Katie asked.

"Nah, as a matter of fact you jus' in time c'mon in," Derek smiled opening the door wider.

As she drifted further into the rooms corridors Derek secretly admired her curvaceous frame. She wore fitted dark blue jeans, platform wedges and a white sleeveless blouse. Mariah's Carey "Dreams" fragrance filled Derek's nostrils.

"Derek I wanna' apologize for the other day."

"Don't mention it." He waved dismissingly.

The spacious suite was complete with sleek vintage furniture, a 50" flat TV, and a faux mounted fireplace. To Katie astonishment, the suite was empty.

"Well don't jus' stand there, go 'head make yourself at home. The guy's a be here any minute," he said before disappearing from her sight. Katie started to protest, but with Derek's assurance that Fray would soon be arriving she begun to relax taking a seat on the suede sofa. Derek re-entered the room carrying a bottle of Cherry Ciroc joining her on the sofa. He placed the bottle of Ciroc along with two empty glasses on the coffee table in front of them. He used the remote to turn up the boxing commentators pre-fight broadcast.

"Would you like a drink." he gestured to the bottle of vodka.

"No thank you." She quickly replied.

Derek cracked the seal pouring himself a drink. After sitting through a half hour of boring miscellaneous fights there was still no sign of Fray, Katie began to grow restless.

"Can you call Fray back for me please?" Katie asked for the umpteen time.

Placing his glass down with a thump he picked up his cell phone dialing numbers, hoisting it to his ear. Ever since he and one of his mistresses joined Fray and Katie in Puerto Rico he secretly grew eyes for her. After learning of Unique's threesome with the duo he was almost certain Katie would do the same if propositioned right. He pretended to be listening to a ringing phone, he then removed the phone from his ear tossing it back on the table top.

"Dat nigga shit still goin' to voicemail." He lied.

"Well, I best to be goin' then. This was probably a bad idea anyway." She said standing to leave. Derek reached over grabbing her wrist.

"Shawty you ain't got to leave. You can hang out wit' me." He sneered

"Nah, 'dats a'ight it's getting late anyway." She replied trying to break free from his grip.

"Shawty why must we continue to play these cats and mouse games. I'm the macaroni wit' all the cheese. Fray jus' my lil man. I can buy you, and fly you anywhere you wanna' go. I gotta stack for you right now." he bragged.

Speechless by his disrespectful outburst she now realized she had been bamboozled.

"Really Derek?" She looked down at his hand that was holding her arm. "Nigga you got me fucked up, getcha nasty ass hand off me!" she raved.

It took a silent prayer for her not to haul off and spit in his face. She had never been subject to this kind of disrespect.

"*Let go of me!*" she snatched away. Derek hopped up from the couch grabbing her from behind.

"I know you want me." His breath was hot on her ear, and neck he reeked of alcohol.

"*Derek get the fuck off me your drunk!*" Katie struggled.

"C'mon shawty you know you want this dick. Stop playin' games," he said fondling her ass and breast. Derek wasn't taking no for an answer. "Shawty you either gon' give me this pussy, or I'ma take it," he said tossing her back on the couch forcing himself between her legs, pinning both her hands above her head.

"*Derek please stop your hurtin' me!*" She tried wiggling free.

"I thought you liked it rough." He smiled leveling his face with hers in an attempt to kiss her. Katie quickly turned away. If she planned on making it out safe, and unscratched her best bet was to play along she thought. Trying not to cry she pressed her lower bottom against the bulge in his pants. Derek was shocked by her sudden movement. Figuring she was getting the hang of it, he loosened his grip on her wrist.

"You ain't gotta take it I'll give it to you," she whispered.

Her sudden willingness won him over. He released his grip entirely sticking his gross tongue in her mouth.

PRESSURE BUST PIPES

"Mm." Katie let out a forced a moan still buried underneath his smothering frame. Derek slid his hands underneath her shirt freeing her breast from her bra, sucking on her nipple. With tear filled eyes, Katie used her right hand to reach for the half-filled Ciroc bottle. Tightening her hold on the bottle she swung it connecting with the back of his skull.

"Ahh...Bitch!" He rolled on the floor holding the back of his head. Quickly scrambling to her feet she delivered another blow to the top of his head, followed by another!

"You fat fuck!" she screamed, crying hysterically before running out the door. She pressed the elevator button desperately trying to get away.

Ronnie had just entered the hotel's lobby with Kitty on his arm. They both decided to end their night at a hotel after the club. *Bing!* The sound of the elevator doors opening got their attention. They were nearly run over by a frightened woman, "What the...," Ronnie did a double take recognizing the woman in a haste.

"Aye Katie." He called out, but she never broke her stride as she jetted out the hotel!

"Who the hell was that?" Kitty asked stepping into the elevator behind him. The elevator opposite of them opened! Ronnie's jaw nearly hit the floor before his elevator doors closed.

Back at Pebblez house, Fray slept peacefully on his back in her bed. The four-play he delivered last night was so amazing, it turned into an all-night fuck session, she had to admit the youngster was a beast in bed which is why she was up early cooking breakfast. The smoke detector sounded off as Pebblez accidentally burned the fried potatoes. Fray jumped out the bed naked thinking he was back in the comforts of his own crib, and his security had been breached. His lifestyle caused him to be paranoid. Squinting his eyes from the beaming sun his eyes began to adjust to his environment. An unpleasant aroma burned his nostrils.

Making his way through the cloud of smoke down the hall is where he found Pebblez in Gray leggings, and a midriff t-shirt fanning a towel in front of the smoke detector.

"What'chu in here burnin'?" he yelled just as the alarm stopped. Looking into the kitchen he noticed the fire on the stove was excessively high, and a black skillet was in the sink sizzling with smoke coming from it under running water.

"I was tryna surprise you wit' breakfast." She pouted from behind the island of the standard kitchen.

"What were you fixing?" he asked.

"Eggs!" she whined.

"Awe baby why didn't you wake me. I woulda' helped." Fray smiled pulling her into his arms. "How 'bout we jus' go out to eat?" Before she could reply they were interrupted by Young Jeezy's ringtone.

"That thing been going off all mornin'," Pebblez said rolling her eyes.

"Oh, fa real," Fray responded making his way down the hall.

By the time Fray made it to the room his phone had stopped ringing. Looking through his phone he noticed he had ten missed calls from Sade, and just as many from Ronnie and DeShay. Staring at his phone he could see that she left a voicemail. Fray assumed she and Ashley had gotten into another one of their many altercations. He hit the voicemail button, listening to the messages. The urgency in Sade's voice told him something was wrong.

His mood changed instantly as Sade's petrified voice came

through the receiver. She appeared to be crying and panicking at the same time. It was hard for him to make out what she was saying. Right before the message ended it sounded as if she said Ashley got shot and was in the hospital. Fray nearly lost his grip on the phone. Hoping that he heard the message wrong he replayed it for a second time, which only confirmed that a nightmare had become reality. Confusion and fear took over him, he didn't see Pebblez when she entered the room.

"Boo what's wrong?" she asked with curiosity in her voice.

"I gotta roll," he said worriedly, pulling up his pants, hopping about on one foot putting his other shoe on. "Ashley got hit up last night!" he said in a rush tone his anger growing by the second.

"Oh, my God, is he okay?"

"I 'ont know but chu' need to throw sumthin' on and take me to my car."

Pebblez took off the too small midriff shirt replacing it with one of her Adidas athletic tanks with a built in bra. She slid her bare feet into a pair of running shoes. After turning down her numerous requests to accompany him to the hospital twenty, minutes later Fray was in his car racing like a bat out of hell to the hospital. He nearly had a dozen accidents as he swerved through traffic holding his phone to his ear trying to call DeShay and Ronnie, but neither one answered. This only made him think the worse. Already doing 70mph he turned the wheel right hoping into the emergency lane mashing the accelerator acceding 100mph. He maneuvered the Lincoln along the shoulder to the exit. Five minutes later he was pulling up to Washington Hospital Center. Fray was in and out of the parking lot.

Upon entering the hospital, he found a slender middle age nurse looking through files.

"Scuse me can you tell me what room Ashley Pitts is in?" Fray asked the nurse, she looked up from the stack of paper.

"And you are sir?"

"I'm his brother Sean Pitts." He lied.

With a twist in her swivel chair, she turned to the computer and began typing on the keyboard.

"He's in room 212 Mr. Pitts," she said turning back to the desk, giving him a visitor's badge.

Fray took the elevator to the second floor. Minutes later he was entering Ashley's room. Surprisingly there were no doctors, or visitors standing around Ashley's bed. He laid resting alone with various cords, and tubes connected to his body. Fray approached his bedside softly placing his left hand on his shoulder. His touch woke up a drugged up Ashley.

"You finally made it," Ashley smiled dimly. "DeShay and em' is pissed at chu'."

"Where e'rybody at?" Fray asked.

"They all jus' left, and you know Sade' pregnant I didn't want her up here stressing, so I had DeShay and Ronnie take her back home." Fray mind had yet to shake all the tubes, and beeping machines at his bedside he wanted answers.

"Slim who the fuck did 'dis shit." He frowned.

"Them niggas from up the "City" caught me slippin last night. Tricked me too. Slim dem niggas dressed up, and hit me with one of my own moves." He chuckled faintly closing his eyes in pain.

"Man, I told y'all niggas we shoulda' applied that pressure after DeShay did 'dat shit!" Fray said running his right hand over his wavy hair.

"Yeah, you were right. We were bullshitting we shoulda'

fucked 'dat joint up. If it wasn't for Ronnie, and lil PeeWee dem niggas probably woulda' killed my ass."

"What'chu mean?" Fray was curious to know what PeeWee had done.

"Oh, you ain't heard? PeeWee and Ronnie banged all the way out wit' them, niggas."

"Oh yeah!" Fray said smiling at the thought.

Ashley shook his head acknowledging his question.

"So how long these peoples sayin' you gotta stay in this joint?"

"They was talkin' 'bout next week sometime. The bullet went straight through."

"What'chu get hit wit?"

"A forty-five. Shit burn like hell too." Ashley said weakly.

"Bruh I ain't goin lie. I was panicking like a muthafucka on my way out he-,". The sound of the door opening behind them stopped Fray in mid-sentence. He turned slightly. In walked the 5'2 Katie with her curly locks pulled in a ponytail. Her attire was well coordinated. A short sweater displayed her Love Is Loyalty tattoo on her lower abdomen, Levi denim blue jeans, diamond drop earrings, and brown Ugg boots. There was a hint of concern on her caramel face.

"Oh, my God Ashley I came as soon as I hea-," Katie didn't finish her sentence. She wasn't expecting to be standing face to face with Fray. The look he gave her upon entering spoke volumes. He looked her up and down before casually turning his attention back to Ashley.

"I'ma holla at chu' later homes," Fray said bothered by her

presence, he turned to leave.

Ashley grabbed Fray's wrist indicating for him to stay. Sensing her presence not wanted Katie jumped in!

"Ashley 'dats a'ight I can speak for myself," Katie said stepping further into the room. The two had not laid eyes on each other in months.

"Fray I don't understand. What did I do to make you hate me so much?" Fray was in disbelief by her statement. As much as he tried to suppress his anger he could no longer keep his emotions in check.

"Man, why are you even here!" he snapped. *"You got some nerve showin' up here when you fuckin' Derek!"* he frowned.

Astounded by the hurtful words Katie was unsure how to respond. Out of all the years the two had known each other he never talked to her like that. Not to mention he was accusing her of something she hadn't even done, she now knew how it felt. Grasping at her chest in shock with her manicured hand it felt like she had been stabbed in the heart. The hurtful look on her face said it all. Fray knew his words cut deep as soon as they left his mouth.

"Ho…hold up…wait a damn minute!" she stammered raising her right hand. "Is that what he told you that he fucked me?" she gave off a stern look blinking back her tears.

Ronnie was the one who told Fray about the hotel situation suggesting that they knock Derek off for being disrespectful. Which Fray declined as Ronnie knew he would.

"Do you really think I would do sumthin' like 'dat after all these years!" Katie pleaded.

Fray was unmoved which only cut deeper. She could no longer hold back her tears as she looked up at the man she loved in skepticism.

"Fray he's fuckin lying' I swear!" she sobbed. "Did he tell you he tricked me into believing you were gon' be there? *I swear on my mother he tried to force himself on top of me, but nuthin' fuckin' happened!*" she sniffed, wiping her caramel face with the bottom of her sleeve.

Fray felt conflicted hearing Katie's story because it was the exact same story Ashley had given him a month ago. Nevertheless, who was he to believe? Derek had raised him from a pup. With his pride in the way and being torn between the two, he looked at Katie then Ashley.

"Slim, I'll holla at chu' later," he said walking towards the door bumping Katie on his way out.

"Fray you know what!" she called out to him, "The only thing I'm guilty of is loving a man that's too blind to see the snake in his own back yard," she said just as the door slammed!

WHAT'S BEEF?

The very next morning, Fray was on a mission to end the lives of those responsible for hospitalizing his best friend. With Derek riding shotgun the two cruised down St. Barnabas Rd heading back to the city. Derek took one look at his protégé.

"Man, y'all need to leave this bullshit as beef alone. I mean if it don't make dollars then it don't make sense."

"Say what? man 'dis shit past talk I ain't leaving shit alone!" Fray barked. "First, them niggas put my cousin girl in the hospital, and then they hit Ashley," Fray said turning on Livingston Rd. "I ain't squashing shit big boy I'm about to turn 'dis shit all the way up!"

"Look shawty you like a son to me, and I ain't never told you anything wrong. At the end of the day, you're, your own man so you gotta make ya' own decisions, and I respect 'dat, but sometimes we don't look at the whole picture before we react and then we regret the consequences later. So I'm gonna leave you with something Nietzsche said. Whoever fights monsters should see to it that he does not become one."

He then leaned back in his seat turning the music up leaving Fray to polish the jewel.

With gloved hands, Fray and DeShay tightened the Velcro straps on their bullet proof vest sliding banana-clips in a mac-90, and AK-47 while sitting in Betty's living room. They then pulled out their hooded sweatshirts. Ronnie sat at the dining room table in a t-shirt loading 9mm rounds into a 30 round clip. A loud banging at the door startled them! Ronnie stood from his seat cautiously walking over to the door peeping out its peephole. He soon relaxed unlocking the door pulling it open, "Damn PeeWee why you knockin' like the police?" He said stepping aside.

"I got the car parked outside," PeeWee said closing and locking the door behind him. Fray placed the mac-90 atop the glass coffee table, standing to his feet he walked to the window. He peered at the stolen black Harley-Davidson F-150 truck, looking back over his shoulder he asked, "Where'd you get the truck from?"

"I stole it from on the other side of town," Pee-Wee replied.

He tensed up noticing the cold look Fray gave him. He decided to elaborate more.

"I got it from down the west, trust me we good."

"So what we waiting on?" Ronnie asked slipping on his black latex gloves stuffing his Glock 17 in his waistband. Fray and DeShay picked up their assault rifles, covering them with extra outer garments as they headed for the door.

PRESSURE BUST PIPES

"And jus' where do you think you going?" Ronnie asked looking back at PeeWee.

"Wit' y'all. Y'all gon' need somebody to bust the feds."

"That's what we got Ronnie for." Fray chimed in.

"What! Ronnie can't drive better than me Fray."

"Man, stay in your muthafuckin lane lil nigga. You ain't ready for this gangsta shit." Ronnie frowned.

"Nigga you got me fucked up! You out of all people know my gun gon' go off!" PeeWee spat, referring to the day Ashley got shot.

Fray cut his eye at DeShay to defuse the verbal debate with Ronnie and his protégé. Sighing heavily, DeShay interfered.

"You gon' have to sit this one out lil man."

"But why Shay?" he asked with tears forming in his eyes.

"Cause you's a fuckin' kid and you need to stay in a child's place!" Fray blurted out tired of the back and forth debate.

The crew then headed out the door.

"Damn, holmes y'all ain't have to go on shawty like dat," DeShay said as they stepped from the building. With the lack of love, PeeWee received growing up Ronnie, and DeShay knew how bad he yearned for their companionship. PeeWee finally felt like he had a family with the crew. Out of the four members, Fray was the only one who had not accepted him with open arms.

"Nigga it's because of you his lil ass is even around in the first place. If it was up to me I'd send his lil ass back to school." Fray said climbing in the bed of the truck with DeShay following suit. Ronnie slid behind the wheel of the truck. From Betty's second floor window PeeWee looked down crying as the truck sped away.

Benning Terrace Aka Simple City was dub by the media in the late seventies when an influx of PCP influenced it's residence to become violent. Over the years, the name became a badge of honor instead of a direct insult for its residents. Due to the nice weather, many gathered outside, although it was a red zone area that still didn't stop the tenants from having a good time. The grill was going while young girls played double Dutch and hot scotch. The drive to Simple City from 18 & D street took less than ten minutes. Ronnie drove the supped-up truck past the shrimp boat on the southeast side of Benning Rd. He made a right onto the hill of G street entering the barbaric projects.

Fray and DeShay laid side-by-side on their backs in the bed of the pick-up truck. They stared up at the bright blue sky anticipating Ronnie's signal. Disguising their faces with thick black ski masks they rested their rifles on their chest. Ronnie now had a clear view of the projects, people were scattered everywhere. Amongst those were Bullet and Chucky surrounded by friends. Bullet hands were occupied with a paper plate as he stood stuffing his face with cookout food. Chucky, on the other hand, seemed to be entertaining the crowd.

"Moe, kill my mutha' y'all man anything." Chucky pointed to stuffed face Bullet. "So listen…We snatched 'dis bamma ass nigga outside the strip club the other night, stripped him, and duct taped his hands behind his back and then put his ass in our trunk. Y'all know how 'dis nigga burnt out off 'dat go-go shit." Chucky continued pointing to Bullet. "So 'dis nigga got R.E blastin' the whole time we ridin' out to the nigga spot. I keep tellin 'dis nigga to turn 'dat shit down so we can hear, but 'dis nigga steady bobbin' his head smiling an shit talking 'bout they rockin' ain't they. So after a while you know a nigga ain't got no other choice but to start rockin' to the shit, as we groovin' sumthin' tell me to look back. I look back…y'all ain't goin' believe this shit. Tell me why the nigga we snatched kicked the whole muthafuckin' trunk off! Slim, I see the nigga ass naked haulin' down the highway!" Chucky burst out laughing causing the others to do the same.

"Man fuck y'all," Bullet said laughing as well.

Ronnie knew they were taking one hell of a risk attempting a stunt as such in the heart of Simple City. With his heart beating rapidly he turned off G St and into the cul-de-sac. He was careful not to hit any of the wild running children, as he bucked a U giving himself an escape route. He brought the truck to a stop in front of the building where Bullet, Chucky, and friends gathered tooting the horn twice. With their adrenaline pumping Fray, and DeShay popped up from the bed of the truck like two jack-in-the-boxes aiming their assault rifles. The once smiling faces quickly turned into looks of horror.

Plait! Plait! Plait! Plait! Plait! Was the constant sound of shots being fired. Hustlers cried out as chopper bullets laid them down. Bullet dove to the ground and started crawling underneath a parked car. Never being the one to duck work, Chucky was the only one shooting back as he pulled the trigger to his .40 dipping between cars returning fire! *Boom! Boom! Boom!* Women and children trampled one another as they tried anxiously to run for cover. The onslaught seemed as if it would never stop. Chucky abandoned his place of cover dashing towards a frantic kid scooping him up. With Chucky locked in the sight of his mac-90 Fray started to squeeze, but hesitated at the sight of the wailing child in his arms. His hesitation could have been deadly had he not been wearing a vest.

Chucky wasted no time raising his pistol getting off a quick shot. The hot led hit center mass in Fray's vest sending him sailing backward in the bed of the truck. The impact knocked the wind out of him, Fray struggled to get up.

Seeing his cousin go down beside him, DeShay swung his K in a wrath letting loose in Chucky's direction showering parked cars as Chucky barely got away with the howling kid. Ronnie spotted a police cruiser on the perimeter with its flashing red and blue lights speeding up G street. He immediately put the truck into gear smashing on the gas sending the firing shooters into the rear window of the pick-up truck. The F150 went skidding out of the parking lot in the nick of a time almost colliding with the blaring cruiser as the cops attempted to box them in. Ronnie made a sharp right onto Benning Rd with the squad car on his tail. He switched lanes and bent corners unable to shake the police. Nervously running out of options he stuck his head out the window yelling to the back of the truck, "Man get them people the fuck off me!"

"Fray get up. We gotta get these people the fuck off us before they radio the bird," DeShay said tugging at his at arm.

Regaining some strength Fray struggled to sit up. He armed himself with his half-filled mac-90 aiming it over the truck. He and DeShay opened fire forcing the cops to turn off. Flying down Southern Avenue doing 75 mph Ronnie tried to bust a sharp right at the last minute and crashed! Grabbing their weapons, the trio hopped from the truck making their getaway on foot. Unfortunately, Bullet and Chucky survived the attack unscratched…

Breaking News…

"Good evening I'm Pat Collins, reporting for your channel 5 news. We're standing here live in southeast D.C at the scene in Benning Terrace housing project's where a senseless act of violence has claimed the lives of six people leaving three others in critical condition. What you see behind me folks are faces of grieving family members looking for answers. Now we still don't know what led the gunman here on this sunny afternoon, but what we do know is authorities arrived at the scene while the shooting was taking place, however in their attempt to apprehend the suspects the gunmen sped away in a pickup truck. The

PRESSURE BUST PIPES

chase lasted approximately three minutes before the gunmen opened fire on local authorities according to reports made by law enforcement. Officers later discovered the stolen truck several blocks away from where the deadly shooting took place, however, it's unknown how the suspects escaped after the crash. I'm Pat Collins reporting live."

Fray turned the television off it was his third time today watching the news for updates. He wanted to make sure there were no children harmed amongst the slain, so far none had been reported. Rubbing the fresh bruise on his chest the image of Chucky's weak Nino Brown move replayed in his head. Pulling his prayer rug from the drawer, laying it down, he began to offer salat, "Allahu-Akbar."

WHEN THE BIRDS SING

Katie laid stretched out on her stomach across her queen size bed talking to Unique about her run in with Fray at the hospital. Unique was furious that Katie never told her about the Derek incident until now.

"Nique I had to literally bust his fat ass in the head with the bottle to get out of there," she said shaking her leg on the bed. "And on top of that do you know his fat ass got the nerve to be goin' around lying' on his dick tellin people he fucked me? DeShay called me saying Fray was pissed, and couldn't believe I would stoop so low. Girl, and to make matters worse Ronnie's snake ass just so happened to be creepin' wit' some bitch that night at the hotel when he saw me runnin' out."

"I wish I was dere wit' you. I woulda' cut his ass too short to shit." Unique said bluntly.

"Nique your ass is crazy. I haven't heard dat' sayin' since my mova passed." Katie continued to laugh when all of a sudden the sound of footsteps marching down the hall cut her laughter short. La-La burst through the room door like a madman, Katie sat straight up! Her nose turned up at the smell of alcohol pouring from his pores. One night during their pillow talk she learned La-La deceased father was an alcoholic. Whenever his dad would have a bad day he would get drunk and beat his mother. La-La had become his father continuing the cycle.

"Girl let me call you back," Katie said ending the call.

"Don't get off the phone now. It probably was a nigga anyway." His words slurred as he stood in the doorway.

"Boy please, 'dat was Unique and why are you bustin' in here like 'dat?"

"So why you get off the phone if that was Unique, huh?"

"Because you came in here like you was on sumthin,' and I didn't want her all in my business." She frowned growing annoyed.

"Bitch you think I'm stupid! That probably was that nigga Fray!"

"Okay La-La you drunk and I'm not tryna fight you," Katie said standing from the bed trying to avoid confrontation. She tugged at her tight fitting purple velour shorts attempting to bypass him. Katie's laid-back personality set something off inside him. He grabbed a fistful of her locks, slinging her across the bed.

"Ahh." She cried out.

Before she knew it he was on top of her punching and kicking her.

PRESSURE BUST PIPES

After the petrifying beating, Katie quietly crept in the bathroom to assess the damage to her face. It was the first time a man had ever abused her. Her eye was swollen shut. She began to cry and for the first time she began to question her love for Fray "Is it worth it?" she thought. Not wanting to believe that things would never be the same between them, she quickly pushed those thoughts from her head staring at her bruised eye in the mirror.

"Damn you, Fray." She wept silently.

"Ronnie can you please try to be in here at a reasonable time tonight. I told you the kids love seeing you when they wake up." Teresa stressed the issue. Ronnie grabbed his car keys off the kitchen counter. With all the excessive partying and addiction to the streets Ronnie seen less of his family. He awoke this morning with Teresa standing over top of him irate. It was his turn to take the kids to school. He pulled the covers over his head, but she snatched them back off. She had already taken the kids to school, that was an hour ago. Ronnie now sat downstairs in the living room tying up his butter Timberland's boots. Teresa leaned against the wall with her arms folded across her droopy breast, she was determined to get her point across.

"Ronnie do you hear me. I want you in here at a reasonable time."

"I heard you the first time Teresa damn!" he spat.

He wore gray Sobiato sweat pants and a multicolored short sleeve spring Sobiato hoodie. The Velcro back-brace underneath his shirt hid his two-tone S&W .40. Maneuvering around Teresa's obese frame wasn't going to easy, he started for the door.

"So you jus' gon' block the door. I said I'll be in by nine," he said putting her at ease so he could ease around her. When he stepped on his porch his Rottweiler Hercules rushed up to him, *"Hey Boy!"* he smiled stooping down to pat him. Teresa's husky voice called out to him from the house. From his stooping position, he looked back over his shoulder.

"I knew it was sumthin' I meant to ask you when I got back from dropping off the kids. Do you know somebody who drives a black Charger?" she asked from the doorway.

"Nah why?" Ronnie replied still rubbing Hercules.

"Because I used your car to drop the kids off this morning and I think I was being followed."

"Teresa why the fuck you ain't been say nuthin'? he frowned towering over her.

"Because I wasn't for sure and I didn't want to spook you."

"What did the person look like who was drivin'? you sure it wasn't the police?" Ronnie interrogated her.

"I don't know it had dark tints," she said softly squinting her eyes as she continued to watch the car. "It kinda looked like 'dat one parked right there." She pointed at the tinted black Charger parked directly behind Ronnie's Lexus. Ronnie whipped his head around in the direction of the parked car. The passenger door flew open. Ronnie's eyes bulged at the sight of Chucky upping the Uzi in his hands. He tried pulling his S&W from the back brace, but Chucky had already begun spitting hitting the porch with every shot! Teresa's screams along with Hercules barking and loud gunfire made Ronnie panic.

The dog barking had become obsolete. His gun slipped from his right hand as he shoved Teresa back into the door. She fell to the floor. Not wanting to jeopardize her life any more than he already had, he stayed low running to the end of the porch jumping off, bolting behind the house. He cleared the six-foot brick wall in the

alley behind his house with no problem. Chucky being only 5'6"
was able to climb the wall in two attempts, the Uzi in his hands
slowed him down. He stood on top of the wall firing blindly into
the alley.

The echo of continuous gunfire had awakened Ronnie's
neighbors. Gunshots were almost nonexistent in that area, which
brought cops faster than normal. The first responding unit pulled
directly in front of Ronnie's house. The two uniformed officers
could hear the heavy gunfire coming from behind the house.
Drawing their service weapons from its holsters, they carefully
exited the squad car proceeding with caution. After locating the
source of gunfire, the two nervous officers pushed off the right side
of the house into the alley. They raised their Glocks high at
Chucky's back as he continued to fire unaware of the company
behind him!

"Freeze!" the police yelled.

Without thinking twice Chucky twirled around shooting the Uzi in
their direction. The police dove to the ground. After noticing the
police uniforms Chucky was staggered. He hopped from the wall,
jetted around the left side of the house, and jumped in the car,
Bullet sped off.

PeeWee had just stepped from one of the rundown apartment
building. He had fallen asleep in one of the crew's trap houses. He
puffed on a cigarette exhaling smoke into the night air. He
squinted his eyes as he looked up and down the deserted street. The
visibility was limited from the shot-out street lights. The block was
awfully quiet except for the alley cats and oversized rats shuffling in
the alleyways. After stretching and letting out a yawn he started to
make his way up the block. He bumped into Betty who was

escorting a man in shabby clothes holding a beer can. He had never seen the man in the neighborhood before. Betty's face lit up upon seeing him. she told her friend to stand by while she approached PeeWee.

"Boy, am I glad to see you. Let me get sumthin' for twenty-five," she said dangling a crisp twenty-dollar bill, and a crumpled five.

"Man who the fuck is dat!" PeeWee frowned eyeing the suspicious man.

Over the years of knowing Betty, she never purchased more than one dime at a time.

"Would you stop bein' so damn paranoid he wit' me," Betty said grinding her jaw showing several rotten teeth.

The man in the shabby attire watched their interaction from across the street like a hawk. PeeWee pulled his stash from the crack of his ass, dropping three dime bags of crack into Betty's hand, he took the money. He watched as Betty and the unknown character disappeared around the corner. After pocketing the money, he decided to post up. Out of nowhere two black Lumina's came speeding up the block in opposite directions! PeeWee's heart sank and his eyes grew large at the sight of the unmarked cars closing in on him fast. He didn't give them a chance to exit their cars before he took off running in the opposite direction.

"Police! Police! They shouted in unison after him. PeeWee tried to make it back in the building where he had just come from, but he lost his footing. The officers were all over him before he could push himself back up.

In the meantime, Betty was also being apprehended around the corner for directing traffic. She unintentionally brought an undercover cop to PeeWee, but PeeWee had bigger problems not only did the cops pull his stash out his ass, but they recovered the gun he tried to toss.

The chipped away paint on the old prison bars exposed rust in the fifth district precinct. Two metal benches aligned the graffiti covered walls, and piss stained the seats of the toilets from various overnighters. The smell of the place made PeeWee's stomach turn as he stood at the cell bars shivering. He paced the six by nine holding cell with his arms tucked inside his short sleeve Hanes V-neck t-shirt. It had been over an hour since they processed him, he now wondered what the hell was taking them so long. The jiggling keys coming from a stalky officer got his attention. He walked over to the cell bars to see what was going on. The officer stood on the outside of the tank twirling his keys with an attitude.

"Howard turn around and cuff up, homicide's here to see you." The officer said addressing him by his last name. At the mention of homicide, PeeWee broke wind. He began to wonder if the gun he copped a week ago on the block had been involved in a murder.

"Officer, are you sure you want Howard? I only got a gun and drug case?" PeeWee asked nervously.

"I'm sure kid, now let's go."

Pushing his arms back through his sleeves he complied with the officer's demand. The officer led him up a short flight of stairs, down an extensive hall, and into a dimly lit room. His eyes settled on the two-way mirror that set in the wall to his left. The officer ushered him over to a brown table and chair, which was bolted to the polished concrete floor. A low wattage light bulb dangled over his head just like in the 1960 movies. After taking a seat in the wooden chair the officer uncuffed one of PeeWee's hands cuffing it to the metal ring that had a chain coming from the floor, double locking it.

"The detective will be right with you."

Joe was entering the room just as the officer was walking out. He carried a large evidence bag and a manila folder. PeeWee began sweating profusely upon seeing the legendary detective.

"Sir with all due respect I'm an attorney of the law, and by law, it's illegal to question a minor without his parent's consent," District Attorney Kelly Anderson said, as she and Burnette watched Joe and PeeWee from behind the glass.

"I'm afraid it would do us no good. The only relative we have listed for him is his mother, and she's doing time in Danbury for a violation." Burnett revealed looking in the eyes of the youthful attorney before him.

Dressed in an Olive pants suit, and a white blouse, the Brunette bombshell had her hair slicked back in a ponytail making her prescription specs and dimpled chin noticeable. The petite, pale, green-eyed Amazon looked more like a cheerleader rather than an attorney. Kelly Anderson was barely over twenty-seven and already making a name for herself. Fresh out of law school Kelly Anderson was good at what she did. She played by the book earning the nickname pit-bull in a skirt. When news spread that the cops might have someone in custody in connection with the Simple City shooting, she used her connections to get inside.

"Sir, I'll have you know that I'm strictly by the book."

"Ms. Anderson with all due respect." Burnett sarcastically mimicked her. "The only reason I allowed you inside is because of your father, but this isn't a courtroom we do things a little different around here," He said turning his attention back to the two-way mirror. Joe had already placed the evidence bags and manila folder on the table.

PRESSURE BUST PIPES

"Well...well...well...you must be PeeWee, and if I must say looks like you got yourself in quite a bit of a jam." Joe smiled. "The gun alone could land you five years, and I don't wanna begin to imagine the time judges give black boys for selling crack. So what that being said where'd you get the gun?"

"I found it," PeeWee said.

"You can play all the games you like, but sooner or later I'm gonna get the truth out of you. Your gonna' be singin' like a bird."

"Slim you and I both know there's nothin' you or the judge can do to me. This is my first offense...so cut the jokes." PeeWee said. Joe admired his toughness for now.

"Okay...you got me," Joe grinned. "Unfortunately, if you heard of me then you know I only come out when I'm after someone. So, if you think a lousy gun is what got you sitting in front of me your sadly mistaken son. Trust me the gun is the least of your worries." Joe smiled mischievously. "A stolen F-150 ring a bell?"

PeeWee armpits began to perspire heavily. He didn't know if it was the low wattage light bulb, or if it suddenly got hot. He decided to call Joe's bluff.

"Man, I 'ont know what you talkin' 'bout," PeeWee said.

Joe then opened the manila folder pulling out what appeared to be a sealed laminate print.

"Well, this here says you do," he said sliding the print in front of him that they pulled from the truck. The day of the event was clear. PeeWee recalled not wearing gloves when he stole the truck. He thought back a little harder realizing the trio all had on gloves when they pulled off.

"Man, you can't pin that shit on me. I ain't kill nobody!" he said nervously.

Joe never mentioned the Simple City killings. He knew then PeeWee would do anything to save his own ass. Joe continued to let him hang himself.

"Either you were there, or you stole the truck for someone. Either way, I'm gonna see to it that you fry right along with them unless you tell me what I wanna know."

"Man, I told you I didn't kill anybody I swear!" he panicked playing right into Joe's plan.

"I know you didn't kid. That's why I'm here to help you, but you gotta be willing to help yourself," Joe said playing good detective.

"What I gotta do?" PeeWee asked sounding like a fourteen-year-old instead of the gangsta he portrayed to be. Joe pulled a photograph from the large manila folder pushing it across the table.

"Recognize that guy?"

PeeWee eyed DeShay's mug shot. Coming to him senses he said, "I ain't sayin' nuthin' 'bout him." He snapped, pushing the picture back across the table. Joe calmly got up, walked to the door locking it.

"What's he doing?" Kelly asked curiously from behind the two-way mirror. Her question went unanswered, Burnette continued to watch the interrogation. Pulling his snub nose .38 special from his ankle holster he took a seat across from PeeWee.

"I see you like revolver's," Joe gestured to the evidence bag atop the table. He retrieved the gun, popping out the revolver's cylinder, dumping five rounds on the table leaving one inside. He then spent the cylinder, snapping it shut!

PRESSURE BUST PIPES

"What's he doing now? Kelly looked on in disbelief.

"Joe's a master interrogator just watch," Burnette said.

"You familiar with the game Russian-Roulette?" Joe asked an attentive PeeWee.

"You can't be serious." PeeWee chuckled.

Joe raised his gun aiming it at PeeWee's face.

"Fuck this 'pose to be some kind of scare tactic." PeeWee sat unmoved.

Joe pulled the trigger *Click!*

"What the fuck!" PeeWee flinched taking by surprise. *"Man, what the fuck wrong wit' you, this shit illegal."* He fumed trying to break free from the cuffs. Pee-Wee came to an understanding that the cop was out of his mind. Kelly was already out the office storming down the hall to the interrogation room. She turned the knob, it was locked. She then commenced beating down the door. Disregarding the loud banging, Joe resumed with the interrogation.

"Still think this is a scare tactic? Now who did you steal the truck for?"

"I ain't tellin you shit!" PeeWee said.

Click!

"Aye man, y'all come get 'dis crazy muthafucka!" PeeWee yelled towards the mirror.

"I wanna know who had a hand in the Simple City killings, and I wanna know now!" Joe screamed.

"I can't tell you what I 'ont kn-," *Click! "Help!"* PeeWee hollered falling from his chair.

Joe then towered over him, aiming his gun down.

"There's only three more spins in this barrel kid."

"Your fuckin' crazy man!" PeeWee continued trying to break free from the cuffs.

"Wrong answer." *Click!*

"OH! PeeWee panicked looking up from a helpless position.

"I'm waiting…on second thought. *Click!*

"A'ight, a'ight, I'll tell you what you wanna know. 'Jus don't squeeze the trigger," he said on the brink of tears.

PeeWee had pissed himself. Joe had finally broken him. However, he did last longer than many others. Joe holstered his gun picking up the chair, helping PeeWee back in it.

"You wouldn't mind givin' one of my officer's your statement, now would ya?"

"Nah man, whatever you want," he said wiping away his tears.

"Good," Joe said patting him on the back. Now remember, I'll be watching. He gestured towards the two-mirror.

Kelly was still banging on the door when he opened it. She now stood face to face with the mad man.

"What the hell kind of precinct are you psychos running here? I should be prosecuting you guys and not them." She fumed.

"I beg your pardon." Joe scrunched up his face eyeing the beautiful attorney before him.

"You heard me you maniac. You're lucky I don't have you stripped of your badge."

"Oh, yeah?" Well, I'll have you know it's because of me you're here," he said remembering a time when he performed the same kind of interrogation for her father. Kelly couldn't believe in her wildest dreams that her father would be a part of something like this.

"Alright calm down you two," Burnett said appearing in the hallway, stopping the clash of words.

"And for the record, this old thing doesn't work. I had the firing pin removed years ago." Joe revealed.

The look on Kelly's face was priceless.

"That's what I been tryna tell you, Kelly! Burnette chuckled.

They headed back into the room where they watch PeeWee sang for over an hour. He went as far as offering the detective information they didn't ask, such as who supplied the crew with drugs, various trap houses, where they stashed money along with who picked the drugs up. Yet, he called himself staying loyal to DeShay making sure he kept his name in the clear. He swapped out DeShay putting Ashley in his place at the scene of the Simple City shooting. After gathering all the information PeeWee had to offer, Kelly took a seat while Burnette and Joe stood adjacent to his desk.

"I don't know chief. I still don't think this is enough to get us a conviction in the court of law." Kelly was almost certain of this. "All we have right now is hearsay, and the last thing we need is for these scum bags to hire some hot shot attorneys and prove just that. We still got to be mindful that this kid's fingerprints were the only ones pulled from the truck. So, if you ask me it makes him look more like a suspect," Kelly said.

"Well, what do you suggest we do? Just sit back, and let these murderers continue to roam the streets." Joe interjected.

"Of course not. All I'm simply saying is that with this flimsy evidence we'll be lucky if we make it to trial," Kelly said.

"Well, how about we put this kid back out on the streets…maybe he could get us the evidence we're looking for?" Joe insinuated.

"Wait. are you suggesting that we put this kid back out on the streets to risk him being killed like our other witnesses? If that's what you're inquiring, you can forget it!" she frowned.

Kelly had yet to get over how Joe didn't provide protection to the tournament killer star witnesses. She relied on that high profile case to be the highlight of her career, but it all came crashing down thanks to Joe and his egotistic ways.

"Got Damn it Kelly!" Joe banged his fist on top of Burnette's desk. "We finally have an opportunity to nail these thugs, and you're throwing it all away!" he shouted to the top of his lungs.

"Well, if you hadn't allowed your ego to cloud your better judgment in the first place, we wouldn't be having this meeting now would we!" She fired back.

"Well, excuse me Ms. Matlock for fuckin' up your legacy, but in this career mistakes are the norm." Joe snapped.

"Enough! We're all on the same side here." Burnette said.

Joe refused to surrender.

"Don't bother chief. If you need me I'll be somewhere getting drunk!" he said snatching up his leather vest storming out, slamming the door behind him.

"Well, that went well," she said rolling her eyes flopping down in her seat.

"Must you upset him every time you come here? Despite what you think, he's still the best damn cop this city has," Burnett said.

"Me!" Kelly said pointing to herself as if she misheard his accusation. "Chief, I'm the one who ended up taking the hit from the press for the loss of the two witnesses. So forgive me if I'm busting his balls a little." She shook her head in distress.

"Kelly, word of advice...screw the press! All Joe and I are saying is with this kid on the inside we stand a better chance at building a case. We may even be able to hit them with Rico. You said so yourself the evidence was flimsy." Kelly was left to make a hard decision.

"Alright, but if I agree to this we do things my way. I want twenty-four-hour surveillance on this kid. I want to know what he eats; what time he wakes up in the morning! At the first sign of danger, I'm pulling him out." She said eyeing him without blinking.

"Deal," Burnette said.

THE BLOCK IS HOT

Momma G's door came crashing down! This was the fifth raid Joe, and his team conducted on the crew's operation this week. PeeWee's information was turning out to be helpful after all. They ceased an undisclosed amount of cash and narcotics. Joe was now a man on a mission. Nevertheless, they had yet to land one of the foursomes in custody. Joe rounded up over a dozen low-level workers in the raid who refused to talk. Derek and Fray had just turned onto Momma G's block when the scene of cops startled them. Derek immediately cut the wheel turning into the parking lot. Had the cops waited a minute longer to make their move they would've detained them both.

The two now sat looking up the street as Momma G was lead out to the back of the police cruiser. They waited until the area was clear before putting the truck back into gear. They now drove without a specific destination. With all their spots being targeted at once, the cops were making it hard for them to hustle. The crew was taking major losses as well. Derek had been around long enough to know that something fishy was going on. As they drove down East Capital St, Derek was furious over the loss of money he was on his way to get from Momma G's house. He now sat trying to convince Fray that there was a rat floating amongst his inner circle, which sparked a heated argument.

"Man, how the fuck you gon' tell me. I been doin' 'dis shit too long, cops jus' don't stumble across five spots in one-week Fray. One of them lil niggas you fuckin' wit is hot!" Derek stressed.

"Man stop sayin' anything. Slim I know my men personally, and them nigga's a die first before they work with dem peoples. I'm tellin you it's 'dat hot ass detective, he been on a nigga line ever since bodies start dropping." Fray replied.

"Boy, let me tell you sumthin.' Be very careful who you willin' to vouch for out here because I been in the trenches with some of most thorough-est nigga's, but when it came time to stand up to dem peoples in court pressure bust a lot of them niggas pipes!" he said earnestly looking over at Fray.

All the bickering had given Fray a headache, he wanted to change the topic.

"You hungry?" Fray asked changing the conversation.

Derek nodded yes.

"Shid, stop at the carry-out up there then," Fray said. When the light turned green Derek drove past Eastern High School coming up on the miniature size carry- out known as Hong Kong.

"A'ight, buddy you have a good one," Joe said waving to the Korean man behind the bulletproof glass as he exited the carry out heading back to his unmarked cruiser.

"I got your favorite. Garlic chicken and mambo sauce." He motioned to PeeWee who was lying across the back seat of his cruiser. For the past two weeks, this had become their meeting place.

"Thanks, now can I go?" PeeWee asked as he accepted the bag between the seats. The side of his acne face was pressed against the cloth seat as he lay shielding himself from passing patrons, and vehicles.

"In a minute kid, we still have a few more things to discuss," Joe said looking through the rearview mirror making eye contact. "Now, you're doing good but I'm going to need something a little more concrete, like the location of the murder weapons used in the Simple City killings.

"C'mon man, get real those guns were traded off 'dat same day."

"Well, have they by any chance ever discussed who murdered the witness that was scheduled to testify against DeShay?"

"Yeah, when DeShay first came home, but, I 'ont know which witness they were referring too. They never named any names or anything. I overheard Ronnie tellin DeShay one day 'dat Ashley dressed up for one of them." PeeWee exposed.

"What'chu mean by dressed up?" Joe asked curiously.

"You know, like a disguise," PeeWee said.

"Did Ronnie ever say how Mr. Pitts was dressed?"

"Nah, they stop talkin' when I walked in."

"A'ight so far so good," Joe said, "Try to find out which murder Mr. Pitts participated in, and if you can find out who they traded those guns off too." PeeWee nodded his head signifying he understood.

"A'ight, the coast looks clear take a hike" …

Derek and Fray had just neared the carry out when they noticed Joe's distinctive 66' Nova with the two large antennas parked.

"Aww, shit 'dats that hot ass detective right their slim keep goin'!" Fray said frantically waving his hand in the air behind the tint. With perfect timing, the curb side back door swung open just as they were passing. Derek's eyes immediately shot to the rearview mirror as Fray readjusted his position so he could see who was exiting the car.

"What the fuck," Fray said looking at PeeWee pulling his hoodie over his head.

"I guess we no longer have to figure out who been tellin on us," Derek said shaking his head.

Ashley's stomach had healed properly. He had finally gotten the okay from the nurse to move around. Excited, he called up his homeboys the first chance he got inviting them over. The four of them including his newborn daughter Ava sat in his living room. They had been discussing Ronnie's latest run in with death. Fray and DeShay sat a seat apart on the black leather sectional. Ashley sat on the glass coffee table in front of them, rocking his infant to sleep in his arms. A hysterical Ronnie stood raving as he paced the floor.

"Slim, why you so loud? I jus' told you Sade' upstairs sleep," Ashley said.

"Why I'm so loud!" Ronnie repeated with a frown. "*Yeah, I bet her muthafuckin' ass is up there sleep, they ain't shoot your shit up! Man, we out here horse playin' with these niggas. They killed Hercules slim!*"

"Fuck Hercules!" Fray blurted out, DeShay roared with laughter.

"*Fuck Hercules…nah, nigga fuck you!*" Ronnie spat.

"Hol' up, hol' up, man y'all ease up." Ashley interrupted wanting to keep the peace.

"*Nah, fuck all 'dat. Nigga if it wasn't for your muthafuckin' ass freezin' up them nigga's probably wouldn't a made it out my muthafuckin' spot. They ass shoulda' been dead up in 'dat muthafuckin' circle!*"

"Fuck I'm pose' to shoot a lil girl?" Fray said.

"*Nigga, I wouldn't have given a fuck who got hit up 'dat joint!*" An irritated Ronnie spoke.

DeShay was still doubled over in laughter when Fray turned his attention to him.

"DeShay what the fuck you laughin' at? Your lil man out here hot as a muthafucka!" Fray spat.

His deadly words stopped everything. Fray had been trying to hip the crew on PeeWee's involvement with the detectives ever since they entered Ashley's house, but Ronnie's ongoing raving sidetracked him.

PRESSURE BUST PIPES

"Say What?" DeShay said not believing his ears.

"Nigga, you heard what I said. Shit ain't funny no more." Fray smirked.

"Slim you fa real?" Ashley asked cradling Ava tighter.

"Look, me and Fatz caught 'dat nigga gettin' out 'dat hot ass detective car the other day," Fray confirmed.

"Oh Yeah," Ronnie said.

The three of them keyed in on DeShay.

"I took his lil bitch ass in, and he gon' do some sucka' shit like 'dis!" he snapped walking towards the door, but Fray stepped in his path.

"Hol' fast slim ease up!" Fray said extending his arm in front of him motioning for DeShay to stop.

"Get the fuck out my way!" DeShay said still pushing forward. They began to scuffle at the door breaking Ava's sleep. She let out a loud cry! Fray was desperately trying to keep him from crashing out. Sade's voice echoed from the top of the stairs catching them off guard.

"Ashley, what the hell is goin' on down there!" she yelled, *"Why is my child cryin'?"* She came stomping down the steps turning the corner into the living room. *"Give her to me!"*

"Babe I told these stupid ass niggas to be quiet," Ashley explained as he passed a crying Ava to her mother.

"Boy you know I gotta get up and go to work in the morning," she said with an attitude.

"We 'bout to leave out anyway don't even start tripping," Ashley said.

"Awe…they then upset my baby," Sade' smiled looking down at her daughter carrying her up the steps.

"Shay I ain't about to let you crash out again. I need you to have your thinkin' cap on for 'dis one. Now we 'ont know what 'dat lil nigga told them peoples, or if he got 'em watchin' our every move. We gotta do 'dis this shit quietly," Fray said.

The foursome could not believe they were about to plot PeeWee's murder. The truth was no one wanted to be the triggerman. PeeWee was still that snot nose kid who they use to give dollars to, and chase off the block in the past. DeShay began to calm himself.

"Why all the long faces? He broke the code 'dat we live by so now he must pay," DeShay said sadly sitting back down on the leather sectional.

"A'ight 'dis what we goin' do." Fray began putting a plan together.

EVERYBODY GOT A DAY

With Ashley back on his feet, he and Katie had been promising to hook up all week. The two had not seen each other since she ran into Fray at the hospital. With him hustling and running errands their schedules were conflicted, prolonging their get together. Today Ashley happened to be in the area. He figured it would be okay to drop by unannounced. He called Katie and informed her that he was parked outside. They now occupied the parking lot of her apartment complex. Katie chestnut colored locks hung to the middle of her back, she wore a pair of oversized dark Christian Dior sunglasses masking La-La's most recent attack.

"Why you ain't bring lil Ms. Thang! Katie smiled referring to baby Ava.

"She wit Sade's mother 'dis weekend, but I'm a make sure I bring her pass one day 'dis week," Ashley said leaning up against the hood of his Benz.

"Kee let me ask you a question. Why in the hell do you have on those big as glasses, you nocturnal now." He joked.

For a minute she thought he discovered her secret she became jittery.

"You a'ight?" Ashley looked at her with concern.

Katie wanted to tell someone about the harsh abuse she was enduring but didn't know how to. She opened her mouth to speak but nothing came out. She slowly removed the shades. Ashley tried to maintain his composure, but the love he had for her wouldn't allow him to. His temper began to rise.

"What the fuck happened to you!" he seethed.

Katie didn't have to say anything he already knew. He watched her lower her head in embarrassment on the brink of tears.

"You lettin' 'dat nigga put his hands on you? Is that bitch ass nigga upstairs!" he said walking towards the building.

Katie quickly shook her head no catching a tear before it could fall.

"Kee how fuckin' long has 'dis shit been goin' on!"

"Not long." Tears began to fall as she tried catching them.

Ashley was at a loss for words. This was not the same girl he met a while back. She had been robbed of her innocence, caught up in Fray's fucked up world. The move he thought about it, the more he blamed Fray for her current situation. Ashley knew Derek was full of shit since day one, but Fray was too blind to see that Derek had been brainwashing him all along.

"Ashley whatever you do please don't tell Fray," she cried.

PRESSURE BUST PIPES

"Don't tell Fray!" he said with no pity, "Man, look at your face. He ain't the one gettin' his ass beat in there! Why are you puttin' up wit' 'dis Kee?... answer the fuckin' question?" He demanded.

"You believe in love don't chu?" Katie asked wiping her tears. Ashley was dazed by how naïve she was.

"Kee, are you serious right now…you love 'dis nigga!"

"I wasn't talkin' about him. I was referrin' to Fray." Her voice shivered as she tried to keep it together.

Ashley let her last statement set in before speaking.

"Is he threaten' to do sumthin' to Fray?" he asked.

"Yes. That's the only reason why I haven't left because I love Fray too much."

Ashley's anger was now through the roof.

"Kee, leave 'dat nigga before he kills your ass. I'ma about to roll because if the nigga pulls up while I'm here I'ma smash him on sight, and I don't want you to witness that." He gave her a tight hug before hopping in his car pulling off.

Dusk was now approaching as the newly installed streetlights came on. The neighborhood kids were playing a game of tag when the lights came on, signifying it was time to go in the house. With pacific orders to keep 24-hour surveillance on PeeWee, Roger and Mason sat in an unmarked car away from all the action and disarray. Their disguise was a dead giveaway, the tinted Caprice parked on the corner stuck out like a sore thumb on the residential street.

"See, I told chu,' look 'dat joint been parked out here all day. I think 'dats the police," Ronnie said anxiously.

"Slim, I think we should call it off," Ashley said from the passenger seat looking over at Ronnie, whose eyes were glued to the rearview mirror looking at the parked car. DeShay and PeeWee sat posted up on crates around the corner on 18th street out front of the run-down two-story building.

"Whassup wit'chu and Ms. Shelly's granddaughter. You hit 'dat yet?" DeShay asked releasing a cloud of smoke from his mouth passing PeeWee the half of jay of hydro.

"Man, hell nah she still talkin' dat virgin shit. Every time I try she be bullshitting," PeeWee said before placing the blunt to his lips.

"Tell me about it. I remember those days," DeShay let out a laugh being able to relate. Just then, his cell phone began to ring. He reached into the right pocket of his cargo shorts retrieving it, PeeWee watched his every move.

"Yeah," DeShay spoke into the receiver holding up one finger signaling for PeeWee to wait a minute. *"He did what!"* DeShay exaggerated jumping to his feet. Assuming the caller on the other end was delivering some disturbing news, PeeWee jumped up as well. "Man, hol' on right quick, slim you strapped?" DeShay asked removing the phone from his ear covering the mouthpiece.

"Yeah, whassup!" PeeWee replied hyped ready to bust his gun for DeShay at the drop of a dime.

"A'ight, I'm on my way!" DeShay said flipping the phone closed placing it back in his pocket. "Slim, let me see 'dat joint Aisha bitch ass brother jus' jumped out there."

At the mention of a family member, PeeWee felt like he was placed in an awkward situation, without hesitation he lift his shirt exposing the pearl handle on the chrome .380 handing DeShay the gun. With the loaded gun in his possession, he briefly eyed his young protégé with sympathy, it was too late to turn back now.

"I'll be right back," DeShay said slipping the gun into his pocket, walking down the concrete steps heading across the street to his candy apple red corvette. As he neared his car, he fought back his tears.

"DeShay you want me to go wit'chu?" PeeWee yelled at his back from the stoop, just as he was opening the car door.

"Nah. I'm straight," he answered before sliding into the driver seat. He phoned Ronnie and Ashley before pulling off.

"Slim what the fuck we goin' do? Shay jus' hit me and the cops still parked on the corner!" Ashley panicked trying to come up with a solution as Ronnie double-parked the Saab next to the alley. Ashley watched Ronnie pull his brown 9mm from between the seat and console. "What the fuck you 'bout to do?" he asked curiously.

"Jus' follow my lead and get in the driver seat," Ronnie said slipping from the car. He crept down the dark alley. With his heart pounding with every step he peeped his head out from behind the wall. He was right behind the parked police car.

"Are you nuts? Jennifer Aniston is way hotter than Gwyneth Paltrow!" Mason said as he debated with Roger who was eating a jelly donut. Before Roger could swallow and reply gun shots rang out!

"*Holy shit!* Mason yelled ducking his head. Roger looked through the rear window to locate the source of gunfire. Ronnie let off a few more shots in the air. He waited until the Caprice doors opened before taking off back down the alley. A worried Fray heard the gunshots as he sat parked in a remote location. He prayed DeShay hadn't done unthinkable. Within a blink of an eye,

Ashley's number flashed across his phone screen. Fray hit the end button sending him to voice mail, he started the engine on the rented jeep. PeeWee's position had not changed he still stood on top of the stoop. His eyes scanned the empty block, the shots sounded so close. PeeWee's eyes watched the white Jeep Cherokee speed up in his direction coming to an abrupt stop in front of him.

"Slim, hurry up and get in the police round the corner!" Fray shouted convincingly waving him over to the truck, PeeWee quickly hopped in.

"Was' 'dat you jus' bustin' off?" PeeWee asked.

"Nah, I heard the shots too when I was pullin up then I saw the police standin' by the alley," Fray said steering the truck down East Capital highway, making a right on the southeast side of Benning Rd.

"Damn, I 'preciate dat homes I was dirty as a muthafucka too."

"Dat' shit ain't 'bout nuthin." Fray leaned back in his seat making a right onto G St climbing the hill of Simple City. Cruising on the outer perimeter of the projects, they both took notice of the dimly lit parking lot of the circle.

"Fray, that's 'dat nigga who hit Ashley right there!" PeeWee said pointing Bullet out instantly. Bullet was kneeling down beside the passenger door of a blue Honda Accord. Chucky stood on the driver side chatting as well.

"Slim, you got your joint on you?" Fray asked taking his foot off the accelerator glancing over at him. PeeWee started to reach for his waist but quickly remembered he had given his gun to DeShay.

"Damn slim, I jus' gave my joint to Shay! He shook his head from side to side disappointed.

"You tryin' work?" Fray asked turning down a side street

heading back towards Benning Rd.

Bullet and Chucky continued to entertain the two women in the blue Honda Accord they met previously in the club weeks ago.

"You goin' wit me tonight?" Bullet asked the slender big breast redbone in the passenger seat.

"I'll go if she go." She looked over at her friend for approval.

Her friend was a small-framed woman with a pie face. She sat behind the steering wheel sipping on some Grey-Goose and cranberry juice.

"It's whatever wit' me," she smiled looking Chucky up and down.

"A'ight roll 'dis up then, I'll be right back I gotta take a piss," Chucky said passing the driver a bag of weed, and a single back wood before making his way towards the cut of the rundown houses. Fray and PeeWee pulled into the parking lot of the fish market at the bottom of the hill on G street.

"PeeWee, grab that 'dat hoodie out the back seat," Fray instructed as he grabbed the nickel plated .357 revolver from underneath the seat. PeeWee began pulling the hoodie over his head. While doing so Fray opened the cylinder of the gun checking it before snapping it closed. He then passed the gun to PeeWee.

"I'm tellin you now, don't go up there bullshitting. Get one of those niggas and come straight back!" Fray made his self-clear. PeeWee pulled the drawstrings on the hoodie tight camouflaging his face. He then tucked the gun into the sweater pocket before easing from the Cherokee. With both hands in his pockets, he clutched the gun observing the area for any potential witnesses. The coast was clear. He quickly hopped the wall that separated the parking lot of the market and the Simple City circle. Once on the other side, he whipped out the .357 using the trees as his cover.

Bending down in a crouching position he began creeping up the rocky hill moving branches along the way. Bullet was getting more acquainted with his lady friend, playing with her fat pussy through her tight jeans.

"Boy, stop fa' you start sumthin'." She blushed.

Chucky had already started releasing himself when he noticed a silhouette creeping before him. His heart sped up, and his eyes grew larger at the gun in the phantom's hand as he breezed past him. Luckily for him, PeeWee had not seen him. Chucky dripped piss on his hands, and pants scraping the side of his dick with his zipper as he nervously tried to shove it back into his jeans. PeeWee's black Chuck Taylors hit the pavement as he raced towards a squatting Bullet! After sparking the jay, the pie-faced driver turned her head towards Bullet just in time to spot the hooded man speedily approaching the passenger side of the car with a gun. With trembling hands, she dropped the lit blunt in her lap letting out a wrecking scream.

PeeWee had already had the .357 in the air ready to fire! Bullet's heart stopped as his legs gave out on him, he fell back on his ass, squeezing his eyes closed extending his right hand as if he was shielding himself from the incoming attack! *Click!* The gun did not go off. Troubled, he squeezed again. *Click!* and again *Click!* Before he could turn away and run, Chucky was standing right behind him. His steel Desert Eagle glistened under the streetlights as he aimed it inches away from PeeWee's hooded skull. *Ka-boom!* He pulled the trigger. PeeWee was dead before he hit the ground. Hearing the single gunshot, Fray lowered the electric window dropping the live rounds on the ground of fish market parking lot.

● ● ●

PRESSURE BUST PIPES

Later on that night, Joe laid sleeping in his Greek style home when he was awakened from his drunken stupor by the ringing of his phone. He reached out in the direction of the ringing phone with his eyes still closed.

"Hello?" He answered in a heavy voice.

"We got a problem." Burnett sighed on the other end of the phone.

With the distress in Burnett's voice, Joe slowly sat up glancing over at the clock, it was a little past midnight.

"What is it?" he asked wiping the cold from his partially shut eyes.

"We lost the kid Joe."

"I'm on my way."

He hung up jumping out the bed fully awake. Twenty minutes later, Joe was parking his two antenna Caprice on the opposite side of the yellow tape. Burnett greeted him at his door. The place looked to be in a frenzy. Plain-clothes detectives and uniformed officers moved about gathering evidence.

"Where is he?" Joe asked stepping from his car.

Burnett led the way, ducking under the yellow crime scene tape where PeeWee's lifeless body laid covered in a white sheet. His blue hand sticking from under the sheet still clutching the .357. Joe slipped on a pair of latex gloves and kneeled beside his lifeless body pulling back the sheet.

"Does Kelly know about 'dis?" he asked looking down at PeeWee's corpse.

"She does now," Burnett replied noticing a disheveled Kelly

Anderson through a crowd of spectators.

BE MORE CAREFUL

Club Love was the hottest spot in D.C known for hosting some of the biggest celebrity parties, especially on Friday nights. Fray and his crew were searching for a parking spot when they stumbled upon a familiar face. Unique was exiting from the driver seat of a black Charger when they spotted her. They watched her set the alarm from over her shoulder as she sashayed towards the lengthy club line. Decked out in platforms heels, a sheer-gypsy halter-top, and some leather like black leggings. Ronnie looked closer from behind the wheel of his Lexus. He noticed that that was the exact same car used in the shooting in an effort to take his life. They decided to wait her out.

The club lasted until the wee hours in the morning. Tipsy

partygoers poured into the streets of New York Avenue. Flashing lights, honking horns filled the scenery as men shouted from their cars at the half-naked women in catsuits, and leggings scrambling for their vehicles. Unique finally came staggering out into the busy street unlocking the car door, getting inside. They watched her strap on her seatbelt before pulling off. Mimicking her every move, they made a right out the parking lot behind her.

They pulled into the apartment complex several seconds after her. They spotted Unique up ahead stumbling through the doors of her building. Ronnie found an empty parking spot next to the black Charger, he paralleled parked between a metal dumpster and a fire hydrant. Dawn couldn't have come fast enough. Unique was awakened by the vibration of her bedroom walls. The loud blaring voice of the late rapper Tupac boomed through the speakers of her surround sound system. Still hung-over from last night, she rolled over on her stomach placing the pillow over her. When that didn't work she tossed back the covers and headed straight for the disturbance where she found Bullet bobbing his head, rapping along to the music ironing his pants.

"Bullet, turn 'dis shit down! It's too fuckin' early in the mornin' for 'dis shit." She snapped shutting off the system completely.

"Fuck you doin'? You see I was listenin' to 'dat." He looked up at her from the ironing board.

"Nigga you see me in here tryna' sleep!" she yelled before turning around marching back down the hall.

"Man, ain't nobody' tryna hear 'dat shit, and your drunk ass betta' not scratched my shit up last night." He put on his jeans retrieving his keys from the basket.

The foursome could barely keep their eyes open as they sat parked outside. Chirping sounds of early birds cluttered the air.

"Slim, what'chu y'all gon' do? Pebblez been blowing me up?"

Fray said looking at his phone. Just as Fray finished his sentence Unique's building door opened, Bullet came into view.

"There he go right there!" DeShay said tightening his grip on the handle of his Glock 19.

Without further discussion, they all reached for the door handles. Bullet could be heard rapping Tupac's "Tear Drops & Closed Caskets," song aloud as he bopped to his car. Ready to sprang into action with all four car doors open, the crew looked dumbfounded upon seeing two blue caravans racing in their direction blocking Bullet in from the front and back. U.S Marshals in their signature blue and yellow windbreakers jumped out the vans! Snapping out of their trance, they pulled their doors shut, slouching in their seats hoping they had gone unnoticed. The Marshals had already yanked Bullet from his car, slamming him to the ground. He tried putting up a fight, but before he knew it, two hill-bellies jumped on him slapping the cuffs on him.

"Man, what the fuck goin' on!" Bullet shouted turning his head slightly trying to face the Marshals. Ronnie wasn't sure if he should start the engine, or not, he soon realized they had gone unseen. He cranked the engine putting the car in drive gently pressing on the gas. As the foursome cruised by the action, they lowered their windows just enough so that Bullet could see them. Bullet and the U.S Marshals keyed in on the coasting Lexus. Bullet heart skipped a beat knowing he just flirted with death.

"Saved by the muthafuckin' police!" he thought.

BACK AT FIFTH DISTRICT...

The article was headlined "Third Prosecutor's Witness Slain," with Kelly's picture plastered underneath. It was not Joe this time, but

Roger and Mason were the blame. Burnett had to literally get in between Kelly and the Duo, he was almost certain that there would be blows thrown had he not intervened.

"Kelly, would you please take a seat so that we could get on with this." Burnett gestured, taking a deep breath rolling up the sleeves on his dress shirt.

"I'd rather stand!" she spat heatedly pacing the floor.

"Very well then. Roger, the floor is yours," Burnette said.

Roger stood from the conference table loosening his striped tie walking to the caulk board. With short hair and blue eyes, Roger stood to the side so that everyone could see clearly. Derek's picture was posted at the top of the board and underneath was Fray, DeShay, Ronnie, and Ashley. Beneath their pictures were a few low-level guys.

"What is this?" Kelly asked skeptically eyeing the pictures before her as she finally took a seat.

"Roger is gonna fill you in on what we've learned during the course of our investigation, before PeeWee's murder," Burnett said motioning for Roger to begin.

Clearing his throat, he took control of the meeting.

"Alright, what Mason and I have learned during our time being stationed in the neighborhood is that the kid story checked out. We found out that this man here (pointing to Derek's picture) is the brains behind the crew's entire operation. His name is Derek Allen aka Fatz. To our surprise, he doesn't have an extensive rap sheet like we expected. The only thing we could find in his jacket was a sexual assault, which resulted in him doing eighteen months in the feds.

"Wait! He's a sex offender?" Kelly asked confused.

"Well, after reading the report there was no penetration. The woman said he tried to force himself on her in a building, then cut off her panties. Anyway as PeeWee said he controls the drug trade for the crew's operation. Now, we don't suspect that he's involved with the murders."

"Personally." Mason blurted from his seat drawing stares from everyone in the room. "Sorry about that," he said looking off to the side. "Thank you, Mason," Roger said sarcastically. "Now, as Mason just told you we don't suspect that he involves himself personally, but we do believe he orders the hits, which is where our beloved foursome comes into play," Roger emphasized pointing to their photographs. "Now it was hard for us to determine just who calls the shots because they were all hard to read. However, we took turns watching each of them individually and we were able to put together our own profile with the help from sources on the street. We're all familiar with Mr. Mills from the tournament killing." DeShay's recent snapped photo displayed his freshly twisted locks dangling in his face. "Moving right along to Mr. Pitts who seemed to have dodged us during the tournament killing." There was a picture of Ashley getting out of his car. His thick black locks pulled back in a ponytail. "Sources on the street say that he might be the most dangerous one of them all." Roger turned his attention to Joe.

"They do fit the profile," Burnett said contemplating the possibility of the crew's involvement in the Petworth Massacre.

"What about the other two," Kelly asked turning her attention back to the board.

"This man right here is Mr. Ronnie Watson," Roger said tapping on his picture. "He has a juvenile rap sheet longer than this table. When he was sixteen he was shot in the face by a stray bullet, and shortly after he was committed until he was he was 20. He's now currently on probation. Now, this one here we know very little about," he said fingering the picture of Fray as he was exiting the

Majib. Joe was never able to place his finger on what was so familiar about the kid, he continued to eye the photograph. He had a gut feeling that Fray was bad news. During his years of patrolling the neighborhood, he watched Fray transform. Each year his eyes seemed to harden. "No one wanted to talk about this guy. Supposedly, he looks out for a lot of kids and residents in the neighborhood. What we do know is he's the son of the infamous Frank Pascal."

"Wait, the Frank Pascal," Kelly asked with an astonished look on her face hooking her hair behind her ear. Kelly was still in law school when the bust on Frank Pascal organization aired every local news station, it was the biggest case in the city at that time. Joe acknowledged her with a nod. "Wait. Just so I have a better understanding, you think Pascal is using his son to continue his criminal enterprise from prison?" Kelly asked.

"I'll answer that," Mason said raising his hand in the air.

With stringy hair, brown eyes, and a long pointy nose he began to explain.

"That was the angle we were going in at first, but according to PeeWee Frank wasn't thrilled with his son following in his footsteps. Pascal and Mr. Allen apparently had a huge fallen out about it."

"Thank you Mason", Joe said as his eyes met with Kelly's.

Joe knew if they planned to put a stop to the murderous organization everyone including himself had to be on the same page, even if it meant swallowing his pride.

CENTRAL AVENUE...

It was a beautiful day, cars zipped up and down the broad avenue. Businesses and storefronts were all open for business. From the looks of things, Joyce's salon Tropical Roots was doing good after temporary closing after Hulk's death. With the shop doors now open a steady flow of women filed in and out all day. The metallic blue paint gleamed on the tinted SS Monte Carlo that sat parked outside the salon, its sporty wheels were highly polished. Inside, blue lights illuminated the electronics on the dashboard. The seats were covered in rich leather upholstery. Lloyd Bank's hunger for more album seeped through its speakers.

Chucky sat reclined in his seat taking pulls from his cigarette watching the flow of traffic. He looked opposite of the salon where the 57th projects use to be before the government signed off on the demolition. The once ruthless projects were now townhouses. He remembered when the area was a thriving dope and PCP strip. As he sat waiting for the salon to clear out, he wondered what was so urgent that Joyce wanted to talk to him in person. Tired of waiting, he plucked his cigarette before exiting the car. He stepped inside the embellished salon drawing hard stares from the once gossiping women.

"Won'tchu bitches get back to work or sumthin!" He said with aggression.

"Uh-Un no he didn't!" the women spoke out to no one in particularly.

"Nikki where Joyce at?" he asked walking to the receptionist booth. Before the young woman could reply Joyce appeared from the back.

"Look, boy, don't be coming in here like 'dat!" she said playfully. Her brown Louis Vuitton scarf covered her signature Tony Braxton hairstyle. Her plump rear-end looked as if it was going to bust out of her tight fitting True Religion jeans.

"Man you trippin' these bitches in here fuckin wit' me." He

mumbled as he made his way to the back.

"Damn it took you long enough, and where the hell is Bullet? I was callin' his ass for the last two days," Joyce said closing the door to her office.

"Oh, you ain't heard? Slim got locked up last week."

"Damn again! His ass can't catch a break." She gave a slight grin as she shook her head.

"Yeah nothing serious, though, jus' a petty ass violation," Chucky said, "But what'chu wanted to holla at me about?"

"You might wanna get comfortable for 'dis one," Joyce said sitting down behind her desk.

"Whassup?" He said sitting down on the couch.

"A'ight, so you know I took a break after my cousin's funeral. I just felt like I could not go on after 'dat. I knew eventually I was goin' to have to pull myself together. I was in the house one-day jus' chillin' when one of my loyalist clients called me on my personal number. She begged me to do her hair before she went out of town. At first, I thought it was inconsiderate, but being a woman myself I kinda' understood. So I agreed to meet her at her place after she had given me the address. After maybe about thirty minutes of me doing her hair you're not gonna believe you came strutting through the front door?"

"Who," Chucky said sliding to the edge of his seat.

"Ashley," She said grinning devilishly. "Dat' Bougie ass bitch and her nigga didn't even know Horse was my cousin!"

Chucky sat taken it all in before he stood from his seat.

"You a dangerous bitch shawty, fa real." He smiled. "You still remember how to get out 'dat nigga's spot?"

PRESSURE BUST PIPES

SUNDAY EVENING...

The 24-hour Subway sandwich shop was the only source of light on Florida Avenue. Its dreadful location was an ideal death trap. Customers were on high alert to be extremely cautious or to avoid going there altogether. At two in the morning, when up partying all night it was the quickest place to help quiet the stomach-rumblings.

"Hurry the fuck up, I ain't tryna be bullshitting up 'dis joint!" Ashley said as Unique jumped out from the passenger seat of his Mercedes CL600. Ashley sat parked outside the Subway with a death grip around his Taurus 9. Just like any other night, the sandwich shop was crowded. There were about fifteen people in the miniature size eatery. He watched Unique from behind the tinted windows of his car. It had been awhile since the two had last seen each other. It took him nearly a month to forgive her for letting DeShay join in on their fuck session, not to mention DeShay still bragged occasionally.

For some odd reason, he just couldn't let her go. He didn't know whether it was the ass fucking or the head that kept him coming back for more. Unique called him earlier asking to hook up, which he jumped at the opportunity. Unbeknownst to him with Bullet being locked up, and DeShay turning her down, he was her last option. As he sat parked outside on high alert he watched a group of pedestrians walk past the front of his car and enter the shop. A buzzing sound began to come from the passenger seat. He looked down at her seat noticing her cell phone lightening up. Instantly he lift his head looking through the storefront window, Unique was still at the counter placing her order. Ashley focused back on the vibrating phone. The screen read unknown. He hit the talk button answering on the last ring

REX T. PELOTE JR

"Hello?"

He was greeted with the automated voice of the jail operator.

"You have a collect call from…Bullet. Press 1 to accept."

CHUCKY

The newly renovated two-story townhomes had red doors, concrete steps, black hand rails, and assigned number parking spaces. It was the perfect place to raise a child. The sun shined down on the metallic blue paint of the parked SS Monte Carlo. Devin the Dude pumped through the six by nine speakers. Chucky sat behind the wheel scanning the parking lot, blazing a half of blunt of sour diesel lost in his own thoughts. In his lap laid a fully loaded automatic 9mm Calico, he sat waiting on Ashley's arrival. Chucky had been parked since last night, but Ashley never made it home. The rattling of his phone in the cup holder broke his train of thought.

"Yeah?" he answered, flicking an ash into the ashtray.

"You have a collect call from-…," The pre-recorded voice operator began. Knowing it was his partner in crime he smiled ready to press one. Chucky wanted to be the bearer of good news in hopes of lifting his man's spirits while he was in a depressed environment.

"Whassup Slim!" Chucky said excitedly.

"Moe! Where the fuck you been at? I called your ass 'bout a hun'nid times last night," Bullet said.

"I seen all them blocked calls last night too, but it was about three o'clock in the morning that couldn't been you."

"Nigga, 'dat was me! Didn't my mom's call and tell you they moved me over "CTF" the other day?"

"Kill! Shid you get contact visits over there you came off, but she ain't call me. You ain't gon' guess where I'm at?" Chucky said trying to change the subject.

"Man fuck all 'dat', when you see 'dat freak ass bitch Unique smack the shit outta her for me!" he snapped.

"What she do?" Chucky asked.

"Slim, you know she let dat' bitch ass nigga from around D St answered her phone last night!"

"Yeah! Chucky said holding back his laugh.

"On my mutha' 'dat bitch anything. His bitch ass said they geed her and everything."

"Are you serious?" Chucky asked not surprised. "You gotta stop fuckin with 'dat snake bitch."

"Moe, you ain't even got to worry 'bout 'dat no more she cut off, and if she try to pop up over here I'ma knock her ass out in the v-hall!" Bullet said lividly.

"Slim, 'dat nigga purped out like 'dat?" Chucky shook his head still holding back his laughter.

"He went so far as to say he was about to skeet all over my

bitch." He sighed heavily through the receiver.

"You have two minutes remaining" announced the pre-recorded operator interrupting their conversation.

"Don't even stress 'bout 'dat shit. I was tryna to tell you earlier I'm parked outside dem people's house right now!" he smirked.

"Oh yeah!" Make sure you handle that for me."

"You already know." Chucky managed to say before the phone disconnected.

The sky was starting to turn gray as if a storm was approaching. Chucky looked up at the dark clouds through the windshield studying the sky. He took one last pull of his jay and reclined in his seat letting the mellow sounds of Devin the Dude along with his high kick in. He never anticipated that his task would be so time-consuming. Overwhelmed with fatigue from being up all night under the influence, he struggled to keep his bloodshot eyes open. His eyes began to close slowly as he fought to keep them open. That went on for about five minutes eventually he lost the battle falling sound asleep.

"Really Ashley that's how you feel. You stayed out all night wit' some bitch!"

Sade' shouted rolling her neck with her hands on her hips, standing in the bathroom doorway. As soon as Ashley turned the key entering the house she was on his back following him upstairs to the bathroom.

"What are you talkin' 'bout? I fell asleep over Shay house last night." he lied.

The truth was Unique had sucked and fucked him so good last

night the two had fallen asleep at the hotel, and slept all day.

"So why you ain't answer your phone then huh?"

"It died last night, and I didn't have my charger," he said as he turned on the shower.

"Nigga, you's a got-damn lie! You know what fuck you. I smelled that bitch on you as soon as you walked your black ass in here!" ...

The roaring thunder and heavy showers pounding away at Chucky's windows awakened him. The rain created a dark atmosphere making it hard to see. Wiping saliva from the side of his mouth, he strained his eyes trying to see through the heavy rain. Scanning the parking lot, he stopped on the back of Ashley's Mercedes parked opposite of him. He looked up at the digital clock on the dash realizing he napped on the job for over an hour. "Shit!" he cursed slamming his fist against the steering wheel. He started to turn the key and leave when a set of headlights blinded him. He noticed a small strobe light shining on top of the roof, thinking it to be the police he slouched down in his seat.

The sedan stopped at the head of his bumper. His heart drummed so loud he could hear it. He frantically looked for a spot to hide the Calico. Nervous, he peeked over the steering wheel getting a closer look at the illuminating light. He had mistaken the police to be none other than Pizza Hut. The deliveryman's eyes looked down at the receipt then back up at Ashley's door making sure the address matched. Chucky took notice as he reached for the door handle.

After washing off yesterday's stench Ashley twisted the nozzle shutting off the shower. He pulled the shower curtain back, and was caught off guard, Sade' stood there checking his phone in a silk champagne colored robe, it meshed well with her walnut-complexion. The belt was drawn loosely over her flat stomach and tiny waist displaying her black bra and little cleavage. Her hair was still done in the micro braids Joyce did bringing out her cute button nose.

"Fuck you doin!" Ashley frowned stepping out the tub snatching his phone from her.

"Who is she?" Sade' screamed pointing her finger in his face.

"What the fuck are you talkin' about! who is who?"

"Nigga, don't play dumb wit' me I jus' read 'dat bitch text! Ashley shook the remaining water from the new growth of his dreads wrapping them in a white towel.

"You know what? You ain't shit you can go back to 'dat bitch for all I care!"

The ringing of the doorbell startled them both breaking Ava's sleep, she began to cry.

"Who 'dat?! Ashley questioned.

Sade' rolled her eyes, turning on her heels, walking to Ava's room scooping her from the crib.

"Shh! Mommy got you," She said rocking her as she made her way downstairs. Ava began to settle down as she strolled over to the door. She was greeted with a light gust of wind, and a drenched deliveryman cradling a red installation pouch. *"Oh my God!* It's coming down out there you can step in," Sade' said out of courtesy, stepping aside allowing the deliveryman in the red windbreaker, and black cap to enter. Once inside the aroma of meat lover's pizza filled the air. The delivery man couldn't help undressing the beautiful woman standing before him. Taking notice of the blatant admiration, Sade' smiled faintly pinching the top of her robe closed with her free hand.

"How much do I owe you?" she asked snapping him out of his lustful state.

He glanced at the wet receipt taped to the outside of the red leather bag.

"It'll be $17.50."

Reaching into the pocket of her robe she handed him the exact amount.

"Hold on right quick, let me get'chu a tip."

Cradling Ava in her arms, she spun around giving him sight of her round ass. The curve-hugging robe stopped just short of the cuff of her ass.

"Ashley! Drop me five dollars so I can tip the delivery man." She yelled from the foot of the steps.

Ashley had just finished sliding into his night clothes when he heard Sade's voice echoed from the downstairs. He by-passed the twenty-one shot Taurus 9mm handgun grabbing a handful of crumbled bills, searching until he came across a five-dollar bill. He made his way towards the top of the stairs. The delivery man slipped his hand inside the heated pouch gripping the Calico upon detecting Ashley's location. Ashley noticed Sade' wasn't wearing anything but the short silk robe.

"Sade', why the fuck would you answer the door in dat' lil ass robe! Get the fuck up here I'll tip him!" Ashley spat bouncing down the steps eyeing Sade' as they passed by one another. He continued making his way towards the delivery man who had his head down looking at the floor. "Here you go man," Ashley tried handing him the tip. Chucky looked up, locking eyes with him, pulling the Calico from the bag. Ashley heart sunk to the pit of his stomach upon seeing Chucky's face. He quickly turned running up a few stairs before shots were fired. *Tat! Tat! Blat! Tat!* He fell face first into the carpet. He lied bloody and motionless. Sade's screams could be heard from the top of the steps as she watched the delivery man stand over top of Ashley opening fire. *Tat! Tat! Tat!* He looked up at a screaming Sade,' jumped down the steps, jetting out the front door.

The eruption of gunfire disturbed the elderly community, and the heavy rain had yet to stop falling. However, that still didn't stop the residents from gathering with their umbrellas outside of Ashley's residence. The parking lot was now a circus with various media vans and reporters. Red and Blue strobe lights covered the streets as officers move about securing the crime scene drawing yellow tape making a barrier. Meanwhile, Burnett sat behind his desk finishing up paperwork when his 15-inch television aired the 10 o'clock news. Paying half-ass attention, it wasn't until reporters released the name of the victim found slain in the Prince George's County residence. After hearing the name Ashley Pitts his head shot up immediately watching the live footage.

Burnett nearly spilled his coffee on the floor as he reached for the phone dialing his longtime buddy Peter Daniels, who just so happened to be the chief of police in Prince George's County. After informing Peter that they had an open investigation going on the man found slain, he kindly asked if one of his own could come take a look around the scene. An hour later, he awoke Joe from his slumber giving him instructions to the crime scene. Joe's appearance created a misunderstanding amongst the officers as he tried to cross the yellow tape!

"Hey, you get back behind that tape!" The officers yelled in unison.

"What are you doing? Get your hands off me! I was called here!"

Joe explained as he struggled with the officers. A heavyset man with a receding hairline and saggy jaws appeared in Ashley's doorway watching the altercation.

"Let 'em through!" The detective with the deep voice said stopping everything. The offices glanced over their shoulders as if they had misheard him before releasing their grips.

"As you were gentleman."

The potbelly detective gestured with his left index finger for Joe to join him at the top of the concrete steps. "You Joe?" He asked, extending his right hand as Joe closed the distance between them. Joe eyed the man's hand briefly before accepting it.

"And you are?" He seemed perplexed by the unknown officer identifying him by his name. The man's grip was everything but pleasant.

"The names Cobb detective Cobb," he said releasing his grip from Joe's hand. Joe was not a stranger to tension by a long shot. He knew Cobbs wasn't happy about having a detective outside the jurisdiction come in on his crime scene.

"You know, you wouldn't have such a hard time getting into places if you lost the leather jacket, and tried doing something with your hair," he said eyeing Joe disgustingly.

"You wouldn't have such a hard time catching the bad guys if you lost some weight." Joe fired back. "Now would you mind telling me why the hell I'm here in the first place?"

"I'm still trying to figure that out myself. All I know is I have a specific order to let you through."

"Well who's in charge here? Maybe they can tell me what the hell is going on." Joe said.

"You're looking at him" Cobbs winked.

PRESSURE BUST PIPES

Joe sighed heavily in defeat.

"So much for that," he mumbled, "So what's the deal here?"

"Black male possibly in his early-20s suffered multiple gunshot wounds." Cobbs gave the run down.

"Any witnesses?" Joe asked.

"Several actually. When we arrived we discovered a deliveryman locked in the trunk of his car."

"What's he got to do with all this?" Joe asked confused.

"He says the gunmen approached him from behind demanding his work uniform, before being forced into trunk"

"Let me guess. I'll guy ordered take out?"

"Bingo." Cobb boast.

"So, where's the delivery guy now?"

"We took him down the station for questioning. He's still a little shaken up," Cobb said looking over his notes.

"Well should we take a look," Joe said leading the way inside, surveying the scene. The house was in just as much frenzy as the outside. Several officers dust for prints while a crime scene photographer snapped pictures. Paramedics attended to a young woman with a baby in her arms who sat on the sofa, her face was stained with tear from crying. Her champagne colored robe was now covered in dry blood. There were spent shell casing scattered along the white carpet. The red leather installation pouch with the pizza spilled from the box laid at his feet. Bullet holes and blood was splattered on the walls, he then fixed his eyes on a pool of blood in the middle of the stair casing which lead to the sheet covered victim.

"This way," Cobbs blurted snapping him out of his observation. Joe reached into his back pocket retrieving a pair of latex gloves, covering both hands as he followed him up the steps.

"What's her story? Is she's a witness?" Joe asked referring to the distraught woman in the bloodstain robe during his inspection.

"If you want to call her that. She's the deceased girlfriend. We found her with his dead body in her arms, son of a bitch killed the poor bastard right in front of her and his kid."

"You got to be kidding me?" Joe said shockingly.

"I wish I was," Cobb exhaled, "Now would you like to do the honors?" He asked lowering his eyes to the sheet-covered victim. Without hesitating, Joe kneeled next to the corpse and gently pulled back the white sheet. His eyes nearly bulge from their sockets as he recognized the lifeless victim instantaneously. He now knew why Burnette sent him there. Ashley's lifeless body was flat on his stomach. His head turned to the right with his eyes wide open. Joe's mind began to drift off. "How does it feel to get a taste of your own medicine son of a bitch?" He thought while holding back the sheet. He didn't realize his face now wore a smirk.

"You know this guy?" Cobb asked, eyeing him attentively. Before he could reply, they were interrupted by a voice of a single officer standing at the front of the door.

"Sir there's a woman here requesting that she be let inside, she says she's with him," he said pointing up at Joe. The thought of Kelly Anderson standing outside made Joe drop his head in frustration, rising from his knees, he ripped off his gloves.

"Now, you hold it right there. I wasn't given orders for two of you." Cobbs frowned stopping Joe in his tracks as he neared the front of the steps.

"Would you relax? I'll handle it. In the meantime, why don't you have that bag, and pizza box dusted for prints." Joe replied.

"Is that our guy in there?" Kelly asked.

"What's left of him," Joe replied.

Cobb cleared his throat in an attempt to be introduced to the beautiful woman.

"Can I have a word with you in private," she said with an attitude disregarding the heavyset man beside him.

"Maybe next time big fellow!" Joe said patting Cobbs pot belly stomach before dipping under the yellow tape, the two then headed over to his 66 Nova.

"This better be good you just interrupted my investigation," he said once inside the car.

"You know for a person that agreed to be partners on this you would think that you would bring me along for the ride," she said without blinking.

"It kind of slipped my mind," he said nonchalantly.

"Yeah I bet," she said in disbelief, "Well I did a little investigation of my own," she smiled.

"Oh really?" Joe asked.

"Yup, you know something has always hunted me about PeeWee's murder. Call it what you want, but maybe it's the image of seeing his 14-year-old body laid out on the pavement, or maybe it's the fact that I still can't get over the resident's accounts of only hearing one shot the night of his murder, which we all agreed sounded kind of strange from the get-go. So I decided to contact the forensics specialists that was in charge of the evidence in that case. I had him run the ballistics on the gun pulled off PeeWee's body, and you're not going to believe what I found out? The ballistics test came back showing PeeWee's gun was never fired at the time of his murder, now that explains the resident's testimonies." Her last statement made hairs on the back of Joe neck rise.

"What is this some kind of sick joke? I watched them pull that empty gun out of the kid hand myself." Joe spat.

"Joe listen to me. I know this all sounds kind of crazy right now, but what if somehow the group found out PeeWee was cooperating and staged is death?"

Joe sat thinking about what was being presented to him. The sound of shrieking tires coming to a halt had Joe on high alert! Ronnie brought the Lexus to a full stop. The trio bolted from the car bum rushing the police barricade! Other than their recently snapped photographs, and the one time they faced DeShay in the courtroom this was the first time Kelly encountered them altogether. Kelly and Joe sat watching from across the parking lot while all hell broke loose at the foot of Ashley's door. Numerous police officers restrained the hostile men from entering the house.

The sudden commotion coming from outside the house snapped Sade' out of her silence. Recognizing the voices, she rose from the sofa cradling Ava in her arms rushing towards the door! She found DeShay yelling and struggling with the Husky detective at the foot of the stoop. There were over a dozen officers restraining Ronnie, pinning his back to the trunk of a squad car. Fray lied face down on the pavement with two officers jamming their knees in his back, Sade' watched not knowing what to do.

"*Man get the fuck off me!*" DeShay cursed at the officers.

"*Oh my God! stop! stop! That's my family!*" Sade' screamed hysterically from the doorway on the verge of tears again. With the woman's sudden presence in the doorway, Cobbs turned his head slightly towards the porch. DeShay broke free of his grasp, pushing him aside, dashing up the concrete steps passing Sade' on his way inside the house! Cobbs recovered, but it was too late. DeShay was now on the staircase kneeling next to Ashley's lifeless body, everything around him seemed to fade. DeShay wasn't sure if he wanted to pull back the white sheet, and discover who he already knew was underneath. His hand started to take on a mind of its own as he snatched the sheet back revealing Ashley's bloody face. His body went numb, he let out a roar that could be heard throughout the complex!

"We better get to the bottom of this, and fast otherwise we might as well bring out more body bags," Joe said hearing the cries as he started the engine.

The city's night lights brightened up the front of the police headquarters. Uniformed officers filed in and out of his doors. After Ashley's body was hauled off to the city's morgue, the detectives forced Sade' to go to the precinct for questioning.

"Look, how many times I gotta' tell you? I ain't see shit! I was in the shower." She boasted.

"Well I'm just trying to make sure I got all the facts here," The detective said.

"We been over dis' a thousand times already, am I under arrest If not I'm ready to go!"

Fray sat grief-stricken parked across the street in Sade's SUV. For the first time in his life, he was without his best friend. He looked through the rear view mirror at Ava who was sleeping quietly in her car seat. He figured it was too much excitement for her in one night. Seeing Ashley's replica made him force a half smile. He felt like breaking down for the umpteenth time tonight, but instead, he held back the tears. The opening of the passenger door got his attention as Sade' entered not saying a word. Her eyes were puffy and swollen from crying. Fray reached over giving her a hug, and a kiss her on the forehead before guiding the truck away from the precinct. After dropping Sade' off Fray phoned his cousin.

"Man where the fuck you niggas at? Sade' jus' described the nigga to me who slumped Ashley. It was 'dat bitch ass nigga "C" from of the city," Fray said through clenched teeth using Chucky first initial because of the phone.

"Oh yeah," DeShay said, "Say no more holmes."

The line went dead.

Gunshots rang out as another corner hustler on the episode of the Wire was killed. Pebblez watched re-runs on the 60-inch flat screen TV that was mounted on the wall. She sat on the beige leather sectional couch, fresh out the shower, twirling her damp hair around her finger, as she talked to Gigi on the phone. The electric fireplace burned at a low flame which gave the spacious living room a romantic feel. The hundred-gallon saltwater tank filled with rainbow colored baby seahorses complimented the room.

"Girl I 'ont know where the hell his ass at, he never stayed out this late before. I'm about to hop in my shit in a minute and slide through D street," Pebblez said into the receiver. As soon as the words left her mouth, she heard the locks turning on the apartment door. "Girl speaking of the devil here his ass comes now. I'ma holla at chu' tomar," she said standing from the sofa. Fray stepped into the dim setting with his 2001 new balance. After dropping Sade' and the baby off at her cousin house, he drove her SUV back to his place.

"Where the hell you been at!" Pebblez said with an attitude, her manicured hands rested on her thick hips. Ignoring her question, he gave her a cold stare heading down the hall into the master bedroom.

"I know you hear me talking to you!" She was directly on his heels. He turned the light on.

PRESSURE BUST PIPES

"Ashley got killed tonight," he said just above a whisper. Pebbles gasped.

"Oh my God babe! I'm so sorry, are you all right?"

He kept distance between them extending his right arm, as she tried to embrace him. He got on his knees looking underneath the bed, pulling out his Heckler & Koch .45, grabbing the 21 shot clip placing it inside the butt of the gun, chambering a round.

"What'chu 'bout to do?" She asked watching his every move. When he didn't reply she stood in front of the bedroom door guarding it.

"Man watch out!" He frowned sucking his teeth trying to move her aside.

"No baby please don't do this!" She whined.

"Pebblez get out my fucking way," he said in a calm voice trying his best to keep is cool. He had already made up his mind to avenge Ashley's death, even if it meant spending the rest of his life in prison.

"What about me!" She sobbed. *"I stay up in the middle of the night worrying whether you're goin' walk through dat' door."*

"Man I ain't tryna' hear 'dat shit! Watch out." He shoved her out the way, opening the door.

"Fray please don't go!" She cried out just before the door slammed. Pebblez fell to her knees crying uncontrollably.

LOST LOVE

Today was the day of Ashley's funeral. Steve Young church was jammed packed, you would've thought a celebrity was being buried, but a hood legend in his own right. Fray and Katie took it the hardest. This was the first time the two had laid eyes on each other since the hospital. His presence brought her some relief, God knows she needed it from all the drama she gone through in the last year. Unique attended the funeral as well showing her support.

"Ashes to ashes dust to dust! Rev. Steve Young ended the ceremony. The hundreds of mourners walked past the casket taking red roses, saying their final farewell to Ashley at Glenn Wood Cemetery. The stubborn rain had come and gone leaving behind trails of wet grass. Fray stood alone off at a distance watching the many spectators through tear filled eyes hidden by dark shades. His toned frame dressed in black linen and red black Prada loafers. Fray couldn't leave his best friend, seeing him lying in the casket in the church was hard enough.

Parked up on a hill from the burial site, Katie sat behind the wheel of her Volvo crying non-stop as well. She too preferred to be alone and remember Ashley the way she last saw him. Seeing people began to make their way uphill hill she sat upright from her slouching position, dabbing at her puffy eyes with a Kleenex. When she looked down the hill, she noticed Fray standing off to the side of Ashley's casket. For the first time today, grieving acquaintances giving their sympathy wasn't swarming him. Katie decided to make things right between them, she couldn't imagine what he was going through. She pulled a fresh Kleenex from the glove compartment exiting her car.

Besides her puffy eyes, Katie looked stunning in a black curve-hugging sleeveless jumpsuit with white panel detailing from Osman by Osman Yousefzada, and a pair of black pumps adding a few inches to her height. Her black locks were pinned up revealing her high cheeks, and flawless Caramel complexion. She ran her manicured hands over her jumpsuit smoothing out imaginary wrinkles before starting downhill. As she got closer she contemplated on what she should say. Fray continued to stare at Ashley's resting place in sorrow, tears steadily flowed beneath the rims of his shades.

"You look like you can use some tissue," The soft voice said at his back. The familiar voice made him smile, he turned around. Katie was still just as beautiful as the day he met her. "Hi," she said handing him the tissue with her French manicured hand.

"Thanks," He said in a voice barely above a whisper, raising his shades dabbing at his face.

There was an awkward silence between them before Katie worked up the urge to break the ice.

"I don't even have to ask how you're doin' right now. I know how close you two were, Ashley was just as important to me as he was to you."

Fray stood motionless, his stare fixed on the ground it was too early for him to have that conversation.

"Look I'm not goin' stand here and pretend to know what you're goin' through, but a part of me died with him too," she said catching a tear before it could fall. Fray didn't deny that her intentions were pure he knew how close she and Ashley had become. "I guess what I'm tryna' say is, you still have a friend left in me, and if you ever need someone to talk to my number is still the same."

Fray looked up for the first time locking eyes with her.

"Yeah I would like that," he smiled.

Katie returned the smile as she walked off to an awaiting Unique.

After dropping Fray and DeShay off to their vehicles, Ronnie rode home in silence. This was the first time today he was alone. Cruising down Minnesota Avenue stopping at a red light his mind began to drift. He worried about Fray. He had always been so determined to beat the odds of the streets and not become a statistic. Over the years, Fray shared his dreams of one day going legit, pulling them all out of the streets, and bringing Katie along with them. It was a vision that only Fray seen. That dream now seemed to die along with Ashley. Ronnie saw something in Fray's eyes today that he never saw before, defeat.

Fray was the only one from the crew who had never been to

jail but from the looks of things he was preparing himself mentally if that day ever came after he would avenge Ashley's death. Ronnie knew Fray's hunt for Chucky would not stop until he settled the score. Although the four of them were all close, Fray and Ashley had always been the closest. The blaring of his phone snapped him out of his thoughts.

"Hello?" he answered.

"Where you at?" The caller said.

"Shid on my way in the house."

"Damn. I was tryna' catch you before you went in. You can't swing by."

"Naw man it's been a long ass day. I can hook up with you first thing in the morning. What'chu was tryna do the same thing?"

"Yeah."

"A'ight that's a bet," Ronnie said ending the call.

Fray cruised the south side in a daze listening to the late Tupac "I ain't mad at you." He had already circled the Simple City projects twice after parting ways with Ronnie and DeShay. However, he still wasn't about to call it a night just yet. He decided to take Katie up on her offer, he couldn't stop thinking about her and how beautiful she looked today. Glancing down at his phone he hesitated before grabbing the phone dialing her up.

"Hello?" Katie answered sweetly.

She didn't bother looking at the screen as she pulled it from her black Dooney & Burke rectangular clutch.

"Can you talk?" Fray asked.

Right away she became voiceless. Katie's stomach tightened, it had been a while since she heard the squeaky timbre of his voice over the phone.

"Uh yeah I was 'jus laying down," she said.

"My bad, I didn't wake you did I?"

"Nah you didn't," she said turning down the television.

"So how you been Katie?" He asked trying his best to hide the fact he was just as nervous as she was.

"I been a'ight I guess…thanks for asking. How 'bout yourself?"

"Minus the circumstances. I'm hanging in there," he said sadly. "Are you in for the night?"

The phone became mute.

"If you are I understand."

"No! She blurted out. "I was jus' a little caught off guard dats all. Do you know how to get out here?"

"Yeah I'll be there in twenty minutes," Fray said.

When Fray arrived at her apartment she quickly slipped into a tight-fitting turquoise velour Be-Be sweat suit, with a matching cap. The night started out as friendly conversation, but as the night went on old flames started to spark, heating things up between them. They ended up continuing their night at a Hilton hotel suite. Inside the penthouse, the carpet was tan and plush. White leather furniture, floor to ceiling windows, and an electric fireplace. Its king size bed was covered with Egyptian cotton sheets, and two Mahogany colored end tables on both sides of the bed. The 42" TV was mounted to the wall, the mellow sounds of 90's R&B escaped from the television speakers.

"So what made you decide to call after all 'dis time?" Katie asked leaning back with both her palms pressed on the bed behind her. Fray took a deep breath before answering. He continued looking out the window scanning the cars in the parking lot.

"It's been a long time Kee. You know after you left for the first time in my life I felt empty inside. Sorta' like I lost my way. I remember you asked me awhile back was 'dis life worth it? I was so young and naïve at the time 'dat, I thought I was different from everybody else who played 'dis game. I really thought I could beat all odds. All 'dat changed the day you walked out. Now with Ashley gone." He paused as he fought back his tears. "I now realize 'dis life was all bullshit!" he lowered his head disguising his tears.

Katie sat bewildered by his eye-opener. For years, she had been trying to get him to invest his money and pull him away from the streets. His response was always the same, "Jus' a lil bit more."

"You know it's not too late," she said wrapping her arms around his waist.

"I'm sorry for not believing you," he said turning around in her arms.

She buried her caramel face in his chest.

"I'm sorry too," she said sniffing.

The brutal beatings she was forced to endure by the hands of La-La, faded away with his touch.

"Jus' give me one more chance. I promise I'm goin' get us outta' here. I jus' need a lil mo' time." He kissed her forehead, delicately stroking her back. The suite was now filled with their sniffles and the continuous sound of R&B.

"A'ight all you love birds out there! 'Dis' next one is to get'chu in the mood, you rockin witcha' your girl Justine Love on W.P.G.C 95.5! Xscape's "Understanding" came alive through the airwaves, this was the first song they ever shared together.

PRESSURE BUST PIPES

What I need from you is understanding

How can we communicate if you don't hear what I say?

What I need from you is understanding so simple as 1-2-3

Understanding is what we need…

They stood gazing into each other's eyes. Katie locked her arms behind his neck balancing herself on the balls of her feet initiating the kiss. Fray leaned into the kiss kissing her back. They locked lips for several seconds before Fray pulled back in hesitation.

"You sure?" he whispered, thinking about the new man in her life. Katie slowly reached down grabbing his bulging manhood.

"I'm sure," She said.

Without further ado, they shared a passionate kiss. He slowly undressed her exploring every curve, she seductively crawled on the bed spreading her legs eagle style. Fray licked his way from her toes to her tunnel of love, teasing her, tracing his tongue along her inner thighs. Katie loved every minute of it. She closed her eyes giving him the opportunity to have his way with her tonight. He let his warm tongue stab at her clit sending chills up her spine.

"Mm." she moaned, as soon as her juices started too seeped down her thighs. In one swift motion, he penetrated her. *"Uhh!"* She cried out from the pain. She had to relax her pussy muscles in order to get used to his size again. Everything felt perfect as she straddled him. "Umm oh yes." He was hitting all the spots that hadn't been hit in a long time sending her body into ecstasy. "Ah!" Her body clasped on his. He gave her body what it had been yearning, for the rest of the night he held her in his arms as they drifted off into a deep sleep.

Meanwhile, Pebblez and La-La both paced their own floors. La-La with a bottle of 1738 in his hand could not believe Katie would be so dumb, and stay out all night. Pebblez, on the other hand, had been crying all night. She found herself rushing to the window every time a set of headlights shined through her living room windows. Katie woke up the next morning from a terrible nightmare, La-La had killed her. She was relieved when she realized she had still been in the arms of the only man she had ever loved. As special as the night was, he was still with Pebblez. She looked over at him who had been sleeping serenely, she smiled, if only she could tell him what she had gone through without him.

She gathered her things stealing one last look at him before placing the hand written note on the pillow, she walked out without so much as a good-bye. The sound of Fray's alarm clock on his cell phone had awakened him. He ran his hand along the side of the bed were Katie once slept. He raised his head only to find a note that she had left behind.

Fray, last night brought back feelings inside that I already knew exist. I just want you to know that I never stopped loving you. If only you knew how much I sacrificed to protect our love. I love you so much, that's why it would only hurt me more if you were to choose Pebblez over me, so instead of me living out the pain, I'd rather not know your decision.

Love Always, Kee

He crumbled the note in his hand tossing it across the room. Had he known she still felt that way about him, he would've been kicked Pebblez to the curb.

"Top of the morning," Ronnie said entering the kitchen where he found his sons eating at the kitchen table, and Teresa standing over the stove stirring grits.

"You want something to eat?" Teresa asked still stirring the pot.

"Naw, I'm good, I'm kinda in a rush."

Teresa didn't bother to protest knowing he was off to see his P.O. He then walked to the living room pulling the duffle bag from the closet where he stashed it last night. The bag contained the thirty pounds of Marijuana that Rick requested last night. Ronnie was secretly doing business with Rick behind the crew backs. After adjusting his gun on his waist he kissed Teresa, and his son's goodbye before leaving out. Ronnie placed the bag in his truck and lowered himself into the driver seat. He turned the key in the ignition, turned on the radio, and pulled off.

To his surprise, K St wasn't crowded which was unusual making it easier to find a parking spot on the busy street. He placed his gun under his seat and fed the meter before heading inside the building. Mr. McCant was on the phone sitting behind his desk when he entered. The pair shaped man gestured from him to take a seat before ending his call.

"Nice of you to join me, I thought I was going to have to put out a bench warrant for you," Mr. McCant said checking his watch.

"Morning traffic," Ronnie replied knowing he was only five minutes late. Mr. McCant removed his wire-rim glasses, leaned back in his chair, placed both hands behind his head.

"Mr. Watson I see you haven't had any re-arrests in four years that's impressive."

"I guess you can say I been stayin' out the way." Ronnie forced a smile.

"You know I would've believed you had I not received this paper this morning," Mr. McCant said sliding the faxed paper across his desk.

Ronnie read over the shocking contents, his was bewildered.

"It states you served a confidential informant twelve pounds of marijuana on one occasion, and eighteen on another. You want to tell me about that?"

Ronnie turned in the direction of the opening door, wearing a wide grin on his face Joe stood with two uniformed officers. In both hands, Joe held the duffle bags from his car, and the other officer showcased the loaded gun from underneath his seat.

"Fuck Man." Ronnie cursed himself as they cuffed his hands behind his back. After learning Rick was the informant Ronnie tried calling DeShay once he arrived at the jail, but to no avail, he then tried calling Fray who answered on the fifth ring. After sitting patiently through the phone's recording Fray pressed 1.

"Hello…Ronnie man, what the hell is going on? What the fuck happened!" Fray's voice came alive.

Since his arrest Ronnie dreaded the hour he would have to come clean to his friends. He sighed before beginning.

"Where the hell is Shay? I been tryna reach him all morning."

"He and Aisha went out of town. They should be back sometime this week, but what's up?"

Ronnie began running down the events.

"Slim, we told you not to fuck wit' that hot ass nigga…damn Ronnie!" he hissed. "So what your lawyer talkin' bout?"

"Shit ain't lookin' too good especially wit' all my priors. All together they got me hemmed up wit' sixty pounds, plus I'm a convicted felon in possession of a firearm, not to mention the violation. My lawyer said I'm lookin' at bout twenty years." He exhaled loudly. The phone became silent. Fray couldn't picture losing another friend.

"Hello…Fray you still there?"

"Yeah, yeah I'm still here. I'm just fucked up at you for not listening."

"Tell me about it, but look you got the ability to even the playing field."

"Say no more. I got you," Fray said just before the fifteen-minute phone call was up. How was he to break the news to Teresa and the kids? One thing he knew for certain, Rick was going to pay with his life. After Fray finished the call with Ronnie he dreaded going in the house after staying out all night. He sat in the car for an additional five minutes trying to come up with a believable excuse. The more he thought about it, the more he relived the special night with Katie. He smiled to himself before exiting the car, he figured the cuss out would be worth it.

"Well, well, look who decided to come the fuck home!" she sprung from the couch throwing a vase at his head as soon as he closed the door behind him. He literally had to duck out the way of being hit. She immediately got in his face, smacking him, throwing punches, as she questioned his whereabouts.

"Man what the hell is your problem!" He barked restraining her.

"You're my mutherfuckin' problem where you been at all night!" She screamed.

"I fell asleep at DeShay house last night."

Smack! She smacked him again.

"Try again. Aisha was the first place I called last night."

He looked at her with hatred in his eyes, still clutching his cheek.

He turned around and headed for the door, Pebblez was right behind him.

"That's right nigga, run like the lil' boy that you are, you can't handle a woman like me anyway! She cried.

He stopped dead in his tracks.

"I'm runnin' to keep myself from killing you in this mutherfucka right now," he said before slamming the door.

Katie rode in silence in the back seat of the cab. It pained her to walk away from Fray like that. She got so caught up in the moment last night, she cursed herself for not going home, she was sure to take a hell of a beaten. The apartment building looked more like a dungeon rather than a peaceful duplex that it really was. She still couldn't believe that it had only been a year ago that she went from coming home to the man she loved, to now a man she hated with a passion. It was now time for her to face the music. She prayed La-La would be too drunk to notice she hadn't been there all night. Unbeknownst to Katie, La-La had been watching from the window the moment she got out the cab. Before Katie could put her key in the door, he snatched it open looking like a raging bull.

"Bitch where you been!"

"I... I... I." she stammered.

He cut her off by violently grabbing her by the throat, jerking her inside. *"Ahh."* she cried. He was choking the life out of her, her eyes were rolling in the back of her head.

"La-La stop. You're gonna' kill the girl." His drinking partner Tae tried to intervene. As soon as he let her go her body crashed to the floor, she gagged.

"Now bitch. I'ma ask you one more time where you been?" he seethed.

PRESSURE BUST PIPES

"I spent the night over Unique's house, please just leave me alone!"

He took a step closer.

"Bitch stop lying. You been out hoeing! I saw you when you got out the cab!"

He reached down grabbing a fist full of her locks dragging her into the bedroom.

"I'ma treat you like a hoe!"

"No, La-La please stop...let me go!

She screamed praying Tae will come to her aid. He threw her onto the bed.

"Please don't do this to me." she cried.

"Don't do what! Your trifling ass didn't even have enough decency to take a shower. I smell the fuckin' cologne on you, take your clothes off!" he yelled.

"No." she screamed!

She felt his weight shift from the bed. While still holding her down with one hand he reached for the gun he kept under the mattress. Katie knew it was now or never, she clawed at his eyes. She was quick on her feet as she made a run for the door. He tripped her sending her crashing head first into the dresser. She blacked out.

CLOSED CASKET

"Fray what the fuck is up wit'chu? I hollered at Ronnie he said he been tryna' reach you, and why haven't you handled that yet?" DeShay said from the driver seat of the rented Dodge Magnum. Fray sat in the passenger seat lost in his own multiple thoughts. He reflected back on the heated conversation he had with Derek over the phone. He thought Derek would be happy to hear about his plans of leaving the streets for good, but instead, he ridiculed him. After getting the negative feedback from Derek, Fray debated whether he should tell DeShay his plans.

Fray had also been trying to get in touch with Katie, he wanted to tell her how he really felt about her, but she still hadn't answered the phone. The thought of her loving La-La more weighed in, he quickly dismissed the idea not wanting to picture Katie with another man. The smoke from DeShay black & mild caused him to start choking. His lungs tightened as he reached for his asthma inhaler.

"My fault holmes," DeShay said cracking the window.

"Shay, we been told him not to be hollerin' at 'dat hot ass nigga Rick on those terms anyway." Fray shook his head. "But anyway I was on my way to Jumah Friday when Ronnie called and gave me Rick's address. An hour later I was pulling up at his spot. I scanned the parking lot and all that shit before parking next his BMW. I hid behind his car, when he finally made it to his car, I crept around the other side. I guess he heard something because he turned around fast as shit, but by that time I was already aimed in finger on the trigger. He started begging, then I noticed he was wearing a djellaba. I didn't even know the nigga was Muslim, I just couldn't do it end of story."

"Slim, fuck all that you chose to let this nigga breathe over your man freedom? I'ma tell you now, If I run across that nigga, I'ma smoke him, I don't give a fuck about him bein' Muslim wit' his hot ass," DeShay spat.

"Shay, man look if that's what you wanna do then fine, but Ronnie fucked up this time. I ain't killin' no Muslim like I told y'all nigga's before," Fray said calmly. "By the way, I'm done wit' dis' shit cuz."

"Oh so all of a sudden shit gets too thick for you, you decide you wanna' leave a nigga for dead? Holmes, what type of sucka' shit you on, what pressure bust your pipes or somethin'?"

"Never dat!" Fray replied.

"Well, what is it? I know it ain't 'dat bitch 'dat got'chu ready to walk away from your patnas!"

PRESSURE BUST PIPES

"DeShay, you know me better than anybody. I thought you would be happy for me getting away from 'dis shit. This isn't livin'! eventually, we gon' end up jus' like Ronnie or Ashley jus' anotha nigga dat hustled out here on these streets. Cuz, I got a plan 'dat a pull us outta' the streets forever," Fray said through pleading eyes.

"Man, I ain't tryin' to hear 'dat piece makin' shit! Look around you. We wasn't born with white picket fences nor silva' spoons. This is who we are point blank period, ain't no other way! I ain't goin' out like Ronnie, or Ashley and if I do I'm takin a whole lotta' niggas wit' me!" DeShay barked.

Unique was shopping at the mall updating her wardrobe when her cell phone rung. Looking at the screen she smiled.

"Hello hey baby," she answered.

"You have a collect call from...Bullet, press 1 to accept."

She listened to the recorder play out before she pressed 1.

"Hello!"

"You a trifling ass bitch! He spat.

Shocked by his sudden outburst Unique was unsure how to respond.

"What are you talking about now Bullet?"

"Bitch, don't play games with me you know exactly what I'm talking about!" his voice getting louder as the conversation continued.

"No, the fuck I don't know what you're talking about. Are you gonna' tell me what I did, or keep accusing me?" she said becoming more frustrated wishing she had ignored the call.

"Oh yeah, 'dats mighty funny 'cause I coulda sworn I talked to the nigga Ashley on your phone 'bout two weeks ago." At the mention of Ashley's name Unique swallowed hard. *"And what's 'dis I hear him and one of his men 'pose to geed you?"* he waited for an answer.

"What! Boy, you got me fucked up," She said guilty not knowing what to say next. For the life of her, she couldn't think when Ashley had the chance to answer her phone. Bullet knew when she was lying because she would become very defensive. Unique couldn't see herself without him as she began to cry.

"Bullet let me explain that's not true baby I swear."

"Oh, shawty you can miss me with all that fake ass crying, you lucky I'm not home I would've killed your ass right along with that nigga."

(click) the phone disconnected.

Unique tears began to flow as she finished up her shopping. She called Katie to inform her on what just happened, with Katie not answering the phone she hopped in the Charger, gunning down the highway, heading towards Katie's house. Just, as Unique was pulling up La-La was storming out of the building with his eyes protruding from the sockets. He ran to his jeep, hopped in, and sped off so quick his tires spun on the wet pavement!

"What the hell?!" Unique frowned quickly throwing the car in park. She ran to the building, taking the elevator up, she turned the knob walking in.

"Oh my God no!" She screamed.

Unique found Katie unresponsive, she called 911.

"Oh my God! please, please do sumthin!" Unique voice cracked. With her hands covering her mouth, tears poured down her face as she watched her best friend lay in the back of the speeding ambulance.

PRESSURE BUST PIPES

"Ma'am your gonna have to step aside we're not getting a pulse!" said the redhead paramedic. Unique watched helplessly as the paramedics tried reviving her.

"What's happening!" Unique screamed hysterically.

"Fray and DeShay had been trying to come up with a way to get Chucky, but it seemed like after Ashley's murder he went hiatus. Fray heard through the grapevine that Hulk's cousin Joyce owned a salon on Central Avenue. After doing his own investigation he got all the information intended. Fray and DeShay put two, and two together strategizing their plan for the next few days, they started scoping out Joyce's every move.

"Man, where the fuck she at?" Fray frowned as he lowered his phone from his ear hanging up. He had still been desperately trying to get a hold of Katie.

"She prolly still sleep holmes." DeShay suggested, making a right by Iverson Mall, bucking a "U" making a right into the parking lot. He pressed lightly on the accelerator searching for an empty parking space. With Fray still sporting yesterday's attire, the two decided to hit up the mall to find something to wear.

"Nah she playin' games, Kee don't sleep 'dat hard holmes," he said.

"You tryin' slide pass her joint when we leave from up here?" DeShay offered, scanning the lot for a parking space. With all the spaces occupied, DeShay double-parked in front of the "Up Against the Wall" clothing store. Seconds' later the store door opened getting DeShay's attention.

"Got damn dat' bitch phat as a muthafucka!" DeShay said hitting Fray's shoulder just as he was about to step from the car.

They watched Joyce switch across the lot with a hand full of bags. The two had decided to take a few days off from shadowing her, giving her a freebie. This was the first time they seen her dressed as such. She wore brown knee high Timberland boots, leather like tight shorts, and a white wife beater. Her round ass clapped with every step as she neared the tinted Monte Carlo, she tugged at her shorts pulling them out of her pussy.

DeShay started to beep the horn to get her attention but stopped when the passenger door on the Monte Carlo opened. Fray and DeShay had to blink twice as they watched Chucky walk around to the front of the car, and get in the passenger seat while Joyce got in the driver seat. Katie's words suddenly echoed in his head, *"Fray you promised you were done."*

"Slim which one you want?" DeShay asked referring to the guns.

"Give me the pump!" Fray said ignoring his conscience.

Armed and ready with a vengeance in their hearts, a police cruiser pulled into the parking lot. *"Hol, Police!"* Fray yelled peeping through his mirror just as DeShay was exiting the car. They sat nervously with their adrenaline racing, Chucky drove by them fleeing from the lot.

"I swear slim, don't let dat' nigga get away," Fray said looking back watching the cop's activity. DeShay cranked the engine pulling out the lot headed in the same direction as Chucky. Twenty minutes later Chucky was pulling in front of Joyce's salon.

"Are you sure you got everything?" Joyce asked sadly turning to face him in her seat, she always looked at him like a little brother.

"Yeah, I think so, if not fuck it," he said running his hand over his curly red hair. His face had been all over the news for the last three days. The cops were able to match his prints taken from the pizza bag left at the scene of Ashley's murder. He knew it would only be a matter of time before someone tipped the police off, so he decided to have Joyce do some last minute shopping for him before he relocated.

"Shay pull up there, on that side of the street!" Fray pointed to the empty spot near the alley. "You 'ont got no hood or nuthin' in 'dis muthafucka?" Fray asked looking around in the back seat.

"Nigga 'dis a rental! We 'ont need all 'dat shit on anyway," DeShay said looking around the busy street as he chambered a round into the barrel of the tec. "I hope 'dis bitch don't jam. Fray you ready?!"

Chh-Chh! Fray let the cocking of the pump do his talking, they both slid from the car...

"Make sure you call me as soon as you get there, I'ma miss you," Joyce cried as she hugged him. She stepped from the car wiping away her tears. Chucky sat watching her through clouds of weed smoke as she went inside the salon. He started to pull off, but the ringing of his phone grabbed his attention.

"Hello?" he answered.

"You have a collect call from," ...the pre-recorded operator begun, after letting it play he accepted Bullet's call.

"Moe, whassup? Bullet greeted him.

"Ain't shit fool chillin', out front of Joyce shop right now. I'ma 'bout to roll out in a minute, though, y'know a nigga gotta lay low for a while," Chucky said.

"Yeah, I'm already hip. I saw 'dat shit on the news. Aye check dis' out before you roll, I need you to do me one last favor?"

"I'm listenin?" Chucky was all ears.

"I need you to hit 'dat bitch Unique's head for me!"

Chucky's brain took a minute to process his request. He loved Bullet unconditionally, but with time running out he wasn't trying to take that risk.

"Moe! Y'know them peoples on my line out here. I can't move around like 'dat."

Fray and DeShay began making their way across the street towards the blue Monte Carlo, with their heads down, they tried their best to conceal their individualities and weapons. The intense conversation Chucky was having with Bullet distracted him.

"A'int no time for me to do no shit like 'dat," Chucky stressed to him when he turned to look out the driver side window. He became dumbstruck as he watched Fray rundown on him aiming the pump! The phone slipped from his hand as he tried reaching for his gun. *Boom!* Chucky let out an ear-racking screech. *"Arrgh!"*

"Hello, Hello!" Bullet hollered into the phone.

The eruption of the shotgun blast sent the crowded street into pandemonium. DeShay ran up on the passenger side unloading the Tec. *Tat, tat, tat…Boom…tat…tat…Boom, Boom!* Chucky's body jerked in complete disorder as they pumped him full of led. *Boom, Boom!* Fray fired the last two slugs into his head splitting it open like a watermelon! After DeShay finished finger fucking the trigger, he looked over at Fray, who signaled it was time to vacate the premises. They ran to their car making a getaway. Once the fire ceased Joyce hopped to her feet from underneath the receptionist.

"No!" She screamed looking out the window at Chucky's car.

THE PAST

Joe was pissed as he stormed out to the parking lot to his "66" Nova with Kelly lagging behind. He had yet to mention his reason for being irate. Kelly figured she would get it out of him later. In the meantime, she was finishing up a call with Roger and Mason as she climbed inside the car.

"How did I not see this? After all these years, it was right there in my face!" Joe fumed, pounding his fist on the steering wheel. The way he moved *everything*! It was all right there." He said more to himself than to Kelly. His cheeks were flushed with red.

"Would you give it a rest," Kelly said disrupting his outbursts.

"Look this isn't over just yet so try to keep your head on straight," Joe said as he settled down and buckled his seatbelt before cranking the engine heading to their destination.

Bullet sat alone on the floor in his dark cell. His only source of light came from underneath the gray metal doors where he sat immobile and numb. He stared at the old photos of Chucky, Hulk, and himself as he reminisced. The chaplain pulled him out hours ago informing him of Chucky's death. There was a light tap at his door. The elderly female officer who wore too much mascara greeted him through the small window on his door.

"Harris."

"Whassup!" Bullet answered.

"Get dressed theirs some people here to see you."

After being shackled with the leg irons, and belly chain Bullet was escorted to the visiting Hall. Judging by the way that they were dressed he could tell they were cops.

"Who the fuck are you!" Bullet frowned.

"Would you like to take a seat first?" Mason asked.

"Nah I rather stand! Now answer my question. Who the fuck are you?" Bullet asked again.

"We work for homicide," Roger said flipping out his badge. "We happened to be investigating several murders none of which is involving you, but I'm quite sure we'll be able to get some dirt on you as well, that is, if you're not willing to help with our investigation. Now do the names Ashley Pitts, Ronnie Watson, DeShay Mills and Fray Pascal ring a bell?"

"Never heard of 'em," Bullet said not budging.

"Cut the crap! These guys are responsible for murdering two of your friends, one of which we pulled from a car earlier today, and I must tell ya' it wasn't a pretty sight, but we do know Chucky was the one who done Mr. Pitts," Roger said not buying Bullet's story.

PRESSURE BUST PIPES

"Like I said never heard of 'em." Bullet then turned to leave.

"Let me guess. You're going to leave Chucky out to dry just like you did Hulk!" Mason blurted at his back.

Bullet angrily swung around! His eyes were cold.

"Man, fuck you! Find somebody else to point the finger at." He snapped before shuffling out the door.

IVY CITY PROJECTS...

Joe and Kelly slowly rolled up the trash-strewn street where dozens of fiends wandered about like zombies. It was still hard for them to believe that someone actually lived there. Its brick chipped building had falling into partial decay. With the concrete steps eroding, the residents improvised by tying milk crates together making steps to travel in and out of the building.

"Wait, wait...Slow up 2114 right there!" Kelly said pointing to the last building on their right. The building addresses was spray-painted black. Joe pulled next to the curve glancing at the wandering fiends.

"Stay close to me," Joe said cutting his eye over at Kelly.

As they entered the dim, piss stench four unit building, his hand fell to the butt of his holstered .38 revolver. They climbed one flight of stairs knocking on apartment four.

"Who is it?" the gentle voice yelled upon hearing the light tap at the door.

"It's the police."

The dynamic duo heard the door being unlocked. A radiant face of a teenager peeped through the cracked door.

"Uh...Yes?"

She looked confused as she looked Joe over twice. Joe flashed his badge confirming his identity.

"You must be Helen?" Kelly smiled politely at the young person. Helen was taken aback by the blonde hair woman addressing her by her name. There was a heavier female voice shouting from behind Helen.

"Girl who 'dat at my damn door 'dis time of night?"

"They say they the police," Helen said glancing back over her shoulder at her mother.

"The police? Well, what the hell do they want?" She said appearing in her housecoat, and a head full of rollers. She was a spitting image of her daughter except older, she too looked Joe over twice.

"May I help y'all?" She asked in a curious manner.

"Are you Ms. Smith?" Kelly asked flashing a warm smile.

"Yes, I am."

"Do you mind if we step inside?"

"What's 'dis about?" Ms. Smith asked.

"Your daughter," Joe said rudely.

In the dark night, Fray flew past the Pepsi-Cola plant on Kenilworth Avenue, his headlights shining brightly on the pitch-black road. He didn't know why, but for some strange reason, he felt avenging Ashley's death would bring him some kind of solace. Only it didn't. He hadn't shared this with DeShay, but as he pulled the trigger, Chucky's bloody face seemed to flash the image of his first victim. It was as if he was killing him repeatedly.

PRESSURE BUST PIPES

The truth was every kill seemed that way, which haunted him for years. As he pushed the Lincoln to Katie's crib, he tried calling her again, but to no avail. He heatedly tossed the phone to the passenger seat as he bared off in the right lane. A crushing feeling formed in his chest and many thoughts raced through his head. Had Katie merely given up on him, and given her heart to La-La? Out of the blue his phone rang, figuring it to be the love of his life calling back, he didn't bother to look at the screen.

"Hello?" He answered enthusiastically.

"We need to talk," said the caller on the other end of the receiver. Fray rolled his eyes wishing the voice belonged to Katie instead of Pebblez. He tried his best to camouflage the disappointment in his voice.

"Talk about what?" He said as he turned on his left blinker waiting patiently for the passing cars to pass.

"Look, are you comin' home tonight? I really need to talk to you." Pebblez replied just as he turned up Katie's street. Flashing red and blue lights bounced off his windshield as cops canvassed the area. Assuming it was a roadblock, he slammed on brakes drawing countless stares from the officers and scattered spectators. He put the car in reverse, whipping it into an empty space, shifting the car into gear, and vanishing from the scene…

For the time being Katie laid unresponsive in the intensive care unit with Unique in the waiting area in tears. She lost a lot of blood along the way, not to mention her head injury caused her brain to swell. The doctors were talking about flying her to Washington Hospital center where the surgeons were better equipped for trauma.

To Joe and Kelly's surprise, the Smith's residence was cleaner than they had expected. Its compact living room consisted of family portraits scattered along the wall, with dull hardwood floors, and cheap furniture.

"Sorry for the intrusion ma'am, but we really need to have a word with your daughter," Kelly said hooking her hair behind her right ear.

"Well, y'all still haven't told me what this is all about. I mean it's not every day that cops show up on my doorstep," she chuckled then abruptly cut it off.

"We were hoping Helen could help us tie up some loose ends in our investigation."

"Oh, is 'dat right? Well, tell me, detective, what does my daughter have to do wit' any investigation?"

"Your daughter may be the only one who can identify a murder suspect, and if so she better spit it out!" Joe said still in a bad mood. Helen began to perspire heavily as she was forced to relive that dreadful day. For years, she tried to get rid of those horrifying memories that lived with her every day. She could never forget the distinctive smell of the blood on her face.

"Helen please talk to us were only here to help you," Kelly said softly.

Helen was now on the brink of tears. Seeing her daughter become uncomfortable with the detective's questions Ms. Smith stepped in.

"Look, we really wish we could help you guys, but we don't know a thing about any old murder. Now if you guys don't mind showing yourselves out, we were just getting ready for bed," she said placing her hands in the pockets of her gown.

"Who said anything about an old murder?" Joe's voice was

curious. It was then he and Kelly knew Helen's mother was protecting a secret as well. Ms. Smith walked to the front door and held it open.

"Good night detectives," she said just as they crossed the threshold of her front door. Kelly double backed now facing Ms. Smith.

"Ma'am. I know you're probably thinking this guy saved your daughter's life, but murder is murder and is not right. We believe this person has killed numerous people since then and only Helen can help us put a stop to this. Just something to think about. goodnight Ms. Smith," Kelly said as she walked off.

The downtown city was busy with blue-collar pedestrians and hot dog stands. On the second floor, Kelly stood looking out her office window. The investigation was starting to take a toll on her mentally and physically. Her receptionist's voice came alive over speakerphone.

"Ma'am I know you said to hold all your calls, but you didn't say anything about visitors. There's a woman here to see you."

"Do me a favor would you? Tell her I stepped out for the day," Kelly said picking up the receiver.

"But ma'am she says is important."

Kelly dropped her head still holding the receiver with her left hand.

"I'll be right there." she let out a deep breath.

When Kelly entered the lobby she was surprised to see Ms. Smith standing there.

"Hello Ms. Smith, how may I help you?" She asked hesitantly.

"I thought about what you said, so here I am."

Fray awakened to his ring tone "Many Men." He laid there with his eyes still closed with Pebblez tucked away in his arms, her head was laid across his bare chest.

"Mm, you goin' get 'dat?" She asked groggily with her eyes still closed. Fray looked over at the digital clock it read 7 am he frowned answering.

"Yeah?" he answered still half sleep.

"Youngster what the hell you still doin' in bed! I Thought I told your ass to meet me at the shop at eight," Jeter screamed through the receiver.

"Old man, you do know its seven o'clock right?" Fray said in an agitated tone.

"And...so! It's gonna' take your ass an hour just to get dressed, and then another hour for you to bring your ass over here. Dats' why I'm waken you up now!"

"Man, I thought you said the check wouldn't clear till next week." Fray yawned. Jeeter let out a light giggle.

"I see you don't have a clue about how banks work. They give you a projected time frame, they cleared it today!" Jeeter shouted with joy.

It felt like a barrier had been lifted off his shoulders, Fray was in awe at the good news. He knew this day would come, the feeling was surreal, the never-ending tunnel didn't seem so far anymore.

"Congratulations baby boy you got the shop! I'm on my way to the sunshine city!" Jeeter screamed excitedly. "No more ducking cops and ill fiends, no more sleeping around in the trap houses without changing clothes for days just to get a buck, most importantly no

more flirting with death," Jeeter gave him a reality check. "Hello, Hello… youngster you still there?"

"Yea, I'm still here Mr. J I'm jus' processin' it all," he smiled.

"Well, you should be. I'm leavin' you a gold mine!" he boasted.

"Thanks again Mr. J for everything," he spoke with gratitude.

"Don't mention it, now hurry up and get over here and pick up the keys."

After hanging up, Fray leaned over and pecked Pebblez on the cheek, then sat up placing his feet on the cushioned rug.

"I still need to talk to you Fray it's serious," she said.

"Later. I got sumthin' important to take care of," he said walking towards the bathroom.

His avoidance of her was starting to become frustrating. When he came home last night she was already sleep. She took a deep breath and rolled over. Fray started to turn on the shower when a loud banging at his front door stopped him! Pebblez cringed at the pounding as well.

"Fray would you get 'dat Please!" she covered her head with the pillow. It was obvious she didn't share his same interest as to who in the hell would be at their door. He stepped from the bathroom looking at Pebblez as she lay in bed.

"You expectin' somebody," he asked suspiciously. Before she could reply their door came crashing down followed by yelling! With no time to think, he raced to the foot of his bed frantically reaching underneath the mattress for his pistol. As soon as he gripped the handle he felt the cold steel pressed against his temple!

"Uh, Un, I wouldn't do that if I was you," Joe growled.

Fray had been so caught up in the moment he didn't hear the intruders identify themselves as police. Fray slowly pulled his right hand from underneath the mattress, raising them, surrendering.

"Give me one good reason you little prick why I shouldn't blow your brains all over your pretty girlfriend," Joe said through clenched teeth cocking back the hammer on his revolver. With the sheets held up to her face, Pebblez looked on in horror!

"I got you now you piece of shit, get 'em outta here!"

DC JAIL

The court bus had just pulled from behind the sandy colored brick building. Rattling chains, chatter, and diesel fuel combined crammed the air. The prisoners listened as incoherent voices came over the escorting officer's radios. The two escorting officers then stood from their seats as the bus came to a stop.

"Alright, gentleman single file line!"

One by one, in three-piece shackles they rose from their seats exiting as instructed. The building structure was equipped with dense windows making it impossible to see in, or out. Some of the prisoners were first-timers, terror was written all over their faces. The huge, rusted, steel gate closed in front of them making a loud metallic clanging sound. They were then ordered to strip!

Once Fray was free from his shackles he stood taking in his surroundings, from the graffiti on the walls to each individual inmate. He heard many war stories about prison life, he was now about to experience it firsthand. The place reeked of strong urine. Many untold stories lived within those insane asylum walls, which very few wanted to discuss. For those who managed to survive the chaos was never the same after witnessing brutal rapes, and bloody knife fights.

Fray stood preparing himself mentally for the degrading strip search. "Lift em' up. Let's see the bottom of your heels, bend over, squat, cough," said the male Dick watching correctional officer. Fray passed the strip search with flying colors. He took a shower in R&D (Receiving and discharging) and was issued an orange jumpsuit and a hygiene packet. Once all the inmates went through the same process they were led to a closed white steel door with a bronze handle. There were two wooden benches sitting opposite of each other creating a narrow path to the doorway. A small holding tank set off to their right encased with Plexiglas windows tan bars and another steel door. Fray looked up when he heard the back door open opposite of him, Ronnie stepped inside, with a huge smile he began making his way over to the bars of the holding tank.

"Ronnie Whassup!" His squeaky voice piercing the noisy turbulent. He was still unaware of Ronnie's betrayal. Ronnie turned in the direction of the voice. They were separated by the prison bars, as always Fray's expressions were hard to read. Not wanting to risk being spit on, or sucka punch through the bars Ronnie made sure he kept his distance.

"Aye...whassup slim?" Ronnie's eyes looked back and forth nervously.

"Damn holmes come closer to the bars, you act like you 'ont know a nigga or sumthin." Fray frowned taking in his awkwardness. Ronnie studied him for a minute assuming Fray knew nothing he preceded with caution.

"My bad, my shit been on guard over 'dis joint, it took me a minute to recognize who the fuck you was," he said stepping closer to the bars.

"Man, I can dig it. What block they gotcha in?" Fray asked.

"Shid, nigga I jus' jumped the moon. They 'bout to send me to C.T.F."

"Oh yeah…? *Damn!* I was tryna get around you too," Fray shook his head in dismay.

"What your shit lookin' like? 'cause your face been all over every TV in 'dis bitch," Ronnie asked.

"Man," Fray said dropping his head. "They finally got 'dat lil broad from the alley to make a statement on a nigga. Can you believe 'dat shit? After all these years." He frowned.

"You bullshitted. I told you, you shoulda' smoked her lil ass," Ronnie said with a bogus concern.

"Trust me. If I knew she was gon' do dis shit, I woulda' left her ass back there," he snapped angered by his decision.

"What'chu lawyer talkin' 'bout?" Ronnie asked.

"I ain't even hollered at him yet, he sent somebody else to represent me today."

Ronnie was relieved by his response.

"You talk to DeShay yet?" Ronnie continued trying to pick Fray's mind.

"Nah, not yet, but you already know 'dat bitch ain't goin' make it to trial," Fray said.

Ronnie lowered his head as if he was pondering his own mistakes,

Fray knowing him all too well decided to speak up.

"Yeah you fucked up," Fray said sadly.

They both knew there was nothing either he or DeShay could do to get him out of his situation. Ronnie never raised his head to look Fray in his eyes again. The feeling of guilt started to set in. Fray stuck his right hand through the bars grabbing his shoulder.

"Hold your head in here slim. Never let 'em see you sweat. You already know me, and DeShay goin' hold you down on the outside till there's no more breath left in our bodies, no man left behind remember," Fray smiled weakly.

Ronnie could no longer suppress his tears as they gushed forth. The back door slid open,

"Let's go, Watson. I gotta get you across the catwalk before the count," the slender female correctional officer with the long tresses said. At that moment it was hard for Fray to let go, he knew this would probably be the last time they would ever see each other.

"I love you bruh," Fray said.

The two held each other's stares for some time before Ronnie mumbled it back.

Derek marched back and forth in his living room in front of the television. His conscience was eating away at him as he watched the reenactments on the news of Fray's arrest. Only eight years in the game and the kid had already grown tired of scratching fiends and unnecessary bloodshed. A cycle that he himself never managed to escape. At first, Derek thought the pressure of the treacherous streets had gotten the best of him, but the more he analyzed Fray's situation he realized just how wrong he had been. The youngster stuck to the script and applied every lesson he ever taught him. Fray was determined not to be trapped in the never-ending cycle.

PRESSURE BUST PIPES

After shutting off the television, Derek raided his mini-bar. His mind wandered to the three keys of heroin taped underneath his kitchen sink. Putting three keys in DeShay hands was definitely out of the question, he knew how much DeShay despised him. He tossed the Hennessey back pouring another. He would be lucky if DeShay paid him for one.

PRINCE GEORGE'S HOSPITAL...

Unique had been staring out Katie's hospital window, the thunderstorm was headed straight their way. Katie remained unconscious in the intensive care unit with doctors and nurses attending to her daily. The swelling of her brain had gone down, but her condition was still the same. Every day Unique would come to Katie's room in hopes of finding her awake, only to be turned away in disappointment. Making her way back over to Katie's bed, she took her limp hand into hers. She leaned in planting a soft kiss on her forehead, picking up her jacket starting for the door. Katie's heart monitor grew louder. Thinking something was wrong Unique stopped dead in her tracks. What she saw astounded her!

With a call marked urgent, Kelly summoned Joe to meet her at the 555 building. She didn't bother to brief him. With his anxiety growing by the second he weaved in and out of traffic. It took all of 15 minutes to reach his destination. The historical 555 building is where friendship, family values, and Ethnic street codes were broken. It was located just a few blocks away from the courthouse, however, its remote location was coincidentally tucked away so that the passing eye could not see its employees coming and going. It also served the purpose to protect the identities of government informants.

After feeding the parking meter, Joe entered the building flashing his credentials for the guard by the metal detector, he proceeded to the elevator taking it to the seventh floor. The medium size conference room was decorated to government standards with gray and blue carpet, a United States flag dangling from the wooden pole stuffed inside a bronze anchor, and a rectangular shape table with six black swivel chairs. Kelly sat facing the door at the head of the table. Joe came barging in as if he was missing the excitement.

"How nice of you to finally drop in," she smiled slyly setting aside the troubling thought for a second. Joe ignored her sarcasm as he took one of the chairs on her left.

"So what's this all about anyway?" He asked wiggling out of his cut-off sleeve leather jacket.

"You first Joe," she said calmly.

It was more so a demand than asking. Joe knew the topic from the other night would come up again. Unfortunately, after Ronnie's revelation, Kelly felt there was something Joe was hiding. She watched his body sink into the chair and his eyes trail off. His mind started to replay that dreadful afternoon that changed everything.

"All right," he sighed loudly. "At the time of Ross murder, I was working narcotics. To make a long story short, the evening he was gunned down I happened to be overseeing a buy and bust operation in the D St. area. We had been scoping the neighborhood all afternoon, but there wasn't a soul in sight. That is until we rounded the corner of 18th St. the place looked like something straight out of New Jack city. There were fiends everywhere, and the closer we looked we spotted a guy whose face I couldn't make out at the time, standing out front of an apartment building conducting hand-to-hand sales.

After seeing that I decided to call off the sting. I took every precaution necessary and radioed it in then it happened! One of the dope fiends pointed us out. We thought that we had the suspect cornered, boy was we wrong." He let out a fake chuckle. "I'd never forget how he looked up before taking off. When I was in the field, I had eight men assigned to my unit. My goal was to make sure each one of my men returned home to their family's safe after every operation. I never wanted any of them trying to play hero and go after any of those psychopaths alone, so I happened to be the lucky man awarded the task to go after him. I chased the suspect down a damp alley where I lost sight of him. I was in the process of searching everywhere when the sergeant over me radio for help. Needless to say, I abandoned my assignment my failure to apprehend the suspect caused Mr. Ross his life. Because of Ronnie's testimony I now know the truth," he said sadly. Kelly's face showed no remorse.

"Look at it this way Joe. At least, you stopped the abduction and rape of a little girl, now that's gotta count for something."

"Yeah, but your' forgetting one thing. I'm not the one who killed him."

"No. You're not, but had you not chased Pascal down that alley who knows how many more victims Mr. Ross would've added to his list."

 Now it was Kelly's time to bring Joe up to speed. She informed him that they would have a guest joining them shortly. Several seconds later Ronnie and Mr. Dumas entered the room taken two seats opposite of Joe and Kelly. Kelly waved the Marshal off before resuming.

"I believe you two already met?" She motioned to Joe and Mr. Dumas.

The two acknowledged each other with a slight nod. She slid Mr. Dumas's a large manila folder who in turn carefully scanned through it. The file contained autopsies of the alleged crew's victims, and plea deal the government was willing to offer in exchange for Ronnie's testimony.

"You're a piece of shit you know that," Joe spat.

"Likewise." Ronnie winked.

Joe turned his attention back to Kelly.

"I'd let his ass fry if you ask me!" Joe said.

"But no one asked you! Mr. Dumas cut in. "Kelly, I understand how this work, but given the fact my client is willing to close fifteen murder cases has to count for something."

"*Fifteen!*" Joe blurted out. "You gotta' be kidding me right?"

"Mr. Dumas I can't possibly make that kind of call, and even if I tried I don't have the final say," Kelly said.

"I suggest you make that call because otherwise my client isn't saying a thing until we agree on those terms. You now have until 1 o'clock. I have another hearing to attend." He glanced down at his watch in an arrogant demeanor.

"Pascal! You got a legal visit," yelled the officer in the block. Mark Rashad was the best lawyer in the city that money could buy. He was a tall slender man with a dark complexion, a handful of grays and a close shave. With a winning track record, he practically stepped into the courtroom as if he owned it, not to mention whenever he felt it necessary he would slide his most trusted clients the names and addresses of the government witnesses.

"Whassup Mark," Fray said as he entered the room.

They sat sectioned off from the rest of the visiting hall. The monitored bubble faced them with two officers watching their every move. Fray and Mark could see the entire visiting Hall as the other convicts sat across the way on the phone behind the Plexiglas chatting away with their loved ones.

"Well I have good news and I have bad news, so which one do you prefer first?" he asked.

"Give me the good," Fray said as he braced himself for what was to come.

"Well, I still don't see how they can convict you with this crap and the bad…" He slid him the envelope. "I'll leave you to look through the contents. I'll check back in with you in a week," he said walking to the door waiting for the officer to buzz him out. Back in his cell, Fray had been reading Ronnie's statement for the thousandth time as if something was going to change. He couldn't believe Ronnie would betray him like that. Fray thought back to something his father told him years ago "Your closest friends can be your worst enemies." He was now a firm believer in that saying. Ronnie had told them everything he didn't leave a stone unturned.

It was Wednesday, visitation day, and Pebblez was looking gorgeous for her man. With her signature big hair, she rocked a tight long sleeve cream-colored Calvin Klein sweater dress, diamond studded earrings, and some black three strap Mary Jane heels. Her presence was attention-grabbing. Some women scolded their men for having wandering eyes. She handed the officer in the bubble her visiting slip before taking a seat. With her right leg crossed over her left, she switched her position in the chair showing him a side shot of her plump rear end. Fray smiled upon seeing her. The orange and green Kofi covered his waves complimenting his orange jumpsuit, and his gray New Balance. Pebblez stood up making her way over to the empty phone.

"Hey, babes!" Pebblez smiled cradling the phone to her ear.

"How are you holdin' up?"

Fray let out a deep breath.

"Look around me. Whatchu think?" he snapped.

Pebblez knew this was his first time in prison, so she could only imagine the thoughts running through his mind.

"So, what your lawyer talkin' 'bout?"

"Some shit I ain't even tryna talk about right now," he said.

"Like what!" She protested.

"Not now Pebblez okay. I got a lot of shit on my mind. You holla at DeShay?"

"Yeah, he told me to tell you sumthin' like Cowboy showed up right in the middle and that it was a no go. He said you would know exactly what he meant by that."

"Shit!" He spat dropping his head.

With Helen still breathing, he felt the prison walls closing in on him.

"What's wrong?" Pebblez asked confused and concerned.

Not wanting her to know what was going on he switched the subject.

"Look I need you to do me a favor."

"Anything," she replied.

Fray took a long look at her while he contemplated his next question. With the heat now on DeShay, he had no one else to turn too.

"Can I trust you?" he said bluntly.

"Are you seriously gon' ask me some stupid shit like 'dat!" she frowned.

He felt a little more comfortable with his next question.

"I know." he sighed. "This place just got me feelin' like I can't trust anybody."

"Fray you already know you can trust me. I love you," she said sincerely. "I have something I been needing to tell you, Fray I'm…"

"Tell me later." He cut her off. "I need you to go past my apartment and empty the safe before the lease runs out."

Pebblez was shocked! Just as he predicted she would.

"Say what…wait a fuckin minute," she said raising her right hand in a halting position. *"When the fuck did you get a new apartment? Because the last time I checked we lived together. So I guess 'dis the spot you was using to hide your lil bitches!"*

"Man kill all 'dat. It's not what'chu think. I ain't never told nobody about 'dis spot. It's where I stash my money."

Pebblez stared him down. The truth was he never told anyone about it, except Katie.

"So how do I get the keys…"

TERRITORY

Unique couldn't stop her tears from falling as she stood rocking Katie side to side in her arms. Katie had finally awoken from her unconscious state. Her memory was a blur. She remembered Fray smiling as he held her in his arms. She also remembered entering her apartment and La-La dragging her down the hall, that thought alone brought back the pain. For the first time since she had awakened, she became frightened. "What if La-La had done something to Fray?" she thought. Chills took over her body in fear.

"You scared the life outta' me. I thought I would never see you again!" Unique sobbed snapping Katie out of her trance.

With the thought of Fray becoming unbearable she ignored the sharp pain in her chest, she cupped Unique's chin slowly elevating her head to eye level. She used both thumbs to smooth away her tears.

"Nique. Where's Fray?" Her voice was still weak.

At the mention of Fray, she could tell something was wrong by the look or Unique face.

LAUREL MARYLAND FOX REST APARTMENTS...

The sun was slowly fading when Pebblez pulled into the parking lot, and just like Fray said 2201 would be the third building on the left. After parking, Pebblez walked to the building in search of apartment #10. She approached the door with soft knocks. When her knocks went unanswered, she wiggled the key in the lock that she had taken from Fray's key ring. The place was sparkling clean, it was gorgeous. Afghani carpet, a 72-inch flat screen TV, and white Italian leather furniture. This only fueled her curiosity. As long as she had known him, she never knew Fray to have opulent taste in furniture. "Maybe one to his bitches decorated the place," she thought.

She was just about to move forward when she spotted several pictures of Fray and Katie on the walls of the living room. It was the way he looked at her while holding her in his arms. Deep down inside she knew he was still in love with her. He never looked at her that way, and she had to admit they looked so happy together. At that moment, she wondered if he had been playing her all along. With the back of her hand, she caught a tear. Instead of standing around moping she pushed ahead entering the bedroom closet, pulling back the carpet, removing the loose floor boards.

DC JAIL...

PRESSURE BUST PIPES

The cellblock was packed. There were a hundred and eighty inmates assigned to a unit. That was a hundred and eighty different personalities all crammed in one box. It was like throwing gasoline and igniting a match. The smallest thing could trigger a deadly reaction such as the telephones and showers. Fray sat immobile in the common area looking at the buttons on the wall phone, with the receiver sitting in his lap. He had been trying to reach Pebblez for the past two days but no gain.

Today was no different as reality started to set in that he had been double-crossed. Everything he worked so hard to keep came crashing down with Pebblez disappearance. The thought of being broke was suffocating. And if things couldn't get any worse, Mark had just left from dropping off Ronnie's grand jury testimony. Fray was in so much of a daze, that he didn't hear the inmate in the back of him trying to get his attention. Eventually, the inmate grew tired, walked over tapping his shoulder.

"Bruh, you goin' use 'dat phone?" he asked.

"Don't it look like it?" Fray said looking up at him.

"Oh, my bad. I thought you was just sittin' here," the inmate tucked his tail and walked away. Fray started to punch in Pebblez number again, but thought better of it and called DeShay in its place. DeShay let the recording play all the way through.

"Sup cuz?" he answered, traffic noises filtered in his background. Fray let out a depressing breath.

"Same ol' shit slim. Another day in this madness."

Fray was holding it together. DeShay could hear the irritation in his voice. He too had been in the same predicament before, so he understood his struggle. Even though it seemed like all hope was lost with Helen now in custody, he still wasn't about to give up on his cousin.

"Try to maintain your composure in there slim, it gets greater later," DeShay said.

"Man, Insha Allah," Fray mumbled using the Islamic term of God willing.

"Aye let me ask you somethin' slim. You actually read that shit on Ronnie, or is your lawyer just speculating?" DeShay found it hard to believe that Ronnie was a rat.

"Nigga, how many times I gotta tell you shit real. Do I have to spell it out for you?" Fray lost his cool.

"Slim, it ain't that I 'ont believe you. It's just hard for me to see slim doin' some shit like 'dat."

"Man, you just blew me wit' 'dat shit fa real. Anyway, I was callin' to see if you heard anything from that bitch Pebblez?"

"Now, why would she be callin' me?" DeShay said sarcastically.

"You ain't goin' believe this shit. That bitch just got a nigga for two-hundred stacks!"

"What! Nigga stop playin'!" DeShay said in disbelief. *"Man, you gave that bitch access to your money? Yous' a ol' sucka for love ass nigga fa real,"* DeShay said.

"I really ain't tryna hear 'dat shit Shay. If you see that bitch you already know what it is!" Fray spat.

"Say no more. I gotcha."

"Your call has been disconnected goodbye," the operator said. Fray hung up the phone returning it to its base. The thought of all the risks he took to obtain his money came rushing back to him at once.

"Pascal!" yelled the female officer walking the tier. He frowned looking up.

"Don't look at me like that. You got a visit," she said handing him his pass. At the mention of him having a visit, he wondered if he should call DeShay back and call off his decision. "I'll just send word to slim later," he thought. He stepped in his cell and threw on his v-hall attire, several minutes later he was stepping out into the corridor heading in the direction of the visiting hall.

"Boy, hurry up that girl been here since count," said the sergeant working the door.

After handing him his pass Frayed stepped inside the v-hall. He was shocked to find Katie sitting there instead of Pebblez. Her locks were curled and pinned up stylishly. Wearing a gray above the knee sweater dress, and black Ugg boots she waved and smiled as she stood. However, Fray didn't share her same enthusiasm. His expression was dull as he took a seat in front of her separated by the Plexiglas. For the first time since meeting her, he had mixed feelings. They locked eyes for what seemed like an eternity, neither knew where to begin.

"Hey," Katie said blushing.

Fray remained stone-faced.

"Man, what'chu want?" he frowned.

Katie knew it was going to be hard to explain.

"I know you're probably wonderin' where I been."

"Save it shawty you don't owe me nuthin.' I understand you fell in love wit' slim. So please do me a favor and don't ever come up here again. I'm through playin' your game." His words felt like a sharp sword cutting deep as well as the coldness in his eyes. Katie was trying her hardest to blink back the tears, but the more she looked into his eyes she could no longer contain them. His opinion meant everything to her. She sat there at a loss for words.

"Exactly what I thought!" he stood up to leave.

"Fray please!" her left hand darted to the glass.

He stood there for a brief second contemplating if he should walk away, or hear her out.

"You got five minutes," he said.

Before saying another word, she looked from him to the crowded visiting hall, no one seemed to be paying them any attention.

"Fray I been in a coma all this time." Tears streamed down her pretty face. "The morning I left you, La-La was at home waiting for me."

Now, it was he who was at a loss for words. His soul grew dark for the man who hurt her.

"Tell me everything and don't leave nothing out." He demanded.

For the next several months the two were inseparable again. Katie made sure she was at every court date, visit, answered every call, and not to mention she ran the shop in his absence. His trial date was approaching fast, and as promised, she remained firm by his side. There were times when he thought she was going to up and leave only to have her pour it on even stronger, they even toyed around with the idea of marriage. Fray had just finished offering the night Salat when his cellie stormed the cell. He was fresh off the juvie block but was very advanced beyond his years. He had a lanky frame, mocha complexion, long medium sized locks and a full mustache. They had been cellies for the past nine months and Fray had really grown to like him.

"Nigga you 'ont know how to knock? you almost ran up on a snag!" Fray joked folding his prayer rug.

"Nigga please." Anlo chuckled slapping the air. "But, on some real shit, you ain't goin' believe who they just brought in here?"

Fray's first thought was Ronnie. If so, he would not hesitate to butcher him.

"Your man La-La," Anlo smiled answering his own question.

He and Fray had grown so close that Fray confided in him about La-La and Katie. Fray's eyes lit up, as his mind started replaying all the dreadful encounters Katie had filled him in on.

"Oh fa real, what cell they put 'em in?"

"61, and it's away from the cameras," Anlo said.

What Anlo didn't know was the only thing on Fray mind was murder.

"A'ight bet. Let 'em get comfortable I ain't goin' move on him tonight."

The next morning Anlo awoke to the sound of the toilet flushing. He looked over to find Fray suited and booted washing his hands at the sink.

"Damn slim. You up already what time is it?" he asked sleepily.

"Four o'clock," Fray answered.

He watched Fray lift the mattress, and take the flat piece of steel he carved from underneath his bunk. The tip of the shank was sharpened to a needle point. Fray didn't have to say a word, Anlo was up and on his feet in no time.

"So how you tryin' do this?" Anlo asked waiting for instructions. "You sure you wanna be a part of 'dis?" Fray asked.

"Trays up men trays up!" yelled the detail inmates as they rolled in the food cart. The C.O working the bubble unlocked all the doors on the block letting the men out for breakfast.

"They got that garbage out here shawty," said La-La's cellie as he pulled on his jumper heading for the door. He was serving misdemeanor time for a crack pipe. La-La was dead tired. His days of clubbing and drugging had finally got the best of him.

"I'm good. You can have 'dat shit if you want," La-La said from his bunk.

He was fresh off the streets and was in no rush to stuff his body with prison food. The TV rooms and general area was full in no time. Once the inmates received their trays, they scrambled around for a seat. With their focus sat on cell 61, Fray and Anlo blended in with the crowd. They slipped past the security bubble, and down the steps startling La-La's cellmate as he came out.

"What the...," Fray placed his finger to his lips warning the person to be silent. Fray exposed the knife causing the man to fearfully comply. "Beat it," Fray gestured with his head. Anlo took his position by the door. Fray crept inside finding La-La in bed snoring stretched out on his stomach. He then shut the door halfway behind him. With his right hand gripping the knife tightly, his eyes burning with fire as he looked down at him, in one swift motion, he plunged the blade into his shoulder!

"Argh!" La-La screamed out.

PRESSURE BUST PIPES

Fray stepped back. He wanted La-La to see his executioner.

"You like beatin' women," Fray said with anger.

La-La's eyes widened at the sharp object in his attacker's hand! He was tempted to plea, but seeing that the man had kill on his mind he thought again. He then lunged at him from his bunk! Fray ducked the wild haymaker he tried to deliver and slammed the knife into his gut-grabbing a hold of his shirt. He flipped the knife bringing it down connecting with the top of his head, red mist shot across Fray's face. La-La's blood only seemed to ignite the savage beast within as he plunged the blade into his right shoulder. La-La ignored the pain. He bum-rushed his way past Fray taking one in the back as he made it to the door.

Anlo stood guard on the side of the door with his back pressed against the wall, with his arms folded across his chest. He could hear the scrapping going on inside. He was anxious to slide in and join the action a few times, but Fray pacifically told him to stay out of it. His head turned towards the door when La-la flew out like a bat out of hell. His reflex reached out, and grabbed him, putting him in a chokehold and pulling him back in! Fray looked like a mad man holding the knife. His jaws were covered in blood as well as his jumper. Anlo spun La-La around so that Fray could finish him. Fray stabbed him in his stomach repeatedly with no intentions of stopping. Anlo realized that he might have gotten into move than he had bargained for.

"Aye chill slim...you goin' kill 'em!" he yelled as he released La-la to the floor. Anlo grabbed Fray pulling him towards the door. Before they knew it, La-La was crawling on the tier leaving a blood trail behind. The C.O called a code blue for assistance seeing the bloody man on the floor.

The graduates roared as graduation caps flew high in the air! The celebration was off the chains. It took eight long months, but the young police recruit finally did it. Derek wasn't pleased with his sister becoming a police officer, because of the life he lived, and although he missed her graduation she couldn't wait to share the good news. She thanked her family and friends for attending the ceremony, then quickly made in an exit towards her car. The drive to D St took 15 minutes with light traffic. As she pushed her Toyota Solara up the street past the rundown houses and slums, she was reminded of the sacrifices her brother took in order to give her a better life.

When she pulled up, there was a large gathering of people crammed outside the neighborhood liquor store. She lowered her window, she didn't recognize any of the hard faces, in fact, the only person she would have recognized standing amongst the crowd was Fray. Derek made sure he kept his family separate from his street associates, but with Fray it was different he looked at him more like a son. The group of young hustlers watched the decelerating car come to a stop before them. Assuming it was a sale one of them jumped up before the others could react, rushing the car!

"Sweetheart how many you want? We got dubs the size of pillows," said the young hustler holding out the bags of weed in his hands. He wore black field boots and a black hoodie. Rachel looked at him with a frown. She made a mental note to speak with her brother on how he was running his block.

"Get 'dat shit away from my car. I 'ont smoke! I was just lookin' for somebody," she said rudely shooing him away with the back of her hand.

"Damn you ain't have to say it like 'dat. All you had to do was say you wasn't tryin' to cop. Stuck up bitch," he mumbled.

"Lil boy who the fuck you callin' a bitch!" she shot back.

"I'm callin' you a bitch, bitch!" he barked.

"Yeah, aigh't we a see. I got your bitch."

Rachel rolled up her window and sped off.

Katie had just pulled up on D St, she spotted DeShay amongst the crowd coming out of the neighborhood liquor store. He was happy to see her. He pulled out his black & mild before crossing the street in her direction.

"What slim talkin' 'bout?" He asked sliding into the passenger seat. She had just come from visiting Fray.

"Boy, I 'ont know what I'ma do wit your cousin." She shook her head.

"Why you say that." He questioned.

"Because his fuckin ass went to the hole, so now his damn visits is on the screen." She said frustrated.

"What he say happened?" he asked surprised.

"That's the problem...he didn't! she said in a calm voice as she looked at DeShay. "One of my sister's boyfriend's work over there, he said he supposed to stabbed somebody."

Their attention was diverted towards the store as Derek's truck skidded to a stop. When Rachel finally got a hold of Derek, she told him about the altercation she had with the boy sending him berserk. They watched Derek exit the truck storming towards the youngsters posted up outside the store. With no warning, he struck one of them to the ground and commenced stomping and beating him.

"*Oh my God!*" Katie said in shock.

DeShay hopped out the car, crossing the street bypassing Derek's running truck. He locked eyes with the passenger, the woman looked to be about his age or a little older. Rachel sat with her hands in her lap watching DeShay approach her brother from behind. She lowered the window in an attempt to ease-drop on the commotion. Lil Greg was on his hands and knees with a bloody mouth trying desperately to get away.

"Nigga, if you ever disrespect my lil sister again I'll kill you!" Derek said. "And that goes for the rest of you nigga's out here."

He drew back his fist to strike the youngster again when DeShay grabbed it!

"Dats' enuff big fella," he said pulling him off of him.

"Man get the fuck off me! Dis lil muthafucka needs to be taught a lesson."

"Slim chill shawty a kid," DeShay said struggling to restrain the two hundred plus pound bear.

"Nigga, what the fuck you his guardian angel or sumthin? Man, move out the way and mind your own business."

He tried to go around DeShay and continue but was met with a firm stiff arm to his chest knocking him back.

"Nigga, technically this is my business!" He pointed in the back of him. "All these young nigga's work for me now."

Derek disregarded DeShay effort to stop him, he attempted to side step him again.

"Slim ease the fuck up!"

This time, DeShay stopped him with his forearm.

"Man, if you get in my way one more time I'ma disregard, you Fray peoples." Derrick spat.

It was a long time coming, but with Fray absent, he was no longer able to keep the piece.

"*Nigga What!*" DeShay frowned. "*Man, you ol' bitch made ass nigga you could play games out here if you want, and get your shit pushed back.*" he barked lifting his shirt showing the butt of the gun in his pants. "*Fuck you talkin' 'bout you goin' disregard I'm Fray peoples. Nigga, truth be told if it wasn't for slim we woulda' been got wit' your ol' ass!*"

To onlookers it looked like Derek bit off more than he could chew, in a sense, he knew he did. He regretted his choice of words as soon as they left his mouth, not only did he know DeShay was a hot head, but he also knew he had a reputation for killing people where they stood no matter who was around. Derek tucked his tail gracefully. He looked down at the butt of the gun in his waistband.

"You right. You got it shawty," he said holding his hands up in the air backpedaling towards his truck.

NORTHEAST DC

"So what'chu got on?" DeShay said into the receiver of his phone as he lowered himself into his corvette, Unique had been trying to get him to come over all day. Parked outside of the food seven liquor store on the boundaries of Benning Rd, cars zoomed up and down the street splashing puddles of water along the way. He started the engine bringing Scarface to life as it played in the background through the speakers.

"Oh yeah?" He smiled. "A'ight give me 'bout twenty minutes," he closed his flip phone and picked up the half-smoked blunt of haze from the ashtray. Just as he was about to spark up a pearl-white Jaguar pulled in front of him in the parking lot. He knew the passenger right away, but the driver's face seemed vaguely familiar.

"Bitch hurry up. I'm not tryna be sittin' here all day." Pebblez said to Gigi from behind the wheel. She looked around nervously. Pebblez had just come back from Cali to check on Gigi.

"They'll be no witness to this homicide

No re-enactments on the late night news to be re-dramatized All they got is the nigga with the dot in the middle of his muthafuckin head he been shot."

Scarface's lyrics meshed well with how DeShay was feeling at that moment, he finally made out the driver's face through the misty rain. Pebblez had cut her hair short as a disguise, she looked like she had gained a few pounds also. He watched Gigi exit the car covering her hair as she ran into the liquor store. He pulled on his hood and grabbed his Glock from underneath the seat. He got out the car, walked over to the white Jag. Pebblez was so busy playing with the buttons on her radio she didn't see the shadow approaching her. The knock on her window came unexpectedly. She squinted her eyes through the blurred window looking up into DeShay slanted eyes, she automatically stopped breathing.

While the Koreans bagged up Gigi's items a loud explosion startled them, followed by a car horn. Gigi raced out the door, she saw Pebblez head slumped on the steering wheel with her brains blown out.

The next morning, Fray laid on the floor in the middle of his cell doing crunches when the morning officer slid is daily paper underneath the bars. After he reached his thousandth mark, he stood to his feet picking up the newspaper. The front page was centered on the war in Iraq, he skimmed through the pages going to the Metro section. He began reading the article with the familiar background...

DC police are investigating the shooting death of a pregnant woman outside of a local liquor store last night. The shooting occurred around

PRESSURE BUST PIPES

9:00 PM in the 1900 block of Benning Rd., Northeast. The victim was later identified as 31-year-old Pebblez Morrow of Bowie Maryland. She was found shot to death inside her car, authorities are urging anyone with information to please come forward.

Fray let the papers slip from his hand, he tried to recollect any conversations or signs of Pebblez being pregnant. He wondered if that was the reason she kept telling him they needed to talk so desperately over and over. His mind went blank.

"Shawty, 'I'm telling you if you fuck wit' me we can get some money," Derek said.

He had been riding lil boo around for the past hour just as he had done Fray back in the day. However, he knew that the youngster didn't possess that same persona. Derek had in alternative motive.

"No disrespect slim. I ain't tryna get caught up in what you and DeShay got goin' on, but to keep it all the way one hun'nid wit' you, I feel like 'dat a be some snake shit on my behalf to cut slim off just to fuck wit' you when in all actuality 'dat man ain't showed a nigga nuthin' but love since day one," he said with a straight face. Lil Boo was one of DeShay's trusted workers. He was also PeeWee's best friend. With strong facial features and a long chin, it was hard to go unnoticed.

Derek erupted with laughter at his reply.

"Fucks so funny?" Lil boo said.

"Aw, man nuthin." Derek waved him off in between laughs. When he saw he still had lil boo's attention he pulled the truck over.

"A'ight, you sure you wanna hear 'dis?" Derek took his silence as a yes. "It's just 'dat when I look at you I see PeeWee. Blinded by loyalty until he found out the truth." Derek played mind games with the youngster.

"The truth!" Boo frowned not knowing he had just fallen for Derek's plan. "And what might that be?"

"You really don't know do you…He was set up."

"What? Whoever said he was set up cuz." Lil Boo was all ears now.

"I'm tellin you he was," Derek made his-self clear.

"And how do you figure 'dat? Lil Boo asked.

Derek threw the truck back into gear slowly whipping the wheel to the left merging back into traffic, he glanced back at lil Boo.

"An empty gun sounds familiar?" he smiled…

DeShay pulled up to his house around 8:00pm. Darkness filled the once blue sky. He was coming from dropping Fray's trial clothes off to his lawyer for tomorrow. As he sat there looking around his deserted parking lot, the stress of his cousin's trial weighed heavily on him. The one time that Fray really needed him the most he was unable to come through on his end. He laid his head back on the headrest burying his face in his hands. From his windshield, he gazed upon the bright stars. He wondered if there was really a heaven, and if so was Ashley up there. He took a long pull from his cigarette.

His mind replayed old memories of himself and the trio as it did daily, the images of Ronnie upset him he banged his fist on the dashboard. He was still boiling inside about him turning state, and Mark also told him not to be surprised if the government decided to bring an indictment against him as well. With that being said, he attempted to pay the closest people to Ronnie a visit before coming home, only to discover that the government relocated Teresa and the kids, he stepped out into the night. The invisible crickets chirp loudly as he stepped on the porch. His peripheral picked up movement in the bushes on the right side of his house. A chill raced through him and without hesitation, he pulled out his gun!

"Who dat!" DeShay said aiming his gun at the bush, his adrenaline pumping. "Man, you got one second to tell me who the fuck in 'dat bush or I'ma spray that bitch up!" He spat.

"DeShay it's me, Moe!" Lil Boo said stepping out from behind the Bush with his hands reaching for the sky. His clothes were wet and muddy. DeShay frowned.

"Boo, what the fuck you doin' at my house!"

DeShay had brought lil Boo out to his house once, which he waited in the car for him while he ran inside.

"Slim it ain't what you think. Me and lil Greg happened to be in the area when dem' peoples got behind us and chased us comin' back from over some broads house I swear," he said frightened.

DeShay cocked his head to the right as if he was contemplating the thought.

"Where Greg at?" His voice was skeptical.

"Shit man, I 'ont know we went separate ways."

DeShay stared him down before lowering his gun, he had never known the youngster to be on no bullshit, let alone a robber or killer.

"I ain't have nowhere else to run slim," Boo said trying to convince DeShay.

"You sure you ain't got nobody' wit'chu'?" DeShay said raising his pistol again.

"Naw man I swear." He pleaded.

"A'ight, come on in I'ma give you a change of clothes, and then we goin' go see if we can find this lil nigga Greg."

Lil Boo walked up the porch steps, DeShay stopped him at the door frisking him thoroughly. Had Boo been carrying a gun he would've killed him on the spot. DeShay made him kick off his muddy shoes before entering. His crib was laid out. Aisha was in the kitchen washing dishes when DeShay came up behind her wrapping his arms around her waist surprising her. The I-pod music was so loud in her ears she didn't hear him when he came in.

"What I tell you 'bout havin' 'dat shit so loud," he said.

She removed the Sony ear-pugs and greeted him with a warm kiss.

"Shh. Try not to make too much noise I just put her to sleep," she whispered.

When DeShay bent down to kiss her neck she saw movement over his left shoulder.

"Who the hell you got wit' you?" she frowned.

Outside of the original crew, she wasn't use to him bringing anyone home.

"That's lil Boo, Boo come in here right quick! Boo 'dis my girl Aisha, Aisha this lil Boo," he introduced them.

"Hi, you doin'?" Boo spoke pulling the chair from under the table about to take a seat.

"Oh no, you don't. Don't sit in my chair wit' those muddy clothes on," she placed her hand on her hips. She turned her attention back to DeShay. "How long y'all stayin'?"

"We were just leavin'," he smiled grabbing her ass kissing her on the forehead. He ran up the steps skipping a few in between to get Boo a change of clothes. Five minutes later, they were stepping back out the door.

"Is she always that mean?" Boo asked opening the passenger door.

"Nah, she only like that wit' muthafuckas she 'ont know," DeShay said cranking the engine. He then put his gun under the seat.

"Aye, hand me that pack of cigarettes out the glove compartment," DeShay said.

Boo shifted papers around until he located the pack of cigarettes.

"A'int no more in here holmes," Boo said crumpling the pack.

"*Shit!* I gotta hit the gas station first."

Amoco was semi-crowded when they pulled up.

"I'll be right back," DeShay said slipping from the car. Boo looked at DeShay's back as he stood outside the bulletproof window paying for the cigarettes. He reached over and slid his sweaty palm underneath DeShay's seat taking his Glock .40. DeShay made his way back to the car, Boo felt like it was now or never. The thumping of his heart became louder than the A.C, he tensed up even more as DeShay got closer. He started to squirm in his seat, he had never killed anyone before, he secretly wanted to back out. Before he knew it, DeShay was opening the door! He raised the pistol and closed his eyes. DeShay never knew what hit him.

"*Pascal!*"

The banging on the bars woke him out of his sleep!

"Huh?" he answered tiredly to the C.O tapping her keys against his bars.

"The chaplain wants to see you."

"For what?" he asked agitated already knowing it couldn't be good. He sat up bringing his feet over the side of the cot rubbing his eyes. "A'ight give me ten minutes."

"Make it five," said the officer before turning and walking away. As promised the sergeant came back in five minutes strapping him with leg irons, and a belly chain. She escorted him around to the chapel. Chaplain Betty Green was an elderly woman with bi-focal glasses and gray hair, she was sitting behind a black desk when Fray entered.

"Sorry to bring you down here on such a short notice. I just received a call from one of your relatives. I'm afraid your cousin DeShay was killed last night, I'm so sorry dea...,"

Fray never heard the rest, his heart stopped beating. For once he searched for his inner voice to howl, but nothing came out. Life without DeShay was unthinkable. He dropped to his knees and began bawling! The chaplain waved off the officer as he tried to yank him back up by his belly chain. It took Fray some time to get his emotions under control. The chaplain helped him to his feet.

"Sweety would you like to make a call?"

"Yes," he said in a broken voice. "Two if possible," he sniffed while wiping his face with the back of his hand.

"We'll I'll give you some time alone," she said handing him the phone. The first person he called was Derek. Derek and lil Boo sat inside his truck outside of Langston golf course discussing the details when the ringing of Derek phone interrupted them, he answered on the third ring.

"Hello," Derek answered.

"Slim what the fuck happened to my lil cousin last night!"

Fray's voice bust through the receiver. The stress in his voice was evident. Lil boo had no idea Fray was on the other end of the phone. He went back to eating his food like a savage, half-ass listening to the one sided conversation. Derek immediately sliced his hand through the air for him to tone it down. He took note of the straight through phone call, looking down at the screen, at that moment he wondered if Boo covered all his tracks.

"Wh... wh... where you at slim?" Derek asked awkwardly praying that he hadn't been released.

"I'm callin' from the chaplain's office." Derek was relieved.

"Slim, you ain't even gotta say it I already know you fucked up. I'm fucked up too that was my lil man, and I wanna' know who killed him just as bad as you do. I had my ears to the streets all morning tryna find out who was behind 'dat shit, don't trip the streets gonna talk."

The change of Derek's conversation made Boo focus in on the conversation.

"Who 'dat?" Boo asked puzzled.

Derek tried to silence him with a wave but it was too late.

"Who wit' you?" Fray asked intriguingly.

Derek nudged Boo with a frown.

"You 'member lil Boo don't you? He said whassup we 'jus comin' back from gettin breakfast."

There was a period of silence followed by more sobs. Fray thought he could control the breakdown, but the pain he suffered was unbearable. This was something he would never get over he talked through his tears.

"When you find out who was behind this shit kill 'em all," Fray hung up in his ear taking a deep breath punching in the digits of his next call. He listened as Aisha picked up.

"That was Fray and he's pissed," he said as he shifted his truck into gear.

"So! His ass could get it too!" Boo spat.

"Easy there cowboy, let's not go gettin' ahead of ourselves until he shows different. My boy is off limits. Now where were we?"

"I was tellin you 'bout how I had to stash my gun in the nigga bushes because he got the drop on me." Boo relived every event leading up to DeShay's murder.

"Slim, I swear I never knew pulling a trigger could be so easy," he bragged. He didn't realize Derek was boiling inside as he tightened his grip on the steering wheel. Derek could not believe Boo was stupid enough to go through with it after allowing Aisha to see his face. He watched his calculated plan fall apart, knowing it wouldn't be long before Fray contacted Aisha and pieced it together. He thought of countless ways to get out of the predicament. With fury clouding his thinking he managed to hold it together.

"So where's the gun now?" Derek asked.

"I stashed it at my mom's."

All Derek could do was shake his head.

"What?" Boo asked dumbfounded.

That was Derek's breaking point.

"Your dumbass still got the murder weapon! Fuck wrong wit'chu?" he fumed. Boo looked lost not knowing where he went

wrong. *"Look, we goin' go get 'dat!"* Derek spat as he weaved in and out of traffic. Ten minutes later, they were pulling in the alley out back of Boo's mother's house. Derek cussed him out the entire ride.

"Go get 'dat!" He persisted. He waited for Boo to turn his back to open the door before he reached for his .38! As soon as Boo feet touched the pavement, Derek hastily scanned the neighbor's windows making sure the coast was clear before calling him back.

"Aye Boo," he waited for him to turn around. Boo gasped as he stood motionless staring at the pistol. "You fucked up…" *Boom*!

The article in the paper had Fray so enthralled he never heard the officer outside his cell calling for him.

"Pascal," He yelled even louder this time.

Fray lift his head from the paper locking eyes with C.O, he still didn't respond.

"You have a visitor," said the sweaty officer annoyed that he sat there not answering him.

Fray set the paper aside and stood from his bunk, he had been expecting Katie. Katie awaited his arrival in the packed visiting hall. She was dressed in a black fitted blazer, a black blouse that matched perfectly with the dark denim jeans, and black thigh high boots accessorizing it with gold accessories. The whole ride there she wondered how he was coping with DeShay's death, it was bad enough he was still mourning the loss of Ashley, not to mention Ronnie's betrayal. Overall, she could not understand how he managed to remain mentally stable. She blushed as he entered the room.

"Hi you doin' beautiful," he said through the receiver smiling blowing her a kiss.

"I'm good how 'bout yourself? How you been holdin' up?" she asked crossing her leg at the knee. He took a minute before responding.

"Tell you the truth Kee. For the first time in my life I don't know," he said in a low heartfelt tone.

"Have you read the paper," she asked.

He slowly nodded his head up and down. That wasn't the reaction she was expecting.

"Well?" she pressed on eyeing him. "Did you know 'em?" Katie was referring to today's article written about Boo. When the cops responded to the shooting, they found him in the back of an alley suffering from a gunshot wound to the chest. He was rushed to the hospital where they pronounced him dead. Their knocks were answered by Boo's mother who allowed them inside the house. They searched the place from top to bottom until they discovered the murder weapon used to kill DeShay, ballistics showed.

"Yeah I knew 'em," he said unbothered trying to piece it together himself.

"Fray look. I know you always say the less I know the better. Now I'm not trying to insinuate anything, but I find it kind of strange that DeShay got killed right after he and Derek had that huge dispute!" Fray's expression said it all, it was obvious he hadn't heard.

"You didn't know?"

She started to explain everything she saw that day.

OMERTA?

"Order! Order in the court!" Judge Weisberg yelled as he banged his gavel repeatedly. The courtroom was in a complete disarray, the press snapped pictures of lawyers, spectators, and public officials. The media was all over this one.

"Were up kid," Mark said adjusting his tie on his black suit.

The U.S Marshals stood on both sides of the freezing holding cage in the back of the judge's chamber. Fray was dressed to impress. With a tailored Versace suit, Gucci loafers, and Ferragamo personality glasses. Days before the trial, Mark insisted that he cut his beard bringing out his youthful features. He and Mark had gone over everything from top to bottom the night before. Mark biggest concern wasn't Ronnie's testifying that was his least concern, but Helen is who worried him.

"Is it crowded out there?" Fray asked nervously in a shaky voice.

"Unfortunately yes. The media turned this thing into a circus."

"What are our chances?" Fray asked sitting on the iron bench. Even with a jury of his peers, he still found himself on the edge of his seat.

"Look," Mark exhaled loudly. "With these kinds of cases, you can never be too sure. The important thing is getting a good jury, which I think we got. Now do me a favor, and try not to look so got damn nervous when we go in there," Mark said standing up.

The jury had been removed before Fray was allowed to enter. He sat next to his lawyer at the table, the jury was then escorted back in. Fray's focus was all over the courtroom but was cut short upon seeing Katie's radiant face in the middle row with Unique accompanying her. Katie's presence lift his spirits.

"I love you," he mouthed.

The bailiff announced the presiding of the judge which interrupted their stare.

"All Rise!"

Weisberg was a white man with salt and pepper hair matching his robe. The bailiff then motioned for everyone to be seated. Detective Joe was the first of Kelly's witnesses to take the stand. His bizarre attire put frowns on the juror's faces. He looked nothing like a man of the law, he looked more as if he was on the other side of the law. After taking a seat in the chair, he tapped the microphone in front of him to make sure it was on. The D.A rose from her seat tugging at the hems of her pinstripe blazer. She approached the witness chair with a smile, pushing her designer specs up on her face. Her blond curls dangled in the middle of her back. Fray picked up the pitcher of water from the table and pulled himself a glass. He had mentally prepared himself for a long day.

"Detective, how would you describe this murderous 18 & D organization?"

Kelly began her cross-examination.

"*Objection your honor!*" Mark leaped to his feet. "Since when did this become a racketeering trial?" He said.

"Ms. Anderson where exactly is this going?" the judge intervened.

"Your honor may we approach the bench?" she asked.

The mics were turned off, and a device was activated to muffle out the conversation. The heated discussion lasted for about three minutes before Mark returned to his seat with a defeated look on his face. The judge turned his attention to the witness.

"You may answer the question."

Weisberg was a friend of Kelly's father.

"They had no regard for human life," Joe begun. He paused to look at the jury making eye contact with each of them. "In my nine years on the force, never have I ever encountered another group so cunning and dangerous. They caused fear wherever they went. Whether it was intimidating people, killing witnesses the list goes on. That's just to name a few of their violent traits."

There were whispers and grunts amongst the crowd of jurors. Helen's mother was next on the stand.

"Ma'am would you please state your full name for the record?"

"Elain Smith," the woman replied in a raspy voice.

"Ms. Smith if you don't mind my asking, was there ever a time where your daughter's childhood was prematurely ripped away?"

The D.A asked as she calmly paced the carpet-covered floor. Ms. Smith remembered that drastic change in her daughter's life all too well. She tried hard to fight back the tears as she thought back to the day Helen appeared before her in the kitchen covered in blood.

"Yes." she murmured with watery eyes.

"Ma'am...I know this is hard, but can you describe the change for us?" Kelly's voice was pleasant.

Ms. Smith took her time going down memory lane.

"For months, she wouldn't eat. She barely spoke two words to me at a time," she gently patted her eyes and nose trying to keep her mental strain together.

"Now was this totally out of your daughter's character?"

"Yes, ma'am."

"Ms. Smith you never did say what brought on those changes," Kelly continued.

"She was nearly raped." Her voice trailed off as she wept lowering her head to her chest. The prosecutor then did something out of the ordinary. She stepped close to the witness stand and gripped the woman's hand.

"You said she was nearly raped what prevented it from happening?"

"Someone must've heard her screams because they came to her rescue killing the man on top of her."

"No further questions your honor," Kelly said taking her seat. When the woman stepped off the bench she secretly mouthed the words "thank you," to Fray with a genuine smile. Ms. Smith's testimony was so emotional that the judge called for a 20-minute recess. Fray paced the small holding cell in the back of the courtroom. With his arms locked behind his back and eyes fixed on the dirty tile floor, his mind was more so on DeShay murder than his own fate. He promised himself if he made it out of there, Derek would suffer the most torturous death one could imagine. He was caught by surprise to see two Marshal's emerged from the staircase with a shackled Ronnie. Ronnie appeared startled by his presence as well. The Marshals led Ronnie over to the empty cage beside him.

"You really goin' go through wit' 'dis shit, huh slim?" He asked disgustedly. Ronnie remained silent. "I guess you never really know a nigga until 'dat pressure is on," Fray said.

Ronnie stood with his head pressed against the bars he was not expecting to see Fray, at least not until he entered the courtroom. The door leading to the courtroom opened.

"They're ready for you," said the Marshal sticking the key inside Fray's bars.

"All Rise!" Announced the bailiff as the judge walked to his bench. "This court is now in session."

The prosecutor resumed to the floor as Ronnie occupied the witness chair. Fray and Katie both burned holes through him with their furious eyes.

"Look at this 'ol shameful muthafucker. I can't believe his ass used to eat at our table," Katie whispered to Unique.

"Mr. Watson, how long have you known the defendant?"

The DA gestured towards the defense table. Ronnie was hesitant at first, but the more he thought about the time he was facing he decided to go through with it.

"Since 89 we grew up together."

"So is it safe to say that the two of you were friends?"

"At one time, yes," Ronnie cut his eye at Fray for the first time.

"Mr. Watson did you and Mr. Pascal also grow up with two other individuals by the names DeShay Mills, and Ashley Pitts?"

"Yes, sir we did."

"Where they also members of the 18th & D crew?"

"Yes."

"If you don't mind my asking where are they now?"

"They're both deceased," he said sadly.

"Mr. Watson let me direct your attention back to the day Mr. Ross was murdered." She paused to catch her breath. "Did, there come a time that you encountered the defendant."

"Yes."

"What can you tell us about that?"

"I was sleep when Fray came banging on the door at my grandmother's house. He was sweaty and out of breath. He said that he had just kilt' someone."

"Would that person have been Mr. Ross?"

"Yes."

Kelly walked over to her table taking a sip of water before she continued.

"Mr. Watson you wouldn't by any chance know what Fray did with the murder weapon?"

"He swapped it for a new one, something we always did whenever our guns got dirty."

"Mr. Watson when you say dirty, do you mean murder on them?"

"Yes."

"No further questions your honor," Kelly smirked.

It was now Mark's turn to cross-examine the witness. He approached the bench with conceit.

"Mr. Watson, are you the same guy who had thirty pounds of marijuana seized from your car along with a firearm? Mr. Watson, are you the same one who was arrested at the age of sixteen with a firearm in your possession, not to mention doing Juvie life for being a menace to society? and Mr. Watson aren't you the same one who violated your probation?"

Ronnie didn't know if he should answer the questions, he looked towards the judge to bail him out.

"You may answer the questions," the judge confirmed.

"Yes." His response seemed to cause whispers from the jury.

"So Mr. Watson correct me if I'm wrong. You could've pretty much been behind Mr. Ross murder. I mean your criminal record compared to my clients who have never been in trouble with the law, I believe it's very safe to say you're capable of it."

Mark calmly stood in front of the jurors looking at Ronnie.

"But I didn't!" Ronnie snapped.

"How do we know that? You expect us to take the word of a menace." Mark said nonchalantly, cutting his over at the jury. "I guess you're also going to try and convince us that you are testifying at your own free will." Mark was just getting started.

"I...I... I don't understand the question," Ronnie said.

"Well let me rephrase it for you. What kind of deal did you work out with the government!"

"Objection your honor!" Kelly sprung from her seat.

"Overruled!" Weisberg said shutting her down.

Ronnie was baffled.

"Mr. Watson weren't you also confronted by your parole officer for selling 90 pounds of marijuana to a government informant by the name of Rick Lanier, in which you were arrested for on the spot. I'm assuming that's what brought you here to today."

"Yes," Ronnie exclaimed loudly.

"In fact, isn't it right Mr. Watson that you would do anything to avoid a lengthy prison sentence even if it meant lying on your onetime friend?"

"I'm just tryna do the right thing."

"Well, why wait eight years to do the right thing? I mean you would agree that this case is eight years old?"

"Yes," Ronnie said.

"In fact, Mr. Watson had you not been caught for your wrongdoings you would not be here testifying today?"

"To be honest with you no," he chuckled at that question.

"So, you are testifying to get out of jail."

"Yup!"

The courtroom erupted with soft chatters. Kelly dropped her head. Mark had been setting him up all along. He had just discredited Ronnie.

"No further questions Your Honor," he smiled.

Ronnie looked furious stepping from the stand, he and Fray locked eyes. Fray winked at him as the Marshal's escorted him away. Kelly was devastated at Ronnie's testimony. She had to get it together for her next witness.

"Ms. Anderson your next witness please," the judge called out.

"Your Honor I would like to call Helen Smith to the witness stand." Kelly said shuffling through her papers."

The courtroom was completely silent at the mention of the only person who had witnessed him do it, Fray left leg began to tremble underneath the table. His nervous system was jumping. Had the jury noticed the beads of sweat that formed on his forehead, they would have reached a verdict on the spot. Helen took her seat on the stand, this was the first time in eight years that the two had seen each other. Fray kept his eyes low periodically glancing up at the witness stand, he knew his destiny laid in Helen's hands.

"Helen before we began, would you mind me addressing you by your first name we already have your mother's last name down on record?"

"No," her hands had already started trembling. The prosecutor sensed her nervousness. She took a moment to walk over to Helen and comfort her.

"I know this is gonna be hard for you, but try to relax, and take a deep breath. At any moment if you feel like you need to take a break feel free to do so," Kelly said trying to make her as comfortable as possible.

Helen nodded her head agreeing.

"I want to direct your attention back to May 16, 1999. For the record would you mind telling us how old you were then."

"Eleven." her voice split and the tears began to fall. She closed her eyes and took the courtroom back to the dreadful afternoon. It took her 10 minutes to retell her story. When she opened her eyes and scanned the room everyone from the judge had tears in their eyes. The prosecutors then regained her composure stepping closer to the witness bench.

"Helen. Take a long hard look at the defendant sitting across from you," she pointed at Fray. He appeared nervous, but for the first time today he did not break eye contact. "Is this the guy who came to your rescue. The man you saw murder Mr. Elbridge Ross in cold blood?"

Helen stared long and hard at him, he was her hero.

"No." She finally uttered. Her statement surprised the entire courtroom.

"Excuse me!" Kelly said not believing her ears.

She watched her case crumble right before her eyes.

"I said no," Helen said a little louder. Kelly wasn't the only one in the state of confusion. Fray sat shocked as well. He knew Helen recognized him from the moment she sat down, however, with her not identifying him he knew his chances of walking out a free man was moments away.

"No further questions your Honor," she said in defeat as she walked back to her seat flopping down, covering her face with her hands. Mark declined to cross-examine the witness.

"Ms. Anderson I'm afraid if you don't have any more witnesses I'm going to have to send the jury back to deliberate," Weisberg said.

"Your Honor, may we approach?" She asked.

Fray looked perplexed, he looked to Mark for an answer who in turn shrugged his shoulders and proceeded to the bench.

"Oh, I'm sorry...I was just informed that malaise witness has finally arrived."

"Wait a minute! This witness is not on my list." Mark frowned madly shuffling through his paperwork.

"Whoops...what was I thinking?" Kelly said smacking her forehead. "I totally forgot to give you this, this morning honest mistake," she smiled as she handed him a paper from her folder, she handed one to the judge as well. Mark stood stunned as he read over the paperwork. The DA now had enough for their racketeering case. Fray had been watching him the entire time, and from the look on his face, he knew that this couldn't be good.

"Your Honor I would like to call Mr. Derek Allen to the stand at this time! He has been a government informant since the early 90s." Hearing Derek's name everything seemed to stop Fray could not believe it. The man that pulled him off the porch, and introduced him to the game was a rat the whole time. It was now clear how he ducked the conspiracy charge with his father. Fray felt like throwing up watching the man he looked up to like a father walk down the aisle. Derek placed his right hand on the Bible and raised his left.

"Do you swear to tell the whole truth and nothing but the truth so help you, God?" The bailiff quoted.

"I do," Derek said.

Fray dropped his head to his chest.

"Damn Pressure Bust Pipes" ...

"Fray, wake up, wake up man," Ashley shook him forcefully.

Fray opened his eyes and was dazed when he saw his best friend standing there holding his basketball. He jumped up wrapping his arms around Ashley's neck holding him tight. Tears began to fall on the back of Ashley's shirt.

"I missed you so much Ash," Fray said still holding him.

"Miss me," Ashley said confused. "Look, man, we still goin' to shoot some hoops or what?"

SHOUTOUTS

To my lil brother Anlo; you are my heart, Cornell (Tony) Glover; we have been joined at the hip since daycare. I love you brah, Fat-Hall; I couldn't ask for a better friend what's already understood don't need to be said, Gene; you have stood by my side through thick and thin. I love you cuz, Wesley & Jason Sewer; you only get real friends once, Pierre (Purpin P) still crazy as e'muthafucka (lol) I will never turn my back on you. I love you boy, H-Mob; only you have the ability to get under my skin and drive me crazy (lol) even then my love for you doesn't change, Wub; it's been awhile what the hell you waiting on, Dave, Teeth, Tuff Slim; (OMG...LLS) love you slim, Gucci, Donnie, Boo-Boo, Barbeast, lil Mike; love you boy, T.Y; I will never second guess you again, love you boy, Lil one, Man, Big-bad, Red Lavelle, Short, Whitey, Ambray, Big-A, Neal, Love, Blind, K-Roc, George, Mike Mahonie, Muzz, Emoney-bags, Pug, Cyrus, Lil Marvin, D.C, T-Mac, Pop; crutty muthafucka (lol), Chicken, Lil Wayne, Bob, Floyd, Corey, Siquan, Ra-Ra, Roach, Kamal, B.G, Jesse, Lil Steve, Big Boost, Chumps, Shitty, Jeezy, Moo-Man, Fat C, Big Jason, Skittles, Fat Lover, Vials, D.J, Tony Mapp, Beedy, Big Dog, A.D, Curt, Joe Green, T-Roy, Rick, Zo World, Head, Quizzy, Juan T, Black, Wop, Slick , Lil Wee, Big Wee, Gotti, Keyarie, Rocky, Sauce, Face, Momolu, Dennis Outlaw, Shirey, Omar, Terry Williams, Tonio, Nut, B.G, J.V, Pac-Man, Mad-Dog, Sean Branch, Fry, Pretty B, Chaka, Malik, Lonte, Damo, Wayne-Wayne, Lil Shannon, Junior, Big Mark, Bugz, Vito, TyKeisha, South, Dink, Spade, Corn, Price-Bey, Quig, Egg-Yoke, Rot-Not, Storm, Welling ass Steve, Pat, K.D, Juice,...and if I didn't mention

REX T. PELOTE JR

your name please don't be offended. It's a lot of names to try and remember all at once, so shout out to all the good men who names weren't mentioned.